To Tina

ROADSIDE GUIDE to the
OLYMPIC PENINSULA

Official Guide
of the 70th Birthday
Road Trip
Aug 9 - 14, 2018

Happy Birthday
Love Steve.

ROADSIDE GUIDE to the OLYMPIC PENINSULA

Christopher Chapman

Roadside Publishing

All cover images by author.
Front cover photos clockwise:
    View from Hurricane Ridge
    Roosevelt elk
    Third Beach
    Interrorem cabin

Back cover clockwise:
    View from Hurricane Ridge
    Isaac Stevens and Native Americans at treaty signing ceremony
    Salmon along the Soleduck River, near Sol Duc Hot Springs

Manuscript edited by Kris Fulsaas.
Page layout and cover design by Lori Fulsaas.
Final copy edited by Jim Dickmeyer.

Book printed in the U.S.A.

Roadside Publishing
www.roadsideolympicpeninsula.com

DEDICATION

To my very supportive parents, John L. and Elizabeth J. Chapman.
Also to Joe, who was the most patient and supportive.

Table of Contents

Throughout the book, look for special interest places indicated with picture icons that include birding, geology, hiking, history, natural history, photography, scenic views and wildlife.

 Birding   Natural History

 Geology   Photography

 Hiking   Scenic View

 History   Wildlife

PREFACE

I wrote this book to add depth to the experience of traveling the Olympic Peninsula. It is so much more than tall mountains surrounded by tall trees.

What is the history of the place? Who were the first humans to inhabit this incredibly fertile land? Where are they now? What is going on with the land and the forests and inhabitants today? Where are the forests of old-growth trees? What about the salmon, once so plentiful? What is so special about a Northern Spotted Owl? Are there any left? Did the earliest pioneers really travel up and down the beach to access the forests and their homes? How did the U.S. government change the Peninsula? What were Teddy Roosevelt's and FDR's contributions? Is there really evidence for mastodons in Sequim? Who were the Wobblies? Do the Indians still hunt whales with almost ancient technologies?

The book is a sort of travel guide and driving tour. The book starts with the topics that pertain to the whole Peninsula, in Part I, The Big Picture: geology, natural history, and human history. Then in Part II, Olympic Milestone Loop, the book drills down to the finer details of specific locations in the Milestone chapters, which guide you on a circumnavigation of the Peninsula. Each mile along the way is connected to every other mile, but because history, geology, and natural history are never isolated at a specific milepost, Part I provides context for the miles in Part II.

The Milestone chapters start on US Highway 101 in Olympia and direct you in a counterclockwise loop around the Peninsula. But you can start anywhere along the highway: each Milestone chapter is self-contained. The main highway, 316 miles long, is the backbone of the Peninsula. You *can* drive it in one day, but take your time and explore.

You'll also find numerous side-trip options that take you away from US 101 (the Olympic Loop Highway) to explore nearby parts of the Peninsula. Again, you *could* skip these side trips, but they take you to some of the Peninsula's most special places, including Port Townsend, Cape Flattery, Ozette Lake and the North Beach area. Some of these side-trip Milestones are loops; others are out-and-back trips. In addition, each Milestone also might contain a shorter side trip off US 101 to explore rivers and mountain roads to the heart of the Peninsula.

Dozens of excellent books tell you where to spend your money on restaurants, lodging and entertainment, but this isn't that kind of book. I make suggestions on uncomplicated and accessible places to hike, but I provide only the simplest of details, leaving the particulars to the many well-researched hiking guidebooks that are available. I point out some of my favorite places to bird, to view wildlife and to photograph, but serious photographers can recognize a good spot as well as I can. Birding spots tend to be more covert, which is why in the Milestone section I indicate important bird areas (IBAs) and give links, in Appendix E, to the local Audubon clubs that describe numerous other birding spots on the Peninsula.

I write about the Olympic Peninsula as it is typically designated: bordered on the east by Hood Canal, on the north by the Strait of Juan de Fuca, on the west by the Pacific Ocean and on the south by the Chehalis River. But don't let my definition of the Peninsula stop you from traveling east onto the Kitsap Peninsula or south of Aberdeen on US 101. Westport, Willapa Bay and Long Beach on south to the Columbia River are every bit as scenic and interesting as the Olympic Peninsula itself. (Maybe I should write *Roadside Guide to the Pacific Coast* to cover that region.)

The appendices in the back of the book add more specifics. Appendix A, Timeline, is a brief overview of the Peninsula's chronolog–y. Appendix B shows mileage distances between the Peninsula's highlights. Appendix C, Resources, offers addresses of museums, park visitor and ranger stations, and websites of tribes, environmental and naturalist groups, appropriate government agencies, campgrounds, chambers of commerce and tourist sites. You will see numerous birds on your trip and I include Appendix D to assist you. Appendix E has simple tips on how to maximize the photographic potential of your trip. Appendix F lists the national and state registered historic landmarks on the Peninsula.

I hope you enjoy reading this book as you travel and enjoy the unique and spectacular Olympic Peninsula. If you want to correct or add something in the book, please visit **www.roadsideolympicpeninsula.com**. Finally, if you want a guided tour like no other, I would love to lead you—visit my website to contact me.

ROADSIDE GUIDE TO THE OLYMPIC PENINSULA

PART I.

THE BIG PICTURE

It had more the aspect of enchantment than reality, with silent admiration each discerned the beauties of Nature, and naught was heard on board but expressions of delight murmured from every tongue.

—Thomas Manby, junior officer sailing along the Strait of Juan de Fuca, 1792, on the *HMS Discovery,* captained by George Vancouver

INTRODUCTION

The Olympic Peninsula is one of the most special places on the planet. It is home to the nation's largest old-growth forest and the only rain forest in the Lower 48 states. It has more biomass per acre than anyplace on earth. Olympic National Park is a UNESCO World Heritage Site and a Biosphere Reserve.

The Olympic Peninsula is also a place of contrasts. The west side of the Peninsula receives more than 140 inches of rain per year, while the northeastern region around Sequim receives about the same amount of rain that Los Angeles does. The Peninsula is the site of incredible greed, natural bounty and intense environmental concern.

Though the Peninsula's interior and northern coast were completely covered by ice only 10,000 years ago, it has been occupied for thousands of years. In recent times, you couldn't drive all the way around it until 1932. Ozette Lake, the state's largest unchanged natural lake, is located in the northwest corner of the Peninsula, an area that didn't have electricity until the 1960s.

The chapters in this section will enrich your understanding of the Olympic Peninsula's many contrasts and help you understand its ancient past, its flora and fauna, and its human history both prehistoric and recent.

GEOLOGY

The geology of the Olympic Peninsula is some of the most interesting in North America. It is a dramatic example of how landmasses are formed and how they evolve. This chapter could be called "Ice, Water, Gravity and Plate Tectonics." Born below the ocean surface, the Peninsula has been sculpted by those four forces for 50 million years.

Plate Tectonics

The earth's surface is made of constantly moving plates that drift about the planet, constantly bumping and grinding into each other, all driven by the internal heat of the earth and gravity. There are seven major oceanic and continental plates and dozens of smaller ones around the world. When these plates collide, the earth's landforms are created and/or destroyed. A fault line is created at the boundary of two or more plates. It is also where most of the action takes place, geologically speaking.

The Olympic Peninsula is technically on the North American plate, which is moving west. The much smaller Juan de Fuca plate (the eastern edge is about 150–300 miles offshore) is moving northeast to dive under the North American plate. South, off the coast of California is the Pacific plate, which is moving north. Continental plates, such as the North American plate, are lighter than oceanic plates, such as the Juan de Fuca plate.

Plates are not eternal. When they collide, some plates are destroyed by moving underneath other plates, called *subducting*. This is the environment we have just off the coast of the Pacific Northwest. The Juan de Fuca plate seems to be on a suicide course with the North American plate. The pressure created by the Juan de Fuca and North American plates moving together is immense in an area known as the Cascadia subduction zone just off the coast.

The intersection of the North American and Pacific plates is the famed San Andreas Fault line in California. As Los Angeles slides north along the San Andreas Fault, the Juan de Fuca plate could be completely overridden by the North American plate in 50 million years and LA could be a suburb of Seattle.

Plate tectonics have done most of the work in creating the Olympic Peninsula. Eons ago, the rock of the Peninsula was created far offshore and slowly transported to its current location. Some rock was created as part of unknown islands, but the vast majority was produced deep in the ocean. Undersea volcanoes erupted vast amounts of basalt in layers sometimes miles thick. As the basalt was erupting on the ocean floor, it cooled quickly, forming pillow basalt (which can be seen today on the Hurricane Ridge Road). Some basalt cooled above the ocean surface and formed columns; these can be seen along road cuts along Hood Canal.

As the ocean floor moved east, these basalt layers were laid down alternately with layers of sedimentary rock. The sediments came from organic material settling to the ocean floor, debris brought up from the earth's mantle by the geysers along the plate boundaries, and sand and mud deposited by ocean currents.

At one time, the Pacific coast ran on a line about 250 miles east of the Olympic Peninsula, from central British Columbia through Spokane and into southwestern Idaho and eastern Oregon. Small plates, or *terranes,* moved north from Mexico and California and parked against the ancient coast, forming a coastline that is almost recognizable as today's. When the heavier Juan de Fuca plate carrying the future Olympic Mountains reached the North American plate, it submerged under the lighter continental plate. This might have been the end of the future Olympics except for an interesting geologic phenomenon. The lighter continental plate scraped the Olympic rocks off the heavier oceanic plate as the heavier plate moved underneath.

As the Olympic rocks were added to the North American plate, they were wedged into the corner formed by the older North Cascades in Washington State and by Vancouver Island in British Columbia. This wedging into this geologic corner caused the rocks to bow into a horseshoe shape, creating the Crescent Formation (named for Crescent Bay on the Strait of Juan de Fuca, not for the crescent shape of the formation). The oldest rocks are basalt that lies in a horseshoe shape stretching from Neah Bay east to Hood Canal and south and west to Lake Quinault. This 9-mile-thick layer of rock was formed on the bottom of the ocean.

When the Olympic Mountains reached the continent, the layer was pushed into a vertical position, where it sits today. And as the sedimentary rock lying to the west of the basalt reached the coast, it also was turned vertically and now makes up the core of the Peninsula. The new core rocks, being weaker than the basalt, ended up extremely jumbled as they adjusted to their new position in the horseshoe.

The Olympic Range looks almost like an enormous car wreck—and it is. But remember that the time frame of this car wreck is enormous, involving millions of years. The plates are currently colliding at a speed of only 2 inches per year—about twice as fast as your fingernails grow! But the pressure is gargantuan, enough to flip some rock layers

Ribs of Crescent Formation: These sedementary rocks parallel the basalt horseshoe right along the Strait. Created horizontally, they are now tilted closer to vertical.

completely over. Between the forces of the tectonic plates pushing the mountains up and erosion trying to tear them down, the mountains are currently winning.

The ages of the Peninsula's rock span from 55 million years old on the Crescent Formation to 15 million years old at the coast. This helps to explain a lot of the geology. The oldest rocks got here first and have been slowly slammed by younger and younger rocks. That makes sense. But what explains the 144 million-year-old rocks out at Point of Arches, south of Neah Bay? There is speculation that this ancient rock is actually part of the North American continent, exposed by unknown forces.

Ice

As the whole dome of the Olympic Peninsula rose from the sea, it was immediately set upon by processes that gradually reduce every-thing to sea level: ice, gravity and water. Ice is the great bulldozer. The Olympic Peninsula has been assaulted by ice in the form of glaciers for millennia. Currently, it has 9 percent of the continental U.S. glaciers, more than anywhere in the United States outside of Alaska. This is due to the Olympic Mountains' elevation and copious amount of moisture that falls on them. In fact, there are very few areas in the world that have such low-elevation glaciers as the Peninsula has.

When enough snow falls in the mountains that it doesn't melt in the summer, it is called a *snowfield*. When this snowfield becomes large and heavy enough that it starts to move downslope, it is called a *glacier*. Gla-ciers are amazingly powerful. As they move downslope, they gouge out U-shaped valleys. They also gather rocks, which when combined with the weight and movement of the ice, literally shape mountains.

Over the eons, the Olympic Peninsula has been sculpted by the gla-ciers of numerous ice ages. The last ice age to impact Washington State peaked about 20,000 years ago and probably left our state about 10,000 to 13,000 years ago. During this ice age, the Cordilleran Ice Sheet, which flowed south out of Canada, made it as far south as Olympia. It also was forced to go west around the Olympic Mountains by the hard basaltic Crescent Formation and scoured out the Strait of Juan de Fuca before it proceeded to just north of Forks. This ice sheet, along with its many lobes, was instrumental in forming both Hood Canal and Puget Sound. It is estimated that it was 4000 feet high above Port Angeles.

Because of the weight of this enormous continent-sized ice sheet, the land was actually pushed down by as much as 300 feet. However, the sea level was even lower because so much water was frozen in the glaciers; Mount Olympus might have been twice as distant from the sea as it is today. The glaciers originating in the mountains, if not blocked by the ice sheet, extended all the way down to the sea, as the Hoh Glacier did. When the glaciers retreated, the land rebounded.

The rocks the glaciers pick up can be transported far from their source, and are called *glacial erratics*. These rocks, embedded inside the hard glacial ice, help glaciers become efficient earthmovers.

All over the Peninsula a trained eye can see examples of erratics that are Canadian rocks transported south during the many ice ages. These erratics have been found underwater off the coast of the Peninsula and up as high as 3500 feet in the mountains. The erratics could have been dumped directly off the glacier or embedded in an iceberg that floated away. This is the same process that the Alaskan glaciers exhibit when they calve into the sea.

Glacial erratics have been found dozens of miles up the Elwha River, which might indicate that there once was a Glacial Lake Elwha, created by melt water from mountain glaciers and dammed by the Cordilleran Ice Sheet. There also is evidence of numerous shorelines up the Elwha valley, which are very hard to see due to the vegetation. These multiple shorelines suggest that the ice sheet from the north repeatedly dammed the lake, and then the lake repeatedly broke through. (Another example of this process was Glacial Lake Missoula, which formed the Channeled Scablands in eastern Washington by this same glacial damming and subsequent flooding.)

As the ice sheet moved into Puget Sound, all the rivers that normally flowed into Puget Sound were diverted south by the ice sheet. Glacial Lake Russell, on top of what is now Olympia, collected the water before spilling it farther south over the Black Lake area into the Chehalis River. All of this water caused that river to swell to a size that would rival the modern Columbia River; this is why the Chehalis River valley is so large.

Sometimes a retreating glacier leaves behind a large chunk of its frozen self. These chunks are so large that they form permanent depressions called *kettles*. Examples of kettles can be seen 3 miles due north of Sequim in the Pothole region just off of Sequim Dungeness Way. Keep your eye out for out for any depressions in the landscape in that area.

The glaciers also deposit erratics along their sides, called *lateral moraines,* or at their snouts, called *terminal moraines*. Ozette Lake, Lake Cushman, Lake Quinault and numerous other lakes were created behind terminal moraines. The glaciers dug out the lakebeds and retreated, creating a natural dam with their terminal moraine at their most advanced point. You can see the Peninsula's many glaciers with any clear view of the Olympics. The most up-close and expansive view is from Hurricane Ridge (see Milestone 4).

Gravity and Earthquakes

Landslides and earthquakes are also great equalizers. As the glaciers retreated from their U-shaped valleys, the then-unsupported valley walls collapsed to the valley floor. Also, the high amount of rain makes soil very unstable, so there is an enormous amount of slumping. Add a mammoth earthquake or two, and it is surprising that anything is still vertical.

The Peninsula has seen plenty of earthquakes since it resides on the Ring of Fire, a ring of volcanic and seismic activity that stretches from New Zealand north to Japan to Alaska and south to South America. Scientists have discovered several places on the Peninsula where an enormous earthquake struck on January 26, 1700, at 9:00 p.m. They know this because the tsunami that struck the Japanese coast the next day could only have been caused by that megathrust earthquake from the direction of the Peninsula. Whole parts of the Peninsula and Puget Sound dropped 6–10 feet. Scientists estimate that the earthquake registered a 9 on the Richter scale.

An earthquake of that size today would bring the Puget Sound area to its knees, literally and figuratively. We have only to look at the 1964 earthquake in Anchorage, which registered a 9.2, to get a hint of the devastation that Seattle and Tacoma would suffer in the next big one. It is only a matter of when, not if.

Water

While ice acts like a bulldozer, water is a more subtle but just as effective sculptor. There is a lot of water on the Peninsula. The west side of the Peninsula gets more than 100 inches per year. The Hoh Rain Forest

Note Destruction Island in the upper left.

Visitor Center gets more than 13 feet annually. Mount Olympus gets more than 200 inches per year.

This water forms twelve major rivers that radiate from the Peninsula's center. (The radial nature of the rivers indicates that the Peninsula arose as a whole. As the dome rose, the rivers started carving their way to the sea.) The rock and sand that the rivers carry downstream erode everything downhill. The water is doing its best to level the mountains as they rise from the sea, and it won't be deterred.

Another way in which water sculpts the Olympics is when it works its way into the cracks of the rocks and freezes, slowly prying the rocks apart.

On the coast, wave action is another way in which water has sculpted the Peninsula, creating cliffs that rise up to 300 feet from the sea. Many remnants of the former continent, known as *sea stacks,* can be seen from shore. Sea stacks are old sections of continent that the sea has isolated from the shore. Typically they are composed of much harder material than the surrounding shoreline and, thus, resist erosion.

(Hike the Third Beach trail near La Push for some of the most dramatic views on the Peninsula.)

A good example of this is Destruction Island which is about 3.5 miles off the coast (see Milestone 7). Wave action erodes the shoreline at a rate of about 3 inches per year, which indicates that Destruction Island was connected to the coast about 70,000 years ago. The island's elevation reveals its connection to the land. If you draw a straight line along the slightly sloping elevation of the island and continue that imaginary line to the coast, you will see that the island is a natural extension of the current coast.

Glossary: Geology

glacial erratics: rocks picked up by glaciers and transported far from their source; erratics can be dumped directly off a glacier or embedded in an iceberg that floated away

glacier: a snowfield large and heavy enough to start moving downslope

kettles: permanent depressions formed when large chunks of a retreating glacier are left behind and melt

lateral moraine: rocks and debris deposited along the sides of a glacier

sea stack: old section of continent composed of much harder material than the surrounding shoreline that resists erosion and, thus, the sea isolates from shore

snowfield: formed when enough snow falls in the mountains that it doesn't melt in the summer

subduction: the movement of one plate under another

terminal moraine: rocks and debris deposited at the snout, or end, of a glacier

terranes: fragments of Earth's crust that has broken off of its original plate and has become attached to another plate

Olympic marmot

2

NATURAL HISTORY

The Olympic Peninsula has a rich variety of ecosystems stretching from the Pacific Ocean, which harbors gray whales and orcas, to the high Olympic Mountains, habitat for Roosevelt elk and Olympic marmots. Its varied ecosystems are home to twenty-six unique animal and plant species and subspecies, including the Olympic snow mole and the Olympic torrent salamander. The Peninsula can be considered an ecological island that was cut off from the remainder of the continent on and off for thousands of years during the last ice age. Glaciers from the north and the powerful Chehalis River in the south provided both isolation and time in which species became differentiated from their nearby and genetically similar cousins found elsewhere in the Pacific Northwest.

The Coast: Whales

The Olympic Peninsula is ringed on three sides by salt water. To the east is Hood Canal, to the north is the Strait of Juan de Fuca and to the west is the Pacific Ocean. Some of the coastline consists of sandy or cobble beach and reefs, where tide pools are exposed at low tide; other parts have steep, unstable bluffs or headlands that can be impassable at high tide.

All of the plant and animal life in the Peninsula's coastal waters on the Pacific Ocean is protected by the Olympic Coast National Marine Sanctuary. Theodore Roosevelt first proposed this marine reserve in 1907 in an attempt to preserve the nesting sites for more than 80 percent of Washington State's seabirds (see Appendix E, Birding). The sanctuary covers more than 3000 square miles: from the high-tide line onshore out to 30–40 miles offshore, stretching from Cape Flattery in the north to Copalis Beach in the south. The sanctuary is two and a half times larger than Olympic National Park. Inside the sanctuary, you cannot approach to within 200 yards of any islands or fly lower than 2000 feet.

The sanctuary also encompasses the Washington Islands Wilderness. The total land area covered by the Washington Islands Wilderness is less than 1 square mile, but it covers more than 600 islands and rocks and 300 square miles of coastal waters (Destruction Island, James Island, and Tatoosh Island are not included in the sanctuary but have their own visitor restrictions).

The largest of the Peninsula's fauna is the gray whale. These monsters of the coastal waters weigh 80,000 pounds and reach lengths of more than 50 feet. They were once a key component of Indian culture and subsistence, yet in modern times, only one has been hunted and brought to shore in almost a century (see the Makah section in "The Peninsula Tribes," in chapter 3, Original Inhabitants). It is hard to imagine the original inhabitants of the Peninsula paddling offshore in their hand-carved canoes with only spears to hunt these enormous animals.

Gray whales have the largest migration of any mammal. They pass by the Pacific coast twice a year: in March, going north on their way to the Arctic Ocean, and in November and December, going south on their way to breeding grounds in Baja California, Mexico. Now extinct in the North Atlantic, gray whale populations in the North Pacific are estimated to be about 22,000 individuals, down from a historic high of about 100,000 in all the oceans of the world. The Makah and other Pacific coast natives stopped whaling in 1920s when it was realized that the whale harvest wasn't sustainable. Japan, America and other nations continued to hunt gray whales until 1949 when the International Whaling Commission granted the whales protection. To see the whales from shore, find a high promontory on the coast. Cape Flattery and Kalaloch (pronounced "CLAY-lock") are perfect places in March (see Milestone 7).

Orcas, a/k/a killer whales, and humans are the only predators of gray whales. Orcas will harass a gray whale mother and her baby calf until they can take the calf. Adult gray whales themselves are too large for the orcas. Orcas are found in every ocean, numbering perhaps 50,000 globally. They are iconic for Washington State, though there are only about 200 that prowl Puget Sound and the Olympic coast. The best place to view orcas is the San Juan Islands from a whale-watching boat or from Lime Kiln Lighthouse Point on the west side of San Juan Island (technically not on the Olympic Peninsula but nearby).

The most charming animal on the Olympic coast is the sea otter, found only in the waters of the North Pacific. This prized mammal has more fur per square inch on its body than any other mammal, and this luxuriant fur has led to its near extinction. Prized initially for its fur by the Chinese, the sea otter drew fur traders from around the world to the waters of the North Pacific in the eighteenth and nineteenth centuries to gather the pelts to sell in Asia. European sailors initially traded just trinkets with the Northwest Coast natives for the sea otter pelts. Later, they hired or enslaved the natives as hunters until the local waters were depleted of sea otters.

The sea otter trade completely reorganized the local Indian economies. Natives who previously spent time harvesting and collecting food for their own subsistence spent more and more time collecting otter pelts and less time gathering their own food.

Created by Sarah Willoughby, 1885

Early Europeans settlers on the Pacific coast of Washington erected high scaffolds or perched on top of rocks and shot the otters with specially marked bullets. They would wait for the next tide to bring the otter carcasses ashore to claim them. The image here is from Copalis Beach.

Once ranging from Japan to Alaska to Baja California, the sea otter population has recovered from the slaughter to about 150,000 worldwide, one-half of the pre-European-hunting high. Sea otters now exist in only about two-thirds of their historic range and are considered an endangered species in Washington, extremely susceptible to oil spills and water pollution. The Washington coast has about 1000 individuals, which have grown from the 29 that were brought in from Alaskan waters in the early 1970s. (The first attempt at translocating otters failed and all 30 died within a few days. A second attempt a year later took the lessons learned and all of those otters survived.)

Despite their warm fur, sea otters have to consume a fourth of their body weight every day to maintain metabolism and keep warm. Their favorite habitats are kelp beds, where they wrap themselves up in the seaweed, float on their back and enjoy their favored shellfish. They are best seen from the shore from Kalaloch and on the Ozette coast trail.

Other sea mammals to be found in the waters and islands of the Olympic coast include harbor seals, California sea lions, Steller sea lions (see sidebar), and northern elephant seals.

The Steller sea lion is named after Georg Steller, a German naturalist who was commissioned by the czar of Russia to be the medical officer and naturalist on Vitus Bering's second and ill-fated Pacific voyage. The expedition left St. Petersburg in 1738 and reached the Pacific coast in March 1740. In 1741 Steller became the first European to set foot in Alaska, on Kayak Island (southeast of Valdez). Unfortunately, he was allowed only ten hours onshore before Bering pulled anchor and headed for home. Bering died that winter on Bering Island; Steller died in Siberia on his way home. Of the six species named after Herr Steller, two are extinct and three are endangered. Only the Steller jay thrives; it can be seen everywhere in the western Americas from Alaska to Nicaragua.

Steller Jay

A volunteer aiding in the clean-up.

The Olympic beaches, while very remote, are littered with all the flotsam and jetsam that the ocean can deliver. Walking the beach, you can pick up plastic bottles and hard hats, yards of fishing line and colorful buoys, anything and everything that floats. The coastal stretch from La Push to Cape Flattery is the most isolated part of the U.S. coast outside of Alaska, but without the serious hard work of volunteers and the National Park Service, it would look like the worst garbage dump imaginable. The Japanese tsunami of 2011 dumped millions of tons of floating debris into the North Pacific. Due to prevailing ocean currents, the local coast could be the hardest hit of anywhere.

Hood Canal, which lies on the Peninsula's eastern side, doesn't have this ocean debris problem, but it does suffer occasionally from low oxygenated water, which leads to massive fish kills. During the summer, the plankton population explodes due to increased sunshine, long days and ample nutrients. One primary nutrient is nitrogen, which occurs naturally but flows into the canal from human activity, such as leaky septic systems, overfertilization of lawns and runoff from forests and fields. These plankton "blooms" eventually die and sink to the bottom in the autumn. It is during this stage when decomposing plankton consumes so much oxygen that the surrounding waters become *hypoxic,* or oxygen deprived. One of the shallowest areas of the bathtub-shaped canal is at its northern head, so there isn't a natural flushing of waters that you would expect with every tide change.

If Bald Eagles interest you, the Peninsula is a great place to spot them. Look for them at all coastal locations. They are opportunistic carnivores but fish is their preferred diet in this part of world. Neah Bay and Seal Rock Campground, along Hood Canal just north of Brinnon, are prime locations but they are found everywhere. They were removed from the Endangered Species list in 1995 and the Threatened Species list in 2007. While no longer endangered or threatened it is illegal to harm them in anyway.

Bald Eagles aren't "bald" from birth. When they fledge they are brown and mottled with white, especially under the wings. They will keep this coloring until they reach sexual maturity and develop their "bald" plumage, typically at age four or five. They can live to be 20 years old in the wild.

The Rivers: Salmon

The Peninsula is home to an amazing number of rivers. They begin in the Olympic Mountains' glaciers at the center of the Peninsula, radiating in all directions as they run downstream to Hood Canal on the east, the Strait of Juan de Fuca on the north, the Pacific on the west and

Four immature Bald Eagles inside the harbor at Neah Bay

the Chehalis River on the south. The Elwha River runs 38 miles from the heart of the Olympic Mountains due north to the Strait of Juan de Fuca, draining about 20 percent of Olympic National Park. Other large rivers include the Hoh, which runs west from Mount Olympus to the Pacific Ocean, and the Quinault River, which flows southwest to the Pacific.

Perhaps the most iconic animal species of the Pacific Northwest is the salmon, which once were found in every freshwater stream on the Peninsula in bountiful quantities. Today, they have been reduced to less than 10–20 percent of their historic numbers.

In pre-European times, salmon was a mainstay of the Indian diet. Not only were there unbelievable amounts (by modern standards) to be harvested, but they came with regularity in multiple runs per year. The native population density of coastal Washington State rivaled that of

Aztec Mexico prior to Columbus, due in large part to the salmon and the bounty it brought virtually every season. While the Indians were quite adept at harvesting the fish, they didn't take more than they needed. They ate fresh salmon and dried what they required to sustain them until the next run, which might be just a month or two away. All the tribes on the coast and much of the interior had as much salmon as they could eat.

Pacific salmon include five species of true salmon (chinook, chum, coho or silver, pink, and sockeye) and two of oceangoing trout (steelhead and cutthroat). Called *anadromous,* these fish all return from the ocean to spawn in the stream of their birth. The two trout species return to the ocean after spawning, while the true salmon die soon after.

Newly hatched salmon spend a few months to a few years within their freshwater home before heading out to sea. There they spend two to five years circling the North Pacific before returning to the same stream or close by where they were born to spawn and then die. The amazing navigation system that allows them to return to their birth stream is found in their nose. Each waterway has its own smell, and the salmon can zero in on it when it is time to return.

The good news is that their noses aren't 100 percent accurate, and as many as 20 percent will find a different, though geographically close, stream to spawn in. This phenomenon helps increase the genetic diversity of each salmon stream and allows the salmon to populate new streams that might become available to them. The Elwha River dam removal and habitat restoration is counting on this same phenomenon to help repopulate the river. (Salmon are starting to discover streams along the north slope of Alaska in the Arctic Ocean that are becoming ice free due to global warming.)

However, by returning to the same stream, the salmon population of that stream becomes more evolved to handle that specific ecosystem. Salmon are highly evolved to their birth stream. Over time they become what scientists and the Environmental Protection Agency describe as evolutionary significant units (ESUs). Each salmon run is different, and it is some of these runs that have been classified threatened or endangered.

The decline of salmon on the Peninsula and elsewhere around the world can be attributed to the four Hs: hydroelectricity and dams, habitat loss, harvest levels and hatcheries (which affect wild salmon's genetic diversity). The salmons' decline has been caused by a thousand cuts from many masters:

- ✓ General public
- ✓ Commercial offshore fishing industry
- ✓ Indigenous peoples
- ✓ Logging industry
- ✓ Transportation—inland barges and marine traffic
- ✓ Power producers and consumers
- ✓ Agriculture—irrigators
- ✓ Recreational industries

Peak harvest of salmon occurred in Washington State at the end of the nineteenth century. The arrival of European settlers brought new harvesting technologies, increased harvesting success, canning and distribution systems into the area, and the end of the famous bountiful salmon runs was at hand. The good news was that canned salmon was available globally for the first time.

Logging brought habitat destruction, especially in the beginning of the twentieth century. The timber industry would clearcut the forest right to the creek edge; creek water became too hot for lack of shade, and the stream beds became filled with silt from erosion, burying the salmon's required nesting grounds. Sawmills dumped thousands of tons of sawdust directly into the rivers, dramatically changing stream chemistry and smothering salmon nest sites. Pulp mills poured massive amounts of unregulated industrial chemicals directly in the rivers.

Small semi-permanent dams, called splash dams, were erected to help move logs downstream. These dams created a small temporary pond; logs were dropped behind the dams, and when the water level became high enough to float the logs, the whole dam was lowered all at once to float all the logs downstream. The dam was then raised again to repeat the process. The logs crashing downstream would rip out the stream beds, eliminating key salmon nesting areas. The good news was that thousands of people were employed and logs, wood, and paper were readily available both domestically and for export.

The splash dams were a minor inconvenience compared to hydroelectric dams erected in the first half of the twentieth century. The poster child on the Peninsula is the Elwha Dam, which started generating electricity in 1913. The Elwha Dam, erected 5 miles upriver from the coast, cut off more than 95 percent of the river's spawning grounds. The river once hosted all five species of salmon, including enormous 100-pound chinooks. Now only about 1 percent of the salmon return to the Elwha from their historic highs.

The state laws at the time required that salmon runs were not to be interfered with, but Thomas Aldwell, the owner of the Elwha Dam, negotiated to build a hatchery at the base of the dam "designed" to maintain the salmon runs; however, the hatchery was abandoned a couple of years after the dam was completed. The dam also blew out once, and Aldwell just threw in rocks, debris and other riprap to plug the hole. The dam was never licensed to operate because it was never anchored to the bedrock; nevertheless, it generated power for almost 100 years for the pulp mill located in Port Angeles (see "Elwha Restoration" in chapter 7, The 21st Century and the Future).

The absence of salmon from the Peninsula's rivers affects more than just the humans who want to eat them. Salmon returning from the sea are a major source of nutrients for the whole forest. The effects of this nutrient deficit are not well understood, but without salmon, the rivers become less productive since there is less marine-derived nitrogen and phosphate in the rivers and *riparian areas.* These nutrients help juvenile salmon survive. Without spawned-out dead salmon in the river, there are fewer insects and therefore less nutrition for new salmon. And without fish carcasses littering the beaches, there is less food for larger animals such as eagles, coyotes, and bears. These larger animals drag the dead salmon away from the waters into the forest, where the salmon provide nutrients for the whole forest.

The Forests: Elk

Enormous trees are the most popular tourist draw on the Olympic Peninsula. These magnificent temperate-forest ecosystems are the most biologically productive areas in the world. The old-growth forest is a cathedral, with its majestic canopies and dominating green columns. At the same time, it can feel suffocating if you want to see any distance into the forest or even up to the sky above.

What is an *old-growth forest?* In its simplest definition, an old-growth forest is one that has been undisturbed for more than 200 years. It contains standing snags, downed trees, and a multilayered *canopy* with trees of all ages present. There are old-growth forests on every continent. The taiga, or boreal forest, in the far north of the Northern Hemisphere, is old-growth; these forests have been growing for centuries. However, the trees are only 6–12 inches in diameter.

What is it that makes the Peninsula's old-growth trees so enormous? All trees have microscopic pores, called *stomata,* in their needles or leaves. The vast majority of trees open these pores when the rate of evaporation through the stomata is equal to or greater than the tree's ability to sustain its moisture requirements by pulling water from the ground. In the south, if the hot, dry air sucks out too much moisture, the stomata close and the tree stops growing. Up north, the environment is too cold and dry and the growing season is too short. Here on the Peninsula, conditions are just right: Goldilocks weather, not too hot and not too cold, with abundant moisture and plenty of shade from the cooling rain clouds off the Pacific.

The Peninsula's forests have been growing uninterrupted for more than 10,000 years, ever since the climate warmed and the last ice age's glacial ice melted away. The initial glacial-free environment was cold and dry, and Lodgepole pines flourished. (They are virtually gone now from the Peninsula, having been muscled out by the bigger trees and the wetter weather).

The Peninsula is home to fifteen different kinds of evergreens, but the mighty Douglas-fir is the predominant tree; it grows virtually everywhere in the Pacific Northwest (and Rocky Mountains). But the Douglas-fir doesn't have the last word. Forests progress through various stages as they get older, with the types of trees changing with the forests' age.

Red alders were once considered a weed tree to be eradicated since they grow fast in open areas. Foresters now know that without them, nothing grows well. These opportunistic alders are the foundation for all that comes next. The red alder fixes specific nutrients to the soils, nutrients required by all subsequent trees, especially the Douglas-fir. Alders are *shade intolerant,* meaning they don't grow well in the shade, but after a forest disturbance, they help stabilize the forest floor and begin rejuvenating the soil on most sites.

The Douglas-fir is also shade intolerant and starts to grow soon after the alders, until the alders are completely shaded by their taller successors. Then the Western red cedar, Sitka spruce and Western hemlock, all *shade-tolerant* trees, start to dominate. The Douglas-fir, over time, will

Blow down forest

eventually fall over and die, only to be succeeded by the new shade-tolerant trees. However, Douglas-firs have something the shade tolerant hemlocks and cedars lack, a thick fireproof bark. This last stage is called the *climax stand* type: the forest doesn't change much after that unless there is a disturbance. The most predominant trees at this stage are the shade tolerant ones. But the forest never stands still. Eventually, there will be a wind storm, fire, flood or some other disturbance and the whole process begins again with Douglas-fir and alder. If the forest burns, and even the dampest of rainforests are subject to wild fires, the thick fireproof bark of the Douglas-firs helps them survive as the competing shade tolerant species are set back a generation or two.

Old-growth forests are typically very heterogeneous. When a Douglas-fir falls and opens up the canopy, another fir may grow there, or the competing shade-tolerant species may close up the canopy, creating shade and prohibiting the new Douglas-fir growth. Western red cedar

is the longest-growing species, with ages up to 1000 years. Douglas-firs grow to 700 years old; hemlock and spruce can be 400 years old.

The biggest natural killer of trees on the west side of the Peninsula is the wind and fungus. The wind blows down the tree which is immediately set upon by fungus. Western red cedar has a large taproot, which helps it compete by not being blown over as much as the other trees. It also exudes a chemical protection that repels fungal invasions. Fungi and bacteria can change a forest much like forest fires only they tend to target specific species over time. Large fires create forest change quickly; fungi and bacteria do so slowly. Large fires have occurred but, overall, it is too wet for any large conflagration. The largest fire in the 20th century burned from the Lake Crescent area southwest to Forks.

When a tree does fall, it is almost immediately attacked by fungi and insects. But despite this onslaught, it may take centuries before the tree completely disappears into the forest floor. While it is decaying, forest

Note the large trees growing in a colonnade. The nurse log can be seen decaying under all of them.

litter lands on top of the downed tree, providing an environment for new tree seedlings. These new trees eventually send roots down the side of the downed log to the forest floor and continue growing. The downed trees, called *nurse logs,* are not hard to spot: look for mature trees in a row, with a hole where the decayed nurse tree once was. The nurse logs are popular with seedlings since they allow seedlings to start growing 1–10 feet above the forest floor. Stumps can also serve the same purpose.

There is more biomass per acre in an old-growth forest on the western lowlands of the Olympic Peninsula than anywhere else in the world, including the Amazon rain forests. But don't just look up at the towering

trees. Notice that the ground is covered with logs. And if you look close enough, you will see that there are logs lying upon logs lying upon logs, part of the 50 tons per acre of wood litter that covers the forest floor. One-fifth of the biomass is in these decomposing logs, wood litter and underground fungi.

Fungi, yeasts and bacteria are the keystones of the forest. Without them, the forest would be unrecognizable, if not completely barren. These valuable pieces of life assist everything else to grow. Trees need them to gather the nutrients they need from the soil. Specific fungi coat the roots and massage the nutrients in the soil so that the roots can absorb them. In turn, the tree supplies the photosynthetic fuel that the fungus needs. The symbiotic relationship occurs everywhere in the forest. About 20 percent of the forest's biomass is belowground in the form of fungi, yeast, and bacteria. Yet the belowground biology consumes upward of 50 percent of the forest's photosynthetic-generated fuel (Kirk and Franklin 2001). The network of fungal strands passes tree sugars not only to itself but this network also is connected to shrubs and other trees. One of the reasons huckleberries can thrive in dark forests is because they receive sugars from the surrounding trees.

The best places to see the monster trees and wondrous forests are in the river valleys on the Peninsula's west side, especially the Bogachiel, Hoh, Queets and Quinault (see Milestones 6 and 7). All these valleys face southwest and west and get enormous amounts of rain. The Quinault River valley is nicknamed the "Valley of the Giants." It has the world's largest Western red cedar, Douglas-fir, mountain hemlock and Sitka spruce, as well as the largest Western hemlock and Alaska yellow cedar in the United States.

With the Peninsula receiving more than 140 inches of rain a year plus another 42 inches in the form of fog, why aren't its forests a washed-out floodplain? An old-growth Douglas-fir can hold up to 5000 gallons of water in just its canopy (a mature Douglas-fir tree has an acre of surface area in just its needles) and attached epiphytes (nonparasitic plants that grow on another). These epiphytes don't send roots to the ground, but get all their nourishment from what is growing on the tree bark without harming the tree at all. They also get their moisture requirements from the rain and fog. When it rains, they hold onto the moisture as best they can. Between the epiphytes and the tree canopy, when the rain stops, it is still "raining" on the forest floor as the canopy above slowly releases its accumulated water. Also, the forest floor appears to be perfectly designed as a sponge with its piles of fallen logs and debris to absorb and slowly release water. These water "absorb-and-release" strategies assist the forest from washing away.

These big trees and remaining ancient forests represent the final 10 percent of the millions of acres of old-growth that once prevailed before Europeans arrived in North America. It is the old-growth forest that is home to the Northern Spotted Owl. In 1990 the owl became the visible pinch point between timber interests and environmentalists. The Endangered Species Act, signed into law by President Nixon, never proposed saving endangered ecosystems. But with rapidly dwindling old-growth forests on the Peninsula, the owl was also rapidly dwindling. Each nesting pair requires 3000 to 10,000 acres in the Pacific Northwest, and there are only 200 pairs left on the Peninsula (see "Old-Growth and Owls" in chapter 6, The 20th Century).

Other creatures also depend on these old-growth forests. When the Peninsula's first park was proposed, it was named Elk National Park to help celebrate and protect the elk. The Roosevelt Elk (named for Teddy), the largest of the four North American subspecies of elk, had almost been eliminated from the Peninsula. One strange reason for their demise was the demand by members of the Benevolent and Protective Order of Elks, aka the Elks Lodge, for elk teeth for key fobs. The elk population had decreased so much by the early twentieth century that Washington State initiated a ten-year hunting moratorium. Now the population has stabilized to about 4000–5000 in the park.

Elk are the gardeners of the forest, eating almost anything that they can. Without them, the forest would become virtually impenetrable. One seedling they rarely eat is the Sitka spruce. These spruce needles are too sharp even for an elk. The best place to see elk is in the same river valleys as the large trees, especially in the winter. In the summer many elk migrate to the high country.

The only remaining elk predator in the park is the cougar (aka mountain lion or puma). These elusive cats once had a bounty on them. Hunters changed the ecosystem by greatly reducing the number of cougars that fed on the elk that kept the forest at bay. Hunting cougars

was finally eliminated in the park in 1938. Seeing cougars is nearly impossible. They always see you, but you have to spend a *lot* of time in the forest before you will ever spot one.

Wolves, historically the chief predator of elk, were eliminated in the 1920s, also due to a bounty. Wolves have been introduced in neighboring states of Idaho, Montana, and Wyoming by shipping them down from British Columbia. The strategy in Washington State is to only allow them to migrate south from Canada and west from Idaho. There are wolf packs in the North Cascades and the Selkirk Mountains north of Spokane but none on the Peninsula. To reintroduce wolves on the Peninsula, the wolves would have to take a ferry across Puget Sound or come down around through the city of Olympia.

The Mountains: Marmots

The Olympic Mountains are not a particularly high range—Mount Olympus, the highest point, is just under 8000 feet tall—but they are rugged due to huge forests and many glaciers. How do such low-elevation mountains acquire glaciers? Lots and lots of snow!

Timberline in the Sierra Nevada in California is at 10,000 feet, but here on the Peninsula it is 6000 feet, primarily due to the inclement weather. The growing season in the low-elevation sites is virtually all year long, but up high, the growing season is much shorter and drier. The best place to see this mountain ecosystem is from Hurricane Ridge and Deer Park, both accessible from Port Angeles by car.

Up high, the trees are the most prominent vegetation, but gone are the majestic giants of the lower elevations. Here, trees scrap and claw their way to survival. It is not called Hurricane Ridge without reason. Winds buffet everything, making life tenuous. The most exposed trees are stunted and shaped by the wind, called *flagged trees.* You can look at a tree and see which way the wind typically blows. Solitary trees form their own micro-ecosystem. Once one tree gets growing, other trees and vegetation will grow to the leeward of the original tree. Some of these trees, called *krummholz trees,* look more like mutated woody shrubs. The weather is so severe that they can grow to a height of only a few feet above the ground.

Alaska yellow cedar, mountain hemlock and subalpine fir replace the lower-elevation Douglas-fir and Western red cedar. These high-altitude species have short, drooping limbs that allow them to spill all the snow and avoid being buffeted by the winds. Some of these limbs lie against the ground and will develop roots.

In the highest reaches only lowing-lying plants grow. All are perennials because their growing season is too short to allow them to flower, go to seed, and then germinate that new seed the next year. These plants also have leaves and long taproots designed to conserve moisture and get a quick start once the snow melts.

The iconic mammal of the mountains is the Olympic marmot, endemic to the Peninsula. They can be found at 3000–6000 feet elevation. The best place to see them is along the road to Obstruction Point from Hurricane Ridge (see Milestone 4, Discovery Bay to Elwha). They live in burrow communities that can hold up to forty different individuals. Marmots use a distinctive whistle to warn others of danger. Coyotes are their biggest threat, though they are sometimes taken by golden eagles. They begin their annual hibernation in the fall and emerge in May. They are not endangered.

The mountain goat, also found in high elevations, is not iconic but dangerous to humans and disastrous for the park. Introduced in the 1920s near Lake Crescent as a sport-hunting animal, they have thrived inside the park. Unfortunately, the Peninsula is not well suited for these goats. They cause soil erosion and are detrimental to the fragile soils and plants found in the mountains. The goats were subjected to a live capture program during the '80s, which was not a success. Now the only option appears to be killing them from helicopters but the park admin-

istration is working on other options. The population is growing in the park; you could possibly see one near Hurricane Ridge (see Milestone 4), but do not approach—stay a minimum of 100 yards away. These are wild and unpredictable animals. A goat gored a hiker on Mount Ellinor above Lake Cushman in 1999 and killed a hiker on Hurricane Ridge in 2010.

Another popular animal found in the Olympic Mountains is the black bear, which thrives deep in the park. Bears are occasionally visible in the high meadows of Deer Park or Hurricane Ridge feasting on what the summer bounty provides. The mighty grizzly bear has never populated the Peninsula, perhaps due to the Peninsula's isolation.

Glossary: Natural History

anadromous: oceangoing fish born in freshwater that return from the ocean to spawn in the stream of their birth

canopy: the upper part of a forest consisting of treetops

climax stand: last stage in a forest's development when the forest consists of shade-tolerant trees and doesn't change much unless there is a disturbance

epiphyte: a nonparasitic plant that grows on another, getting all its nourishment from what is growing on the tree's bark without harming the tree and getting moisture from rain and fog

flagged tree: a stunted, most exposed tree shaped by the wind

hypoxic: oxygen-deprived; occurs in water when plankton "blooms" die and sink to the bottom, consuming oxygen as they decompose

krummholz tree: a solitary tree that looks more like a mutated woody shrub because the weather is so severe, it can grow to a height of only a few feet aboveground

nurse log: a decaying fallen tree on which forest litter lands, providing an environment for new tree seedlings that send roots down the side of the downed log to the forest floor, allowing seedlings to start growing 1–10 feet above the forest floor

old-growth forest: one that has been undisturbed for more than 200 years, containing standing snags, downed trees, a multilayered canopy, and trees of all ages

riparian area: habitat adjacent to freshwater streams and rivers

shade intolerant: a tree or plant that doesn't grow well in the shade

shade tolerant: a tree or plant that grows well in the shade of larger plants or trees

stomata: microscopic pores in tree needles or leaves that open when the rate of evaporation is equal to the tree's ability to sustain its moisture requirements by pulling water from the ground

3

ORIGINAL INHABITANTS

The first people to enter Washington State and the Lower 48 states probably came down from the north through an ice-free corridor in the interior of North America 25,000 to 40,000 years ago. They likely walked across the exposed land bridge between Siberia and Alaska and on down into the interior of North America. This land bridge, called *Beringia,* was exposed because the ice sheets and glaciers had tied up so much of the earth's water. Sea levels then were 300 feet lower than they are today.

Another possible avenue they may have used to reach Washington State was the coast. There is substantial evidence that humans were living along the coast during that time. Most of these coastal camps are now underwater, but some archaeological sites in British Columbia and southern Alaska do exist. Whichever way they arrived, they began to populate the area within 1000–2000 years after the last ice age's glaciers left.

Pre-European Contact

The Olympic Peninsula, at least its northern and eastern edges, was completely inaccessible up to about 14,000 years ago. The last ice age sent immense sheets of ice down from Canada, some up to 1-mile-thick. This ice plowed into the Peninsula, going south on its western side as far Ozette Lake or even Forks. On the east, glaciers gouged out Hood Canal and didn't stop until they were south of Olympia (see "Ice" in chapter 2, Natural History). When the ice finally receded, the climate was much drier than today; the huge trees we see today didn't begin to grow on the Peninsula until about 9000 years Before Present (BP)—prior to that, it was mostly grasslands.

It is in these grasslands that we find our oldest record of human history on the Peninsula and, perhaps, the state. During the 1970s, while digging a small pond in his backyard, a Sequim resident unearthed a mastodon skeleton. The remains of the nearly complete skeleton had butchering marks and even a spear point lodged into its ribs. The age of this find, to scientists' best guess, is more than 12,000 years BP. The mastodon site maybe the oldest known archaeological site in the state. The mastodon and much more about this find can now be seen in downtown Sequim at the Museum and Arts Center.

Very little is known of these early humans. We know that they used stone tools; some were found at the mastodon site. Other sites indicate that the basic tool kit included spear points, stone knives, and hand scrapers to remove meat from bones. These tools were manufactured from the local stone, more often basalt. These people survived exclusively off of the local plant and animal life. Evidence is far from conclusive, but it appears that these hunters did not kill this mastodon. Perhaps they stumbled upon it drowned or dead from other causes.

Other sites in the state indicate that the earliest inhabitants were opportunistic *hunter-gatherers*. They didn't make permanent camps (at least, no evidence of camps has been found), moving to follow the game and to harvest naturally growing plants. Sites have even been found high in the Olympic Mountains where the only evidence was a small fire scar and/or some stone tools and fragments from as early as 8000 years BP.

The oldest permanent campsite found on the Peninsula is on the Hoko River as it empties into the Strait of Juan de Fuca just east of Neah Bay. It dates to 3400 years old, a time when the Peninsula looked very similar to what we would have found only 200 years ago. This wasn't a year-round site but one used just in the summer and fall, during the heaviest fish runs. Halibut were caught in the strait and salmon in the river. This campsite is unique because it is a *wet site*. The almost exclusively plant-based artifacts were buried in wet mud, where they remained preserved. The artifacts were exhumed by water washing away the mud and immediately submerging them in a preservative solution.

Baskets, cordage, fishing tools, knives and clothing are among the items found. The hats that were found indicate the social stratification. Royal hats had small balls on the top, while commoners' hats did not. Both types were found at the site. The site is also important since it shows the culture lived in a maritime resource–based economy, staying put and building semi-permanent structures while abandoning the hunter-gatherer lifestyle.

As their maritime economy grew, the early Indians started to build more permanent homes. The *longhouse,* measuring 60 feet by 30 feet, was used to house up to six families (mostly extended family members and slaves). The homes were decorated inside and out with art, a recent addition to their culture. The prime example of this culture can be found on the Pacific coast, just 4 miles northwest from Ozette Lake within Olympic National Park. In late 1969, a mud slide revealed a large, buried, permanent campsite that included dozen of longhouses and was first used more than 1000 years ago. This site was buried by another mud slide 500 years BP. The Ozette site has produced thousands and thousands of artifacts, some of which can be viewed at the Makah Cultural and Research Center at Neah Bay.

The Ozette site revealed a stationary population living in long-houses, exploiting the nearby food resources and developing a formalized spirituality. The excavation revealed that all forms of seafood were eaten, along with whale. Deer and elk, possibly hunted in the nearby hills, rounded out their diet. Stone tools had been abandoned and were replaced with ones made from bone and seashells.

Longhouses were the center of activity. They were simply made from cedar planks, constructed to shed the incessant rain and secure enough to withstand the fiercest Pacific storms. Interior fires kept them warm and dried the many fish species, mostly salmon, the Indians consumed.

As the humans became more sedentary, their society became more stratified. Royalty, however they were determined, ruled the tribe. And at the bottom of the hierarchy were slaves. Typically these slaves were captured from nearby tribes during raids or were traded for. (As Europeans encountered the Indians, they captured some Indians, who lived as slaves until they were either rescued or escaped.)

European Contact

The Europeans' first known encounter with the resident population on the Peninsula was in 1775 when the Spaniard Bruno de Heceta dropped anchors off the mouth of the Quinault or Hoh River (see chapter 4, Early Explorers). The native population would never be the same, either economically or culturally.

The Indians clearly wanted what the Europeans had to offer and quickly became enamored with the new trade goods. Over the last decades of the eighteenth century, the Indians started to abandon their traditional lifestyle to concentrate on providing what the Europeans desired: initially, sea otter skins. Prior to European contact, Indians spent hours braiding whale sinew into rope. Now trading a single otter skin would generate all the manufactured rope they could ever use. Indians went from being a totally self-sufficient society to one that depended upon continued trade with the newcomers in a matter of just a few generations.

Before the Revolutionary War, British held to a policy that everything west of the Alleghenies was Indian Territory and that immigration from the east to the west was outlawed. This was the first formal Indian policy in the New World. Everyone "knew" that Indians were inferior, mostly because they weren't Christians, and that their land was for the taking. Holding title to property was completely unknown to the natives. On the Northwest Coast, they did have favorite hunting and fishing sites that were handed down from family to family; however, if the fish were not running, anyone could "trespass."

Each step the Europeans took to the West brought into focus the *"Indian problem."* Policy makers kept wanting to push the Indians west onto lands that the new Americans did not want. Sequestering the Indians onto reservations was supposed to buy time to allow the native peoples to learn the ways of the Europeans and eventually assimilate into the whole society by becoming farmers and Christians. A bigger benefit of the reservation system was to impose European property title laws to the land that the Indians once considered theirs. It was an extension of the policy of either "civilization or extermination."

In just over four generations, the indigenous people went from masters of their domain to being forced upon the numerous reservations that were established in the state in 1856 and 1857. When Washington State was finally recognized as a U.S. territory in 1846, European settlers began to enter the state in greater numbers (see chapter 5, The 19th

Century). Alongside the new settlers was Isaac Stevens, the new territorial governor known as the Great Negotiator. By 1856, all the Peninsula Indians had their orders to move to the new reservations in a series of four treaties.

The Indians on the Peninsula were small autonomous groups of extended family units. They spoke the language of larger groups but had virtually no political system that allowed for one individual to speak for another. Complicating the whole treaty process was the many languages spoken. Not a single American spoke any of the languages of the Peninsula. The Americans spoke English, which was translated to *Chinook Jargon,* the local trade language, then translated into native languages, sometimes with other languages in between. The Chinook Jargon had only 500 words, so the intent or language of these treaties was barely understandable, if at all, to the tribal members.

Stevens and his party weren't really negotiating a treaty as much as dictating one. He reportedly (Hult 1954) opened up talks with these words:

"My children, you call me your father. I, too, have a father who is your Great Father. That Great Father has sent me today to pay for your lands, to provide for your children, to see that you are fed, and that you are cared for. Your Great Father wants you to be happy, to be friends to each other. The Great Father wants you and the whites to be friends; he wants you to have a house of your own, to learn to use tools, and also to have a doctor. Now these things shall be written down in a paper; that paper shall be read to you. If the paper is good, you sign it and I will sign it."

In a matter of a year, Stevens had completed four treaties that encompassed all the tribes of the Peninsula except those of the Chehalis River and Grays Harbor:

- Treaty of Medicine Creek, 1854: Squaxin Island and other south Puget Sound tribes

- Treaty of Point No Point, 1855: Skokomish, Elwha, and Klallam tribes
- Treaty of Neah Bay, 1855: Makah Tribe
- Quinault River Treaty, or Treaty of Olympia, 1855: Quinault, Queets, Hoh, and Quileute tribes

Isaac Stevens would go on to fight in the Civil War. He died a brigader general in 1862 fighting Stonewall Jackson in Virginia. He has two counties named for him: Stevens County in Washington is just north of Spokane; Stevens County in Minnesota is in the west-central part of that state. Also his namesakes are Fort Stevens, Washington, D.C.; Fort Stevens in Oregon; Lake Stevens (just northeast of Seattle); and Stevensville, Montana.

European diseases did more to subdue the Indians than any other cause during the nineteenth century. Historians have speculated that it was Heceta in 1775 who first brought smallpox to the Peninsula. Animals transferred smallpox to humans thousands of years ago when humans started to domesticate animals in the Middle East. Long-term contact with animals gave Europeans more resistance to the disease; American Indians had no resistance. Each successive wave of smallpox, measles, influenza, and other European diseases succeeded in reducing the native populations by up to 85 percent by 1900. In comparison, the Black Plague killed up to one-third of the European population. Prior to European contact, this maritime resource–rich area allowed the Peninsula's original inhabitants to achieve the highest population density of Indians in the Americas outside of central Mexico (Mann 2005).

The Peninsula Tribes

The **Squaxin Island Tribe,** the first to sign a treaty, is known as the People of the Water and live in south Puget Sound. The Squaxin Island

Squaxin Island Tribe's Museum Library and Research Center.

Tribe was closely connected to the tribes to the east, the Puyallup and the Nisqually, and spoke a very similar language. All three tribes signed the same Medicine Creek Treaty, near current-day Nisqually National Wildlife Refuge. At the time of the treaty, the Squaxin Island Tribe comprised all the numerous family groups in the shellfish-rich inlets from Olympia to Shelton. Their original reservation was on Squaxin Island, due east from Shelton. The island, which has no freshwater sources, has been virtually abandoned since the 1950s.

Over time the tribe has migrated to the town site of Kamilche, on the Peninsula southwest of Squaxin Island 15 miles north of Olympia. There they have rebuilt their community, along with an outstanding museum, Squaxin Island Tribe's Museum Library and Research Center. Their children once went to the Puyallup Indian Boarding School but are now taught in nearby public schools. The tribe's Little Creek Casino is the third-largest employer in Mason County.

The numerous tribes and groups of the Hood Canal area were the Twana (now called the **Skokomish**). Their reservation site is at the mouth of the Skokomish River where it empties into Hood Canal. Also known as the Big River People, they signed the Point No Point Treaty in 1855.

This tribe has suffered more than its share of indignities. Where the Skokomish River empties into Hood Canal, a large wetland delta is formed. In 1900 an industrialist from Tacoma purchased the delta property and started to dike and drain it. This property had been the historic source of the *sweetgrass* that the tribal members used for their renowned baskets. The tribe was also restricted from its normal shell-fish-gathering locations by the state of Washington, which claimed jurisdiction of all the tidelands. In the late 1920s, the City of Tacoma built two dams downstream from Lake Cushman on the North Fork of the Skokomish River, dramatically reducing the salmon runs. In 1960 the state took prime waterfront acreage and a historic Indian graveyard to create Potlatch State Park, designated an important birding area (IBA). Most of these issues were resolved when the tribe was awarded a cash settlement in 1965 and with the Boldt Decision of 1974 (see below).

The second tribe to sign the Point No Point Treaty with the Skokomish was the **Klallam** or **S'Klallam Indians.** Their historic home stretched from the northern reaches of Hood Canal west to Clallam Bay along the Strait of Juan de Fuca. They lived in as many as thirty villages, many of them seasonal, on both sides of the Strait. The treaty required that they move onto the reservation on the Skokomish River with the Skokomish Tribe; however, very few of them did.

A large group lived on a bay at Port Gamble. When a lumber company started operations there in the 1860s, the owners offered to provide the building materials for a modest village across the bay at Point Julia. It was not until the 1930s that the federal government formally recognized this group as an individual tribe. Eventually, the U.S. government purchased land on the bluff overlooking Point Julia for the Port Gamble Indian Reservation.

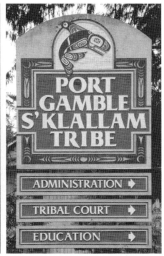

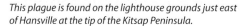

This plaque is found on the lighthouse grounds just east of Hansville at the tip of the Kitsap Peninsula.

The reservation is across the bay from Port Gamble and north of Kingston

The Jamestown S'Klallam, the smallest of the three Klallam groups, also did not move to the new reservation at the Skokomish. Within a couple of decades, the group had purchased about 200 acres north of Sequim and developed their community there. They were never formally recognized as a tribe and were increasingly not allowed to hunt and gather in their usual locations. In 1974 the tribe petitioned the federal government and won recognition, along with a modest land parcel at the southern edge of Discovery Bay for a reservation. They now have more than 1000 acres in the area that is either part of their reservation or held in trust by them.

The **Lower Elwha Klallam Tribe** also did not proceed to the Skokomish reservation after signing the Point No Point Treaty in 1855. They simply went back to where they had always lived and did what they had always done. They too felt the pressure of increased homesteading and Washington State's requirement that only U.S. citizens could fish. It was not until 1965 that the federal government finally created the Lower Elwha Indian Reservation, located at the mouth of the Elwha River, west of Port Angeles.

The Jamestown S'Klallam Tribe community center

Five miles east of the reservation, Ediz Hook creates the best harbor on the Strait of Juan de Fuca. Currently the harbor is rimmed with downtown Port Angeles, a Coast Guard station, an enormous paper mill, a marina, a large shipping facility, and perhaps the site of the

largest Indian graveyard in the country. Recent archaeological evidence points to a continuous human presence on the bay that spans 2700 years. Ancient bones and graves were discovered every time someone built anything at or near the base of Ediz Hook, but development never stopped. When a mill was built next door to the site in 1920, a headline in the local paper read "Squatters and Indian Bones Bother Builders" (Mapes 2005).

In 2004 the state of Washington picked vacant land right at the base of Ediz Hook to construct a dry dock. The Hood Canal Bridge needed a major repair and the dry dock was to be the construction site for the new bridge pieces. Almost immediately after construction started, Indian artifacts and human remains were found. It became clear as construction proceeded that something extraordinary was lying underfoot. Construction was halted, and archaeologists and Lower Elwha Klallam Indians were brought in to determine the extent of the ancient site.

Tse-whit-zen, as the site is called, yielded more than 330 graves with only an estimated 5 percent of the total site excavated. Thousands and thousands of artifacts were found and are currently being cataloged. Construction was permanently halted, and Washington State has abandoned the site. It eventually cost the state more than $60 million. The site today looks like the abandoned construction site that it is. All the bodies have been reburied at the site. All the artifacts discovered are waiting to be housed in the planned museum and cultural center in or near Port Angeles.

Some of the graves and their occupants point to a time of much stress and hardship. Mass graves were found. One grave had a couple embracing. Another had a mother and child. These unexpected finds point to a horrific time in the Klallam Tribe's history: the epidemics brought by the Europeans. The waves of disease were so devastating that often few tribal members were available to bury all the dead, hence the mass graves. Even Lewis and Clark note in their journals the empty village sites along the Columbia River.

At the northwesternmost tip of the United States lies the **Makah Indian** Reservation, home of the People Who Live Near the Rocks and Seagulls. Historically, the tribe was more a Canadian tribe than an American one. They are more closely related linguistically with the tribes from Vancouver Island and farther north than from any on the Peninsula. Their historic maritime homeland stretched from Ozette on the coast to Hoko River east along the Strait and on Vancouver Island. Whaling was a large part of their culture.

John Meares was the first European to reach the Makah, in 1788 (see chapter 4, Early Explorers). There was no trading conducted but

This is the location of the ill-fated Spanish fort

Meares named Tatoosh Island, just off the coast, after one of the Makah chiefs. In 1790 the Spaniards attempted to claim the cape by building a fort, but they abandoned it after four months. In 1855 the Makah Tribe signed the Neah Bay Treaty, giving up more than one-quarter of a million acres in exchange for 30,000 acres and a promised $30,000 per year for twenty years. It didn't help the Makah's negotiating position that one-half of the tribe had been wiped out by the smallpox epidemic two years earlier. The Ozette beach site wasn't added to the reservation until the mud slide revealed it (see earlier in this chapter). Neah Bay remained completely isolated until a road was built from Port Angeles during the 1930s.

A sentence in the Neah Bay Treaty that isn't included in other U.S. treaties guarantees the Makah the right to hunt whales. "The right of taking fish and of whaling or sealing at usual and accustomed grounds and stations is further secured to said Indians in common with all citizens of the United States." Whale hunting has always been a huge cultural event for the Makahs. Their home was adjacent to the migratory routes of both gray and humpback whales. Each whale that was killed provided months of sustenance to the whole tribe. Whaling was abandoned in the 1920s by the Peninsula tribes when whale populations plummeted due to worldwide commercial overhunting. In the latter part of the twentieth century, whale hunting has been severely restricted internationally.

The Makah cutting up a whale in 1910. Photography by Asahel Curtis.

In the late 1990s, feeling a strong cultural urge, the Makahs decided to attempt whaling after a seventy-year hiatus and began the long process of obtaining permits from the U.S. government and the International Whaling Commission, fighting court battles to resume its treaty rights.

After obtaining permission, the Makah killed a whale in May 1999 amid a flotilla of boats full of protesters, media, and the U.S. Coast Guard. The hunt was carried out using old techniques, including canoes and harpoons, and new techniques, designed to minimize the whale's suffering and ensure success. Once the whale was towed to shore, it was cut up on the beach using traditional tools and techniques and the meat was distributed to the tribal members. It was the first time the Makah had tasted whale meat in generations. Though the Makah still have the right to hunt whales in the future, as of this writing, only the one has been harvested.

South of Cape Flattery and west of Forks lies the Quileute Indian Reservation. This tribe gave up more than 800,000 acres of wilderness for a square-mile reservation at the mouth of the Quillayute River and future cash payments and other benefits. They signed the Treaty of Olympia in 1855 with the Quinaults, the Queets and the Hoh. The treaty required that all Indians on the coast move south to the Quinault Reservation. Because of the Quileute Tribe's lack of relationship to the Quinaults, the tribal members just remained where they were. There was little incentive to push them to the new reservation.

The Quileutes were an isolated people. Their language, which is not spoken by any other tribes, is one of only five in the world that lacks the "m" or "n" sounds. They were once related to the Chimakums from an area south of Port Townsend but the Chimakums were wiped out by intertribal warfare. The tribe to the south, the Hoh, is closely related to the Queets and Quinaults. The Makahs to the north speak the same language as tribes from Vancouver Island across the Strait.

At the time of the treaty, Native Americans were not allowed to own property (nor did it occur to them that they should want to), and a local settler, Dan Pullen, tried to develop his own homestead right next to and on top of the Quileute village in La Push. Pullen built himself a small business of logging and fur trading, along with a stately Victorian home in the area. In 1889, while all in the village left to pick hops, someone, most likely the hot-tempered Pullen, burned down their whole village, destroying all the historic ceremonial artifacts. When the Quileutes returned, Pullen was stringing barbed wire around the site as if to claim it.

While Pullen was never charged with a crime, the issue became moot when President Harrison, by executive order in the same year, granted the Quileutes their own 1-square-mile reservation right over their historic village site. Pullen lost his land claims after ten years of litigation and was evicted from the reservation. He was never prosecuted for the arson. (After divorcing Pullen, Harriet Pullen became somewhat notorious herself: during the Klondike Gold Rush, she owned the bar that was the headquarters of Soapy Smith's gang, Skagway's most villainous criminals.)

James Island and others guard the mouth of the Quillayute River on the Quileute Reservation. It is 16 miles west of Forks.

One of the biggest concerns for all the four tribes on the coast is the potential damage from an earthquake and subsequent tsunami. All the reservations are located on low-lying land totally exposed to the Pacific and the Cascadia subduction zone (see "Plate Tectonics" in chapter 1, Geology). This earthquake area is historically one of the most dangerous in the world since it produces *megathrust earthquakes,* which measure 8 or 9 on the Richter scale. A megathrust earthquake and tsunami would literally wipe the reservations off the map. This is the same magnitude of earthquake that happened in Japan in March 2011.

The Quileute, and to a lesser degree the Hoh, are hemmed in by Olympic National Park to the east and are accessed by single-lane roads onto their reservations. The Makah and Quinault have similar problems, as their village sites are almost at sea level. However, these latter two tribes have land that would allow them to move their villages to higher ground if they could generate the resources to do so. The Quileute and

Hoh have no place to go. Federal legislation was introduced in 2011 that allows the Quileute to swap some of their low-lying land with the park for nearby property that isn't so exposed to the dangers.

The **Hoh Tribe,** just 15 miles south of the Quileute Tribe, has recently secured an additional 460 acres on higher ground to the east of their original 443 acres. The original reservation is right at the mouth of the Hoh River. In addition to facing a tsunami threat, the Hoh Tribe's reservation is slowly being washed away by the Hoh River. The river is flooding more often than in the past due to human activity, primarily logging, upriver.

The Hoh tribal members are related by language to the Quinaults and Queets to the south. The Hoh also remained at their historic campsite after signing the Quinault Treaty of 1855. In 1893 President Cleveland formally recognized them as a separate tribe and awarded them their current reservation site.

Quinault men netting & spear fishing at low tide, mouth of the Quinault River, Washington, in drawing made 1886. Created by Sarah Willoughby.

The **Quinaults** were the first Indians encountered by Europeans and the first to draw European blood (see chapter 4, Early Explorers). The Quinaults signed the Quinault River Treaty (aka the Treaty of Olympia) in 1855 along with the Queets, Hoh and Quileutes. The Quinaults gave up 1.2 million acres by signing the treaty (Wray 2002). The Quinault Reservation, at 208,000 acres, is larger than all the other Peninsula reservations combined. The triangle-shaped reservation has a base of 23 miles of unspoiled Pacific coastline and reaches a point at Lake Quinault, which is also part of the reservation.

Three villages are associated with the Quinault Tribe. Queets, which lies at the northern boundary just outside of the reservation, is a small hamlet on the Queets River. Amanda Park is right at the western edge of Lake Quinault. Both communities are on US Highway 101. Taholah is on the coast at the mouth of the Quinault River, at the end of the road just north of Moclips. It is the hub for the tribe, with a population of about 1000. They have diversified from a fishing and forestry economy with their large casino just north of Ocean Shores.

The southernmost tribe on the Peninsula is the **Chehalis.** This group spoke Salish, the most popular language in the Puget Sound (Salish Sea) area. They were made up of the Upper Chehalis and Lower Chehalis. These main tribes were further divided into the Cowlitz, Copalis, Satsop, Shoalwater, and Wynooche groups. The tribes met with Governor Stevens in 1855 in Cosmopolis, south of Aberdeen, but failed to reach agreement when Stevens abandoned the talks, leaving the Chehalis tribes without any reservation. Subsequent negotiations with the federal government led to a 1900-acre parcel in Oakdale, located halfway between Elma and Centralia on the Chehalis River.

Tribes of the Olympic Peninsula

Tribe	Nickname	Location	Language	Connections	Treaty
Squaxin Island Tribe	People of the Water	south Puget Sound near Kamilche	Lushootseed, a dialect of Salish	closely connected to Puyallups and Nisquallys	Medicine Creek Treaty
Skokomish Tribe	Big River People	Hood Canal area at mouth of Skokomish River	Twana, a dialiect of Salish	formerly known as the Twana	Point No Point Treaty
Klallam or S'Klallam Tribe		historically, northern reaches of Hood Canal west to Clallam Bay along Strait of Juan de Fuca in thirty seasonal villages on both sides of the strait	A dialiect of Salish	three groups—Port Gamble S'Klallams (now at Point Julia), Jamestown S'Klallams north of Sequim at southern edge of Discovery Bay, Lower Elwha Klallams at mouth of Elwha River west of Port Angeles	Point No Point Treaty
Makah Tribe	People Who Live Near the Rocks and Seagulls	historic maritime homeland from Ozette to Hoko River east along Strait of Juan de Fuca and on Vancouver Island	more closely related linguistically with tribes from Vancouver Island and farther north	historically more a Canadian tribe than American	Neah Bay Treaty
Quileute Tribe		mouth of Quillayute River	language not spoken by any other tribes, one of only five in the world that lacks the "m" or "n" sounds	once related to Chimakums south of Port Townsend	Quinault River Treaty (aka Treaty of Olympia)
Hoh Tribe		mouth of Hoh River	related by language to Quinaults and Queets		Quinault Treaty (aka Treaty of Olympia)
Quinault Tribe		23 miles of Pacific coastline and Lake Quinault—three villages include Queets, Amanda Park, and Taholah	A combination of Chimakuan (Quileute, Hoh), Chinookan (Chinook groups), and Salish		Quinault River Treaty (aka Treaty of Olympia)
Chehalis Tribes		Oakdale on Chehalis River	Salish	Upper Chehalis and Lower Chehalis tribes divided into Cowlitz, Copalis, Satsop, Shoalwater, and Wynooche groups	no treaty

Treaty Fishing Heritage and the Boldt Decision

All the treaties signed by Governor Stevens contained this phrase: "The right of taking fish, at all usual and accustomed grounds and stations, is further secured to said Indians in common with all citizens of the Territory."

Over the decades since the treaties were signed, Indian fishery rights were slowly withdrawn by state authorities. As fisheries began to diminish due to overharvesting and bad fishery management, Indians were frequently blamed.

During the 1960s and early 1970s, Indians were constantly harassed by state officials, until the U.S. government stepped in and sued the state of Washington. The legal question was this: Could the state of Washington regulate the fishing practices of Indians who signed treaties with the U.S. government?

Until 1974 Washington State authorities increasingly restricted the size of the Indian salmon catch. In 1974 U.S. District Court Judge George Boldt ruled on the case *United States v. Washington,* creating the famous Boldt Decision: "By dictionary definition and as intended and used in the Indian treaties and in this decision, 'in common with' means sharing equally the opportunity to take fish . . . therefore, nontreaty fishermen shall have the opportunity to take up to 50 percent of the harvestable number of fish . . . and treaty right fishermen shall have the opportunity to take up to the same percentage."

This ruling has since been reaffirmed by the U.S. Supreme Court and applied to other treaties and resources. The decision not only handed the Indians 50 percent of the salmon harvest, but required that they have an equal seat at the table in the management of all fisheries. The Boldt Decision has been characterized as one of the most important Indian law rulings ever made and continues to impact Native Americans not only on the Peninsula but across America.

Glossary: Original Inhabitants

Beringia: exposed land bridge between Siberia and Alaska that is thought to have existed 25,000–40,000 years ago

Boldt Decision: ruling by U.S. District Court Judge George Boldt in 1974 in *United States v. Washington* that gave Indians 50 percent of the salmon harvest and an equal voice in fisheries management; one of the most important Indian law rulings ever made; continues to impact Native Americans across America

Chinook Jargon: local trade language with only 500 words

hunter-gatherers: early indigenous people who didn't make permanent camps, moving to follow game and to harvest naturally growing plants

longhouse: simple structures 60 feet by 30 feet, made from cedar planks, housing up to six families (extended family members and slaves); decorated inside and out with art; center of activity with interior fires for warmth and drying fish

megathrust earthquakes: measure 8 or 9 on the Richter scale

sweetgrass: native plant used by Skokomish tribal members for making renowned baskets

Tse-whit-zen: ancient Klallam Indian site at base of Ediz Hook discovered in 2004 during Hood Canal Bridge construction; contained thousands of Indian artifacts and human remains in more than 330 graves (including mass graves), with only an estimated 5 percent of total site excavated; all bodies have been reburied at the site; artifacts will be housed in a museum and cultural center planned near Port Angeles

wet site: archaeological site where artifacts were buried in wet mud, which preserved them

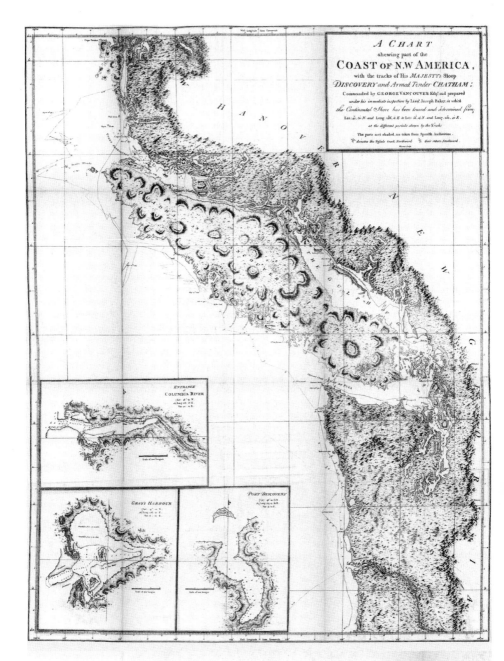

A CHART
shewing part of the
COAST of N.W. AMERICA,
with the tracks of His *MAJESTY's* Sloop
DISCOVERY and Armed Tender CHATHAM;
Commanded by GEORGE VANCOUVER Esq.' and prepared
under his immediate inspection by Lieut. Joseph Baker, in which
the Continental Shore has been traced and determined from
Lat: 45. 30 N. and Long 236. 12 E. to Lat: 52. 15 N. and Long. 232. 40 E.
at the different periods shewn by the Tracks.
The parts not shaded, are taken from Spanish Authorities.
denotes the Vessels track Northward   their return Southward.

ENTRANCE
of
COLUMBIA RIVER

GRAYS HARBOUR

PORT DISCOVERY

London: Published May 1.st 1798. by J. Edwards Pall Mall & G. Robinson Paternoster Row.

Certified to be a Photozincographic copy of "A Chart shewing part of the Coast of N.W. America, with the tracks of
His Majestys Sloop Discovery and Armed Tender Chatham: Commanded by George Vancouver Esq.r and prepared under
his immediate inspection by Lieut. Joseph Baker, in which the Continental Shore has been traced and determined
from Lat: 45. 30 N. and Long 236. 12 E. to Lat: 52. 15 N. and Long. 232. 40 E. at the different periods shewn by the Tracks."
Engraved by Warner _ Published at London May 1st 1798. by J. Edwards Pall Mall & G. Robinson Paternoster Row.

Ordnance Survey Office, Southampton.

EARLY EXPLORERS

Shouldn't the Strait of Juan de Fuca be called the Drake Strait? How about Strait of Juan Perez? Or the Strait of Anian? Or even the Strait of Hwui Shan? There are hundreds of places in the Pacific Northwest named after the famed mariner Juan de Fuca, from highways to schools and lodging. But there isn't much evidence that de Fuca deserves so much fame or that he ever made it north of the Mexico-California border.

Early explorations of the Pacific Northwest by Europeans were for two purposes. The first was finding the fabled Strait of Anian, also known as the Northwest Passage. The Northwest Passage was to mariners and merchants the Holy Grail of sailing routes. It was supposed to save months of sea travel when sailing from Europe to Asia by allowing ships to avoid going around the southern tip of South America. By the end of the sixteenth century, there existed numerous accounts of voyages through the Northwest Passage. We know now the stories were all fictional and that the Northwest Passage was invented by Italian cartographer Giacomo Gastaldi in about 1562.

The second purpose for exploring the Pacific Northwest was for conquest. Europeans wanted to stick their national flag into the ground and claim North America for themselves. The Europeans didn't know

Originally published in 1798

what they were claiming but they knew that they wanted it all. The Spanish were fully in control of Mexico and California and were looking to push north. The British wanted sea-to-sea control from the east coast of North America to the west. The Russians were looking to expand their toehold in Alaska south to California. It was all supposed to have been decided by Pope Alexander VI, a Spanish pontiff sitting in the Vatican, who declared the Pacific Ocean belonged to Spain in 1493. Neither the British nor the Russians were too keen to follow the Vatican's dictate on this issue (or many other issues at the time).

The first nonnative to see the Pacific Northwest and America might have been Hwui Shan, an Afghani Buddhist missionary under the instructions of the Emperor of China. Shan returned from his voyage to the Land of Fusang in 499 after forty years of travel. He probably rode the Japanese Current, which provides a conveyer belt from China and the Far East up to Alaska and down the North American coast. His journals described the people of the Aleutians and his stay in Mexico, or the Land of Fusang. *Fusang* is Chinese for "splendid" or "wonderful" and maybe Mexico was that for him. Historians are not completely dismissive of his story. Unfortunately, he was way ahead of his time or else we would all be speaking Chinese instead of English and Spanish.

The Sixteenth Century: The Spanish and the English

The name Anian came from the Chinese province Ania identified by Marco Polo. Starting in the 1500s the earliest mapmakers and explorers were convinced that California was an island and that Baja California was the southern entrance to the famed strait. Some maps indicated the Strait of Anian was the sea that separated Alaska from Asia through what is now known as Bering Strait. It didn't matter that no one had sailed through Bering Strait until Captain Cook in 1778.

During the sixteenth century, the English and the Spanish were not on the best of terms. Queen Elizabeth of England possibly sent the pirate Sir Francis Drake on a secret mission in 1579 to see if he could find the Strait of Anian. Drake came around the Strait of Magellan and immediately started to plunder his way up the west coast of the Americas. Somewhere in California he disappeared, only to reappear in the East Indies on his way home for queen and country. At home he received the appropriate accolades for being the first sea captain to circumnavigate the world, along with bringing lots of goodies home for her royal highness.

But what did he do between California and the East Indies? He might have discovered what he called New Albion, north of California (Bawlf 2004). Spain and England were almost at war, and the English government didn't want to publicize Drake's exploits for fear of angering the Spanish or indicating that he was on a state-sponsored voyage. All of his official logs and maps were destroyed in the seventeenth century, so his true exploits were never discerned until recently.

Historical discoveries now indicate that Drake was the first to discover the Strait of Juan de Fuca and to sail up the passage between British Columbia and Vancouver Island and the Queen Charlotte Islands, as far north as 57 degrees latitude in Alaska, in what we now call the Inland Passage. Before turning south again, one of his ships was to proceed north into the Strait of Anian (now known as Chatham Strait) and then sail eastward to England. Unfortunately, that waterway ends at Skagway, Alaska. The ship was never seen again though its sailors might have been. Soon after, the name of New Albion started to appear in maps produced in Europe.

In 1590 in Venice, a down-and-out English merchant and promoter, Michael Lok, met a down-and-out Greek mariner, Apostolos Valerianos. Lok was looking to break into the big time, and Valerianos had something big. Valerianos, aka Juan de Fuca, told Lok that he knew where the Strait of Anian was, had been there, and was willing to go back. All it would take was lots of cash delivered to Mr. de Fuca. Lok immediately set to work contacting all of his acquaintances at the English royal court, sure that he would be able to hire Juan de Fuca and make both of them rich. Alas, it wasn't to be. The English were not that interested in the strait at that moment, and besides, they knew the strait was blocked by ice on the eastern end. Also, de Fuca's location of the strait was too different from Drake's to be considered believable.

Juan de Fuca's story is dubious at best. He mentions that at 47 degrees north latitude, there existed a passageway 100 miles wide. The current Strait of Juan de Fuca is only 14 miles wide at its entrance, which is at 49 degrees north latitude. De Fuca claimed that upon his return from his discovery voyage, he petitioned in person the Mexican viceroy and then the King of Spain in Madrid for compensation. No records exist of his appearances. In fact, there are no Spanish records that he ever existed. He claimed he sailed into the strait for twenty days, reached the North Sea, did his duty, and returned back to Mexico. One day of sailing through the current strait would have bumped him into one of the many islands of Puget Sound. In fact, there is no way to go twenty days anywhere once you enter the strait without running aground.

It gets even more interesting when you compare de Fuca's story with Drake's. They almost mirror each other. It appears that one of Drake's men was captured by the Spanish and interrogated. De Fuca might have stolen or had access to the map that the prisoner created for his captors.

The Eighteenth Century: The Spanish, the Russians, and the English

Two hundred years later, the Spanish attempted to solidify their claim to the Pacific Northwest from their outposts in Mexico. The Spanish knew that the Russians were on the move, driven by sea otter furs and imperialism. Vitus Bering sailed twice into the Bering Sea around 1740 from Kamchatka, discovering the Aleutians and southern Alaska.

His second in command had sailed as far south as the Alaskan Panhandle. Also the British had eyes on the West Coast as an extension of their colonialism on the East Coast of North America.

Juan Perez was settled upon as next in line to make the Spanish claim to the Pacific. His outpost at San Blas on the Mexican coast was as far away from Spain as could be. He did reach the northern tip of the Queen Charlotte Islands at 54 degrees, 40 minutes north latitude, about 50 percent up the length of British Columbia, near the Alaskan border in 1774. This is somewhat amazing, since he wasn't that competent as a mariner. He then retreated south to Nootka Sound on Vancouver Island, where he enjoyed peaceful relations with the natives. (Nootka Sound was to become the unofficial capital of the Pacific Northwest for about twenty years.)

Perez was the first European to note Mount Olympus on the Peninsula, which he named Cerro Nevada de Santa Rosalia ("Snowy Peak of St. Rosalia"). He was also the first to note the location of the Strait of Juan de Fuca. The bad news was that Perez didn't do all the appropriate rituals for Spain to claim the Northwest for itself. You can't claim the Pacific Northwest as property of the King of Spain unless you actually get out of your boat and stick your flag in the beach. While very brave, Perez was a mediocre mariner, cartographer, and navigator. He was to die at sea the next year returning from another northern expedition. The good news was that Nootka natives ended up with two silver spoons stolen or traded from Perez, which Captain James Cook would notice four years hence.

Within six months of his arrival, Perez was off north again as second in command to Bruno de Heceta, a more experienced sea captain. They sailed with two other smaller vessels, one of which was captained by Juan Francisco de la Bodega y Quadra. On July 11, 1775, they came to shore at Cape Elizabeth just north of the Quinault River in what is now Washington State. After peaceful trading had gone on for three

Looking north from Point Grenville Point towards Cape Elizabeth

days, Heceta's men finally landed a small boat on the shore. Hundreds of Quinault, hiding in the trees, came forward and killed all seven of the landing party, then hacked the small boat to pieces. Heceta or Bodega y Quadra would later name this spot Point of the Martyrs. It was later renamed Cape Elizabeth. (Point Grenville is south of the Quinault River and Cape Elizabeth is north. Historians are unsure which of these promontories is the original Point of Martyrs.) Credit is given to Heceta as the first to map Washington's coast. And this is the first time any European stepped foot on the Olympic Peninsula and in Washington State.

Besides the minor bit of trading that Heceta did on the Washington coast, he gave the natives the "gift" that decimated them: smallpox. Smallpox would eventually kill up to 30 percent of the natives on the coast within a generation.

On July 29, Bodega y Quadra and Heceta parted company. The original mission was to go to 65 degrees north latitude, find the Russians and take formal possessions of the land. Bodega y Quadra took his 37-foot craft north. Heceta, suffering the Quinault defeat and scurvy onboard, turned south, where he was the first European to note and name the Columbia River, naming it Bahía de la Asunción. Entering the river is difficult even using modern vessels and technology, and Heceta, with his sick crew, could only name the river as they passed by its mouth.

Bodega y Quadra reached 59 degrees north latitude, near the top of the Alaskan Panhandle, on August 15. Finding no Russians, he took possession of all he saw and began his trip south. He finally made it to Monterey forty-five days later and had to be carried off his boat.

Virtually all mariners of this time suffered from scurvy. What they didn't know was that it was caused by lack of vitamin C, which is found in fresh fruits, vegetables, and some meats. Vitus Bering lost his life and almost his whole crew because of it. Perez died from it; Heceta and Bodega y Quadra almost did. The Spanish should have read Captain Cook's logs. Cook figured it out. Though he thought that cleanliness and a diet of sauerkraut was part of the answer, he was fanatical in providing fresh food for his sailors. As perhaps the most accomplished explorer of all time, he roamed the Pacific for years without losing anyone to scurvy.

In 1778, three years after Heceta, James Cook sailed from Hawaii (having left England a few days after the Declaration of Independence was signed in Philadelphia) in search of the fabled Northwest Passage and was on the Washington coast. Arriving at the mouth of the Strait of Juan de Fuca, he wrote in his log "a small opening which flattered us with the hopes of finding an harbour" and named it Cape Flattery, the oldest nonnative name on Washington maps.

What Cook didn't notice was that he was at the entrance to the Strait of Juan de Fuca. He wasn't expecting to find it since he thought that Juan de Fuca's claim was bogus. (The famed navigator had also sailed right by the mouth of the Columbia River.) Cook thought that Cape Flattery was at the mouth of a large bay. He never stepped foot in Washington State and proceeded north to Nootka Sound. It was here that he saw some of the natives wearing silver spoons. Do you remember the silver spoons from Juan Perez? Cook mentions these spoons in his log, and they helped establish Spanish claims to the Pacific Northwest. Cook went on to explore and map Alaska and sailed through the Bering Strait to 70 degrees north latitude, the farthest north any European had yet gone in the Pacific.

It was also at Nootka Sound that Cook traded for a sea otter fur. This would become the final nail in the small animal's coffin. Prior to Cook's discovery, the Russians had the sea otter fur trade all to themselves. After Cook's voyage, the whole world took note. Europeans started coming more often, not for exploration but for the fur trade. Within a few short decades, the sea otter was almost completely wiped out, along with many other sea mammals.

Charles Barkley, a British fur trader, "rediscovered" the Strait of Juan de Fuca in 1787 and noted it on his map, thus sealing de Fuca's posterity. Barkley's wife accompanied him on that trip and became the first European female to visit the coast.

John Meares, another British fur trader, sailed through the region in 1788 and gave the peak the Spanish called Cerro Nevada de Santa Rosalia its name that stuck: Mount Olympus. He also named Tatoosh Island situated off of Cape Flattery after the local Makah chief. Having purchased some land in Nootka Sound on Vancouver Island from the natives, he built a small outpost and the first European ship in the Pacific Northwest.

Unfortunately, when the Spanish arrived again in 1789, they seized all of Meares's assets. This led to the Nootka Crisis, which brought the ownership question of the Pacific Northwest to a head. Remember Pope Alexander VI whose papal bull declared the entire Pacific Ocean for Spain? Unfortunately, the British were Protestant and the Russians were Orthodox Christians, neither of which was inclined to follow the Vatican's rule. And now everyone had a "claim" to the area. The Russians were not in much of a position to make noise but the English and the Spanish were looking for reasons to go to war.

Fortunately, cooler heads prevailed. The Spanish sent Bodega y Quadra and the British sent George Vancouver to meet at Nootka Sound to negotiate the handing over of Spanish holdings at Nootka Sound as part of the larger Nootka Convention signed in 1794. Because of their military weakness, sea otter price declines and the lack of a Northwest Passage, the Spanish signed away their exclusive ownership. The Northwest was to become a free trade area where any nation could develop settlements. Vancouver and Bodega y Quadra established a very cordial relationship and decided to name the island Quadra and Vancouver Island. Very few of the Spanish names for landmarks remain in the present day: unfortunately, the Spanish lost out again, and Quadra was eventually dropped from the island's name. The most prominent Spanish names that have persisted nearby are Port Angeles, Rosario Strait in the San Juans, and Fidalgo Island near Anacortes.

The Spanish were not idle during this time, sending Manuel Quimper in 1790 to further explore the strait and Puget Sound. He performed the "necessary" acts of possession, completely mapped the strait for the first time, and made it all the way to Admiralty Inlet, which leads south into Puget Sound. When Quimper stopped at the Elwha River and Dungeness Spit, he was the first European that the S'Klallam Tribe had ever seen. (The peninsula between Discovery Bay and Puget Sound is named after Captain Quimper.)

Another Spaniard, Francisco de Eliza y Reventa, moved into the area north of the San Juan Islands in 1791, discovering the Strait of Georgia and Rosario Strait and exploring the area around the future city of Vancouver, British Columbia. Eliza y Reventa's map eventually made it into

American hands, which helped the Americans lay claim to the places he saw with the upcoming Transcontinental Treaty of 1819. Finally, in 1792, two more Spaniards were the first to circumnavigate Vancouver Island.

The Eighteenth Century: The English and the Americans

George Vancouver entered the waters off of the state of Washington in 1792. He was sent there to negotiate the final details of the Nootka Convention with Bodega y Quadra. He was also charged with mapping the Northwest all the way to 60 degrees north latitude at the site of Cook Inlet, in Alaska. The commander of the *HMS Discovery* and *HMS Chatham* was only thirty-four years old but already an old salt at Northwest exploring. He was a midshipman with James Cook fourteen years earlier when Cook made it through the Bering Strait.

One of the first things Vancouver did was sail right past the mouth of the Columbia River. Noticing the change in sea cover and even identifying Cape Disappointment, he wrote, "Not considering this opening worthy of more attention." Days later, he met up with Robert Gray, an American trader, who told Vancouver about the river. Thirteen days later Gray would sail his ship, the *Columbia Rediviva,* through the dangerous shoals into what is now called the Columbia River.

Gray was the first American sea captain to circumnavigate the globe. (The first American was John Ledyard, sailing with James Cook.) On May 7, Gray entered Bulfinch Harbor, named after one of Gray's backers. Vancouver renamed it Gray's Harbor, a name that stuck. On May 15, Gray entered the Columbia River. This is very important. Had Vancouver or John Meares, who had also seen the river mouth a few years earlier, entered the river, our political geography might very different from what it is today. Gray's venture on the Columbia River was to prove pivotal when the Americans and English decided how to split up the Oregon Country, with the Treaty of Oregon in 1846. The Oregon Country stretched from the California border to 54 degrees north latitude, near the current southern tip of the Alaska Panhandle and east to the Continental Divide. Gray's accomplishment was critical for the United States to establish legitimacy and to claim at least half of the territory.

Vancouver proceeded to enter the Strait of Juan de Fuca and sail past the first European settlement on the Peninsula. (He labeled the Washington coast "the graveyard of the Pacific" because of its treacherous rocks. In fact, more than 150 ships have been documented to sink in the area just around Cape Flattery.) The Spanish had completed the first European settlement at Neah Bay, right around the corner from Cape Flattery, which Vancouver also sailed past. (The settlement was abandoned after five months.)

One of Vancouver's first stops was at Contractors Creek in Discovery Bay. A sign on US Highway 101 commemorates the event. In his travels, Vancouver mapped and named all that he could see. Puget Sound is named after Peter Puget, who was the most involved in mapping the sound. Whidbey Island was named for Joseph Whidbey, the master of the *HMS Discovery*. Bellingham was named for the controller of the storekeeper's accounts for the British Navy. Mount Baker was named for another of the officers.

Vancouver finally sat down with Bodega y Quadra to finalize the Nootka Convention treaties. Vancouver was presented with Bodega y Quadra's understanding that the only thing the Spanish were giving up was Nootka Sound. Maps later showed that Bodega y Quadra was planning on keeping everything south of the Strait of Juan de Fuca and east of Nootka Sound. Now that they were good buddies, they decided not to decide and both sailed off, letting the diplomats in London and Madrid figure it out. In 1794, both nations agreed to abandon Nootka Sound and all claims of ownership.

Vancouver sailed south to the Columbia River, where he sent a small boat up to the site that is current city of Vancouver, Washington, about 100 miles upriver. It would take Lewis and Clark, in 1805, to complete

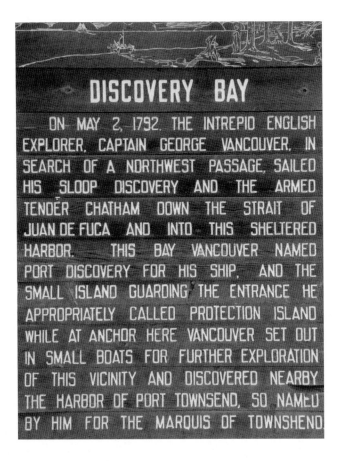

> DISCOVERY BAY
>
> ON MAY 2, 1792, THE INTREPID ENGLISH EXPLORER, CAPTAIN GEORGE VANCOUVER, IN SEARCH OF A NORTHWEST PASSAGE, SAILED HIS SLOOP DISCOVERY AND THE ARMED TENDER CHATHAM DOWN THE STRAIT OF JUAN DE FUCA AND INTO THIS SHELTERED HARBOR. THIS BAY VANCOUVER NAMED PORT DISCOVERY FOR HIS SHIP, AND THE SMALL ISLAND GUARDING THE ENTRANCE HE APPROPRIATELY CALLED PROTECTION ISLAND WHILE AT ANCHOR HERE VANCOUVER SET OUT IN SMALL BOATS FOR FURTHER EXPLORATION OF THIS VICINITY AND DISCOVERED NEARBY THE HARBOR OF PORT TOWNSEND, SO NAMED BY HIM FOR THE MARQUIS OF TOWNSHEND

the mapping of the Columbia River. Vancouver sailed on to San Francisco, Hawaii, Nootka Sound, Alaska, Southern California, Hawaii again, and Alaska again, then home, having completed a very detailed map of the whole coast from California to Cook Inlet in Alaska. Upon his return, the grand dream of a Northwest Passage or Strait of Anian was dead. He wrote, "I trust the precision with which the survey of the coast of North West America has been carried into effect will remove every doubt, and set aside every opinion of a north-west passage, or any water communication navigable for shipping, existing between the North Pacific, and the interior of the American Continent, within the limits of our search."

The Peninsula's First Nonnative Explorers

Year	Explorer	Nation	Voyage
499	Hwui Shan	China	Afghani Buddhist missionary under instructions of Emperor of China spent forty years traveling up and down North American coast from Alaska (his journals describe people of the Aleutians) to Mexico
1579	Sir Francis Drake	England	might be the first to discover Strait of Juan de Fuca and to sail up passage between British Columbia and Vancouver Island and the Queen Charlotte Islands, as far north as 57 degrees latitude in Alaska, now called the Inland Passage
1774	Juan Perez	Spain	sailed to northern tip of Queen Charlotte Islands at 54 degrees, 40 minutes north latitude; first European to note Mount Olympus, which he named Cerro Nevada de Santa Rosalia ("Snowy Peak of St. Rosalia"), and location of Strait of Juan de Fuca
1775	Bruno de Heceta	Spain	sent a landing party ashore south of Quinault River—first time any European stepped foot on Olympic Peninsula and Washington State; all onshore were killed—Heceta named the spot Point of the Martyrs, later renamed either Cape Elizabeth or Point Grenville; first to map Washington's coast; first European to note and name Columbia River, calling it Bahía de la Asunción
1775	Juan Francisco de la Bodega y Quadra	Spain	left Heceta reached 59 degrees north latitude, close to Sitka, AK, then sailed south to Monterey
1778	James Cook	England	named Cape Flattery at mouth of Strait of Juan de Fuca, which he thought was a large bay; sailed past mouth of Columbia River; never stepped foot in Washington State, proceeding north to Nootka Sound

Year	Explorer	Nation	Voyage
1787	Charles Barkley	England	"rediscovered" Strait of Juan de Fuca and noted it on his map; his wife was first European female to visit Washington's coast
1788	John Meares	England	renamed Cerro Nevada de Santa Rosalia Mount Olympus; named Tatoosh Island off Cape Flattery
1789	*Lieutenant Esteban José Martinez*	Spain	seized Nootka Sound
1789	Robert Gray	United States	enters Strait of Juan de Fuca and stops at Neah Bay
1790	Manuel Quimper	Spain	completely mapped Strait of Juan de Fuca for first time; made it to Admiralty Inlet, which leads south into Puget Sound; first European seen by S'Klallam Tribe
1792	George Vancouver	England	entered waters off Washington State while mapping the Northwest to 60 degrees north latitude at Cook Inlet, Alaska
1792	Robert Gray	United States	sailed into the Columbia River on his second trip to the Northwest; entered Gray's Harbor, which he named Bulfinch Harbor
1794	George Vancouver	England	negotiated Nootka Sound away from the Spanish

Glossary: Early Explorers

Bahía de la Asunción: name for what is now the Columbia River, given in 1775 by Bruno de Heceta

Bulfinch Harbor: name for what is now Gray's Harbor, given in 1792 by Robert Gray

Cerro Nevada de Santa Rosalia (**"Snowy Peak of Santa Rosalia**): name for what is now Mount Olympus, given in 1775 by Juan Perez

graveyard of the Pacific: George Vancouver's nickname for Washington coast in 1792

Land of Fusang: Chinese explorer Hwui Shan's name for Mexico in 499

New Albion: Sir Francis Drake's name for the Pacific coast somewhere north of California in 1579

Nootka Convention: 1794 negotiations by George Vancouver on behalf of the British to take possession of the Spanish holdings at Nootka Sound

Nootka Crisis: Spanish seizure in 1789 of the holdings of British fur trader John Meares that brought conflicting ownership claims of the Pacific Northwest to a head

Northwest Passage: fabled sailing route (also known as the Strait of Anian) that was the Holy Grail to mariners and merchants because it was supposed to save months of sea travel between Europe and Asia by avoiding sailing around the southern tip of South America; we know now that the Northwest Passage was invented by Italian cartographer Giacomo Gastaldi in about 1562

Point of the Martyrs: named in 1775 by Bruno de Heceta after his landing party was slain; later renamed either Cape Elizabeth or Point Grenville

scurvy: disease caused by deficiency of vitamin C, often experienced by sailors lacking fresh food in their diet

Strait of Anian: original name for the Northwest Passage

5

THE 19ᵀᴴ CENTURY

The first couple of decades of the nineteenth century were quiet on the Olympic Peninsula. No great sailing ships ferrying Europeans arrived to disturb the status quo, and the Indians went about their business in their own land of plenty (Hult 1954).

Hudson Bay Company

In 1824 the British Hudson Bay Company (HBC) came up the coast from Fort Vancouver to Grays Harbor looking for potential new settlement sites. The HBC would eventually establish Fort Nisqually (just east of Olympia on Puget Sound) in 1833 midway between Fort Vancouver in the south along the Columbia River and Fort Langley on the Fraser River, near Vancouver in what is now British Columbia. The HBC would eventually establish Fort George in Astoria, Oregon, and Fort Victoria on Vancouver Island. All these settlements were strictly designed for frontier capitalism. The aim of the HBC was to tie up the fur trade in the Pacific Northwest.

David Douglas (1799–1834), an adventurous Scottish botanist, came north from Fort Vancouver in 1825 and explored the Chehalis River.

Originally published in 1856

Douglas squirrel, Tamiasciurus douglasii

The energetic Douglas studied natural history all through the Pacific Northwest and eventually died under mysterious circumstances in Hawaii. Until then, he identified hundreds of plant and animal species, and his work transformed English gardens from the seeds of more than 200 different species that he brought home from Washington State. He also transformed the European timber industry with the importation of Douglas-fir, named after him (Douglas-fir is known scientifically as *Pseudotsuga menziesii*, named by Douglas to honor Archibald Menzies, George Vancouver's naturalist). The diminutive Douglas squirrel, *Tamiasciurus douglasii*, is also named after him. The subspecies name of *douglasii* is part of more than eighty species; many were named posthumously.

The Treaty of 1818 signed by the United States and Britain set the majority of today's border between the United States and Canada at 49 degrees north latitude. The treaty also decided not to decide on the area called the Oregon Country (setting it aside for joint occupation by the two countries), which stretched from current California (then Mexico) all the way north to the Russian border in Alaska, roughly bisecting current British Columbia. And it extended east from the Pacific coast to the Continental Divide. This territory included all of the current states of Oregon, Washington, and Idaho and parts of Montana and Wyoming. In the election of 1844, James Polk used the slogan "54-40 or fight!" as part of his presidential campaign. He later compromised with the British by splitting the region roughly in half at the 49th parallel, a continuation of the border from the east from the Treaty of 1818. The Oregon Treaty was signed in 1846.

U.S. Exploring Expedition

In 1838, the U.S. Exploring Expedition set sail with six ships from Virginia for a four-year voyage around the world under the command of Lieutenant Charles Wilkes. Among those on board were biologists, geologists, language experts, artists, and taxidermists. The expedition arrived off the coast of Washington State in 1841, having sailed south and around Cape Horn. After recovering in Discovery Bay, the same bay that George Vancouver had used, Wilkes sailed for Fort Nisqually. There he split the crew. He went overland south to Fort Vancouver and Oregon while others explored eastern Washington as far north as Okanogan and as far east as Walla Walla. Another group canoed down the Chehalis River and charted Grays Harbor.

When the expedition returned to New York, the great national acknowledgment of its achievement wasn't forthcoming. Lieutenant Wilkes was an incredible surveyor but a lousy leader of men. He was described in a later court-martial as being mercurial, petty and tyrannical and was found guilty of one count of illegally punishing his men and then pardoned. Neither the U.S. Congress nor the U.S. Navy bothered to recognize his achievements.

But the U.S. Exploring Expedition helped established the Oregon Country as belonging to the United States. And along the way, Wilkes became the discoverer of Antarctica, the expedition became the first U.S. military circumnavigation of the globe, the expedition supplied the first accurate chart of the Columbia River from the Canadian border to the sea, and the expedition's journals and tons of collected specimens became the origin of the Smithsonian Institution. Wilkes's charts of his travels were still used through World War II. His travels in Washington State helped the United States secure the territory in the Oregon Treaty.

American Settlers

George Washington Bush settled near Olympia in 1845 (see Milestone 1, Olympia to Hoodsport); William O'Leary (1821–1901) became the first white settler on the Peninsula proper in 1848, settling in Grays Harbor. In 1851 the first settlers arrived on the Peninsula's north coast at New Dungeness. Port Townsend and Port Ludlow saw their first settlers in 1852. In 1853 Washington State became a territory and Isaac Stevens, the great negotiator, became the territorial governor (see chapter 3, Original Inhabitants).

Settlers never poured onto the Peninsula; pioneer life there was rainy, isolated, and dark. Without roads, the first settlers stayed near the coast, rivers or lakes and depended on the Indians for survival. (The first road that circumnavigated the Peninsula wasn't finished until 1931.) Supplies were delivered by boats to Neah Bay and Crescent Bay on the strait from Seattle and beyond. There they were ferried to the pioneers close to the ocean or by pack train to those in the interior.

In 1879 Luther Ford and his family drove a herd of dairy cows south from Neah Bay along the beach and up the Quillayute River from La

Push to the future home of Forks, then known as Indian Prairie. The Indians had kept this land as a prairie by burning it periodically. The Forks area was eventually populated with settlers wanting both the tall trees *and* the prairies to use as pasture and farm fields. The prairies were fertile and the timber huge, but there was no way for the produce or logs to get to market. Farm produce was occasionally transported north to Pysht with various degrees of success and hardship. The "road" was barely passable for just a saddle horse, let alone a wagon. The first cattle drive, which drove 150 head all the way from Forks to Port Townsend, took six weeks to make the 100-mile trip. A freight line of packhorses down from Clallam to Forks was started in 1891. It was 1927 before one could drive to Forks from Lake Crescent.

In the 1880s the hot springs on the Soleduck River were "discovered." It took Port Angeles tourists two days on horseback to reach the springs. The '80s also saw some development on Lake Crescent, which peaked in 1889 alongside rumors of the railroad coming all the way to Port Angeles. When the railroad plans collapsed in the '90s, so did the boom at Lake Crescent.

Beaver, the halfway point between the Strait of Juan de Fuca and Forks, saw its fortunes rise as a way station especially as the road improved. It even had its own newspaper, the *Beaver Leader,* and a hotel. The best place to settle was Sequim (see Milestone 4, Discovery Bay to Elwha), with its sunshine, wide prairies, and proximity to the markets of Port Townsend and Victoria, British Columbia.

John Huelsdonk, "the Iron Man of the Hoh," arrived on the Hoh River in 1892 with his new wife, Dora. The trail from Forks was so impassable Huelsdonk had to transport any goods he needed west from Forks to La Push, walk down the coast to the Hoh, and walk up the 30 miles to his homestead. He was legendary for the large weight he could carry. Carrying his body weight was not unusual for him, and, as a packer, he was paid twice the typical wage because he could carry twice as much weight as others could.

Huelsdonk supported his family by packing, hunting and farming. He may have killed more than 150 cougars during his life on the Hoh, but his predation changed the ecosystem of the valley by killing off the main predator of the local elk. This allowed more elk to forage and keep the valley floor open.

However, his family's life was one of supreme isolation. Initially his three brothers joined him, but after "proving up" their homesteads, they left a few years later with the establishment of the Olympic Forest Reserve in 1897, which prevented any new homesteads. Dora left the Hoh valley only twice in forty years, while raising four daughters. It wasn't until the 1920s that US 101 was completed across the Hoh, about 10 river miles downstream from their homestead. And it wasn't until WWII that a road went right to their door. John died at age seventy-nine in 1946, with Dora following six months later. Both were buried on the property. Their homestead is listed on the Washington Heritage Register along the south shore of the Hoh River.

In the Peninsula's northwest corner near and around Ozette Lake, Scandinavians (mostly first generation from Norway and Denmark) tried to homestead. Their mark is still seen by the place names along the lake, such as Tivoli Island, Ericsons Bay, and Jersted Point. They started moving away after their land was included in the Olympic Forest Reserve in 1897. It was a hard and isolated place to scratch out a living. In 1926, a "road" was established from Clallam Bay on the Strait to the lake. And in 1935 one could finally drive a car to the lake. Electricity didn't arrive until the 1960s.

Birth of the Timber Industry

In 1848 the first commercial logging venture was begun on the Peninsula. The *Albion,* an English ship, entered Discovery Bay with the purpose of harvesting spars for sailing ships. It took the crew four months to get eighteen logs on board, with the help of the Clallam Indians. Just prior to sailing away, federal customs officials seized the ship and cargo and later auctioned it all off for twenty cents on the dollar at Fort Nisqually. The ship was then loaded with local foodstuffs and sailed south to San Francisco to help feed the hungry Forty-Niners. The ship was scuttled in San Francisco Bay since the ship's owners couldn't find anyone to sail away. The crew abandoned ship for the goldfields.

The timber industry, especially on the Peninsula, was the dominant industry in western Washington until right after WWII. It began during the 1850s when the region's primary resource was initially exploited. California was a huge market for timber and lumber of any kind due to its gold rush and the burning and subsequent rebuilding of San Francisco. The brig *Orbit* took the first load of logs out of Puget Sound destined for San Francisco in 1850. There was money to be made.

Timber at the dock cost ten cents per board foot in Puget Sound and could be sold for a dollar per board foot in California (a board foot is 1 foot by 1 foot by 1 inch). All Peninsulans had to do was chop timber down at the shoreline and float it to the waiting ships. In 1854, the first viable sawmill on the Peninsula was built at Port Gamble (see Milestone 3, Quimper Peninsula). With a new lumber mill opening virtually every year during the second half of the nineteenth century, the need for ships exploded. The local ship-building industry was born—and boomed. With all the timber and the means to bring it to market, Puget Sound supplied lumber all across the world.

These enormous trees were cut about 6–15 feet above the ground to avoid the triangular base of the tree. First, notches were cut 5–10 feet above the ground, where the loggers could install planks, called *springboards*. Standing on the springboards allowed the fellers to attack the tree with their axes. It wasn't until the 1870s that cross-cut saws (also called misery whips or Swedish fiddles) were introduced (Morgan 1955).

Once the enormous trees were felled, they were cut up, or bucked, into lengths the oxen and mill could handle, typically 24 feet. You can still see these springboard notches on trees all around the Peninsula.

The standard minimum logging crew of the early days lived in a long building that housed the men's bunks and the cook stove. The boss had his own small detached apartment. The oxen were housed in lean-tos. The boss was obviously the top man. Second-in-commands were the teamsters who coaxed the oxen to do the heavy pulling. They were followed by the

This stump is called a nurse stump. Eventually the stump will degrade and the trees will appear to have grown on stilts outlining where the stump once was. The holes in the trunk are springboard notches.

choppers, or fellers, the men who did the dangerous work of cutting the big trees down. Next came the sawyers, who removed all branches and bucked the fallen timber into shorter lengths. Finally, the builders and maintainers of the skid row (see below) rounded out typical logging camp personnel. The cook's importance and prestige rose and fell depending on his cooking skills. Because the crew spent long days working outside in the rain followed by long nights in cramped quarters, the quality and quantity of the meals had a huge impact on morale.

By the mid-1850s, Hood Canal had fifty logging camps (Fredson 1993). But these logging jobs and the conditions were hard. Turnover was high. It was said that it took three crews to fill out a logging camp: one recently hired, one working, and one quitting.

Ox teams, made up of four to eight animals (sometimes 14!), were attached to the bucked logs and dragged as many logs as they could to

Teams of oxen were very hard to handle, especially a team of 14 oxen.

the water—sometimes just one log, other times up to four or five. The paths the oxen used were called *skid rows*. (The term became popular to designate a rundown or poorer part of town. The skid row in early Seattle along Yesler Avenue gave the world the pejorative meaning.) These skid rows were crossed with logs. The grease monkey worked ahead of the oncoming logs applying skid grease, derived from dog sharks found in the local waters.

The initial supply of logs came from homesteaders along the shoreline. If a portion of the forest lacked any clear ownership, often the loggers would go ahead and cut it down anyway. Later in the century, sailors were enticed to go into the forest and declare that they intended to homestead 160 acres. After purchasing the land for $2.50 per acre, the "homesteaders" would then turn around and sell it to the mills and sail away. This is one of the dubious techniques that mills and timber companies used to accumulate thousands and thousands of acres.

A steam donkey and crew.

Timber (raw logs cut from the forest) and lumber products (output from a mill) were shipped all over the world from the large mills at Port Ludlow and Port Gamble and all around Puget Sound. But as with all re-source-extraction industries, the timber industry succumbed to its suc-cesses. The peak production happened in the 1870s and 1880s. Supply of the timber exceeded the demand, and many of the early mill towns became ghost towns.

Railroads and Technology

Timber-harvesting productivity improved with technologies pio-neered in Mason and Grays Harbor counties. The first railroads (albeit an old technology) on the Peninsula began pushing west from Shelton. The steam donkey, which replaced oxen, was first used in the California redwoods in the early 1880s. Due to their portability and power, they were quickly drafted for use in the Peninsula's forests and helped the timber industry penetrate deeper into the forest. The donkeys were essentially just a steam engine driving winches that pulled on a cable attached to the fallen log. They were manned by a choker setter who attached the cable to the log. (The Grays Harbor Community College athletes compete as the Grays Harbor Chokers.) The donkey puncher operated and maintained the steam donkey. The spool tender made sure that the cable gathering on the winch was straight. The whistle punk helped the choker and puncher communicate.

Railroads Planned but Never Built

East Clallam and Forks Railroad

Grays Harbor and Puget Sound Railroad

Northern Pacific Railroad

Oregon Improvement Company Railroad

Oregon Railroad and Navigation

Port Angeles and Everett Railroad
(which was to span Puget Sound on ferries)

Port Angeles Pacific Railroad

Port Townsend and Southern Railroad

Tacoma and Grays Harbor Railroad

Union City and Naval Station Railroad

Union Pacific Railroad

Before the steam donkey, the oxen were the production bottleneck: oxen teams could do only two or three logs per day, so fellers cut only the largest trees. The steam donkey revolutionized the speed at which timber reached the mill. With the more efficient steam donkey, the fellers became the bottleneck, so they started cutting everything, large and small (Fredson 1993).

Railroads plotted tracks all the way around the Peninsula and prom-ised great wealth. The great economic boon of the coming railroads never happened. The nation suffered greatly during the Panic of 1893, but no place more so than the Peninsula. From 1893 to 1897, a quarter of national railroads went bankrupt, and all the talk of local railroads and expanding markets on the Peninsula collapsed. The local popula-tion and property values dropped precipitously. Port Townsend was perhaps the biggest loser, since it had been speculating like crazy with the idea of a railroad connecting it to the south. Peninsula-wide, the equity in pioneers' property almost vanished.

Exploring the Mountains

While a few settlers tried to create lives around the periphery of the Peninsula, the interior was an enormous terra incognita. Indians had been traversing the interior, as evidenced by ancient camps found by hikers and archaeologists. But it wasn't until the 1880s and '90s that the settlers' development started to move away from the coast and up into the interior. The Indians had stories about the massive Thunderbird that inhabited the interior. They also said that there were pleasant valleys and prairies. But until 1885, no European had ever been very close to Mount Olympus. Even today it is a 15-mile hike up the Hoh River before you even start to climb it.

There are many tales of settlers probing the Olympic Range, even some reports of summiting Mount Olympus. The first confirmed explo-ration trip was taken by Lieutenant Joseph P. O'Neil. In 1885 he sailed from his post at Fort Townsend and with six others, eight mules, and one horse landed in Port Angeles. After just over a month making the attempt, and the death of one team member, O'Neil retreated. He had made it farther than any European before him. While some of his team attempted to go up the Elwha River, he led three of his men to the base of Mount Constance on the eastern edge of the mountains where he could view all of Puget Sound. He was summoned by his superiors for transfer to Kansas before he could explore all he wanted, but he wrote of the Olympics in his report, "The day will come when the State of Washington will glory in their wealth and beauty."

The most famous of the early explorations of the interior was the Press Expedition of 1889, sponsored by the short-lived *Seattle Press* newspaper. Governor Ferry, earlier in 1889, said, "A fine opportunity awaits some of Washington's explorers to acquire fame by unveiling the mystery which wraps the land encircled by the snow-capped Olympic Range." The *Seattle Press* read that and thought of selling newspapers, quickly organizing just such an expedition.

Leaving in December from Port Angeles just days after Washington obtained statehood, the Press Expedition took the advice of an expedition member from O'Neil's team and attempted to float a boat up the Elwha. Their guide informed them it was navigable for 30 miles into the interior. First they dragged all the supplies and the unassembled boat up the river 4 miles. After spending weeks building the boat along the river, they abandoned it after about another 5 miles upstream.

At about 18 miles up the river, they entered what is now Geyser Valley, where they thought they heard geysers periodically going off. What they actually heard were the drumming sounds of male ruffed grouse flapping their wings to attract mates. Geyser Valley was truly a paradise, where they found much abundant game and flat land. James Christie, the trip leader, caught 42 pounds of trout in thirty minutes while others complained that the local wildlife were too tame and numerous for a good sporting hunt (Hult 1954). An expedition member took the time to stake out a homestead claim.

On April 29 they reached a pass that offered them the best views of their whole trip. Here they named the whole range for W. E. Bailey, the *Seattle Press* publisher and their sponsor. They also named other peaks for members of the expedition, the governor, and the mayor of the City of Seattle. It was at this pass that they realized they were lost—or at least not where they thought they were. They had wasted ten days by going up the Goldie River, which flowed from the west. At the pass they saw below them the Elwha, to which they had to descend back down.

They started with two tons of equipment, and when they reached the headwaters of the Elwha four months after starting, everything was gone except guns, ammunition, a week or so worth of food, a blanket and the clothes on their back. Fortunately, right at the pass between the Elwha and the Quinault, they were able to kill a couple of bears, which refueled them for the downward trek. Fortunately, they stumbled onto the Quinault watershed.

On the way down, they saw more signs of Indians, similar to what they had seen in Geyser Valley. All of the blazes on the trees and fish-drying racks were obviously very old.

After a hair-raising trip down the Quinault River on a raft they constructed, they finally reached "civilization": they stumbled upon a hunter who was able to provide shelter and food and, within a couple of days, they made it to Aberdeen six months after they started their trip.

They were welcomed as heroes back in Seattle. The *Press* ran the headline "No Evidence of Human Life Except Some Very Old Relics--The Country Comprises one Mountain Range After Another with but Few Intervening Valleys--Many High Peaks Discovered" (Hult 1954). With their return, the dreams of large, fertile valleys and prairies were dead, along with the rumors of lost Indian tribes. These hopes were replaced with the knowledge that the interior, foreboding as it appears from the outside, was indeed very foreboding inside.

Before the *Seattle Press* headlines were published, Lieutenant O'Neil was once again making his way into the interior. This time, he was attempting to transect the Peninsula from Lake Cushman, on Hood Canal at the Peninsula's eastern side, to the Hoh River, on the coast to the west, with a team of sixteen men. They traveled up from Lilliwaup to the lake, past the current Park Service Staircase campground, and up the Skokomish River. The difficulty of this trip can be measured by the creeks that flow into the Skokomish upstream from the campground: Four, Five, Six, Seven, Eight, and Nine streams are barely 1 mile apart, marking the expedition's fourth through ninth nights on the trip. Once they reached the headwaters of the river, the group split up. O'Neil made it out by way of the Quinault River; others explored the Dose-wallips (pronounced "doh-see-WALL-ups") and Duckabush rivers and safely returned to Hood Canal. One group summited Mount Olympus, the first European people to do so. The summit team made it out on the Queets River.

It was in O'Neil's 1896 report that he suggested a national park be created to preserve the Olympic Mountains. Whether President Cleveland ever read the report is uncertain but, in 1897, he created the Olympic Forest Reserve encompassing more than 2.1 million acres. Roughly two-thirds of the whole Peninsula was, with a presidential decree, under federal control. The Seattle Chamber of Commerce called the president's actions "a galling insult" and "an amazing instance of the indifference of the East to the facts, conditions, necessities, and rights of the people of the West" (Ficken 1987). It took a survey team four years to inventory the forest reserve that the federal government had created.

Glossary: The 19th Century

board foot: lumber measurement that is 1 foot by 1 foot by 1 inch

bucked: felled trees cut into lengths of, say, 24 feet

choker setter: person who attached a cable to a felled log

donkey puncher: person who operated and maintained the steam donkey

grease monkey: person who applied grease from dog sharks to the logs comprising the skid row, ahead of the oncoming logs

misery whips: cross-cut saws, a/k/a Swedish fiddles

skid row: paths crossed with greased logs, on which ox teams dragged felled logs to water; popular term to designate a rundown or poorer part of town

spool tender: person who kept the cable straight as it gathered on the winch

springboard: plank installed in notches in a tree 5–10 feet aboveground, where loggers could stand to attack the tree with their axes

steam donkey: a steam engine driving winches that pulled on a cable attached to a felled log

Swedish fiddles: cross-cut saws, a/k/a misery whips

whistle punk: person who helped the choker setter and donkey puncher communicate

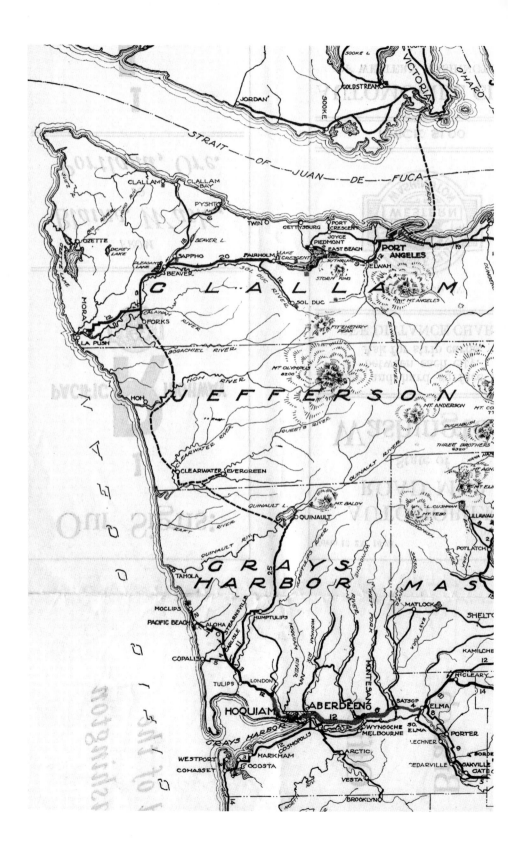

6

THE 20ᵀᴴ CENTURY

President McKinley's Commissioner of the General Land office "looked" at the northwest corner of the Olympic Peninsula and wrote, "This timber was not worth preserving, as it would be destroyed by storms; and it was good for farming." The surveyor's report stated contrarily that the same property was "the most heavily forested region in Washington and, with few exceptions, the most heavily forested region in the country."

Olympic Forest Reserve

The more than 2.1 million-acre Olympic Forest Reserve, established in 1897, was whittled down in size over time by pressure from the local communities and distant powerful interests. About 721,000 acres were removed from the reserve at the turn of the twentieth century. This land was promptly swapped out to a few large corporations, mostly railroads, which were able to trade their "worthless" land they acquired building railroads across the nation for "worthless" timberland in Washington State through the Timber and Stone Act of 1878. Other parcels were homesteaded fraudulently and still ended up with the logging companies.

Originally published in 1919

The government surveyors found only 83 residents in northern Clallam County that lived in the reserve, though there had been more than 340 homestead claims. By 1906 only 1.5 percent of county land inside the reserve was being farmed, as the problems of farming and homesteading persisted into the twentieth century.

With the pressures of the new Olympic Forest Reserve and the continuing struggles of the settlers, the pioneering era stopped in the first decade of the twentieth century. Only a handful of the clearings and buildings that indicate that settlers had ever worked so hard to make a living remain within the park boundaries. The few settlers who did migrate followed a pattern of occupying land for subsistence farming, performing visitor services in places like Lake Crescent, guiding services up the Elwha River, and sporadic mining enterprises everywhere. Virtually all had to take cash-paying jobs with logging companies, the local government or the new reserve to make ends meet.

While there were few residents in the new reserve, the designation essentially killed one of the largest communities at Ozette Lake. Life was tough enough but after the reserve was created, many just left and the community lost its critical mass. Old-time Ozette pioneer Ole Boe wrote in his memoirs, "It is like after the black death in Norway in 1300 when there remained only an isolated human here and there after the pestilence."

But for the Peninsula's boundaries and land use, it was a busy first two or three decades of the century:

- In 1900 President McKinley removed 264,960 acres from the reserve.

- In 1901 the president removed an additional 456,900 acres.

- In 1904 Congressman Francis Cushman, from Tacoma, proposed Elk National Park to contain 393,000 acres. It was voted down.

- In 1905 Olympic Forest Reserve administration was transferred by U.S. Congress, along with all national reserves, from the Department of the Interior to the newly formed U.S. Forest Service under the Department of Agriculture. A few years later the reserve's name was changed to Olympic National Forest.

- In 1908 Republican Congressman Humphrey proposed a game reserve for the Peninsula. It was voted down.

- In 1909 President Theodore Roosevelt created the 610,000-acre Mount Olympus National Monument inside the Olympic National Forest. The primary purpose was to save the elk herds.

- In 1911 President Woodrow Wilson eliminated 50 percent of the national monument.

- In 1916 the National Park Service was created within the Department of the Interior. All national monuments in the country were transferred to the Park Service except Mount Olympus.

- In 1933, the Mount Olympus National Monument administration was finally transferred from the Forest Service and Department of Agriculture to the National Park Service and Department of the Interior.

Again, howls were heard all around the Peninsula as the local citizens once more accused the federal government of not listening to the local community by eliminating the monument from future development and resource exploitation. The Secretary of Interior and the boss of all the national parks was Harold Ickes, an ardent conservationist. He also had the ear of President Franklin Delano Roosevelt and ensured the politics were set up to ease the monument into a full-fledged national park. It took three tries for Congressman Mon Wallgren of Washington State to get a bill passed to establish Olympic National Park.

Olympic National Park

President Roosevelt visited the Peninsula in October 1937. He spent the night at Lake Crescent and lunched at the Lake Quinault Lodge. [history](You too can have lunch in the aptly name Roosevelt Dining Room.) All along the way, he was told the idea of a national park was too extreme or that the park was not big enough. There are indications that he was already in favor of the idea prior to his arrival in Port Angeles where he announced he wanted a park.

On his drive he saw it all: magnificent, intact old-growth forests as well as clearcut acres as far as one could see on that rainy weekend. Driving past such an area he is reportedly to have mentioned, "I hope the son-of-a-bitch who logged that is roasting in hell" (Morgan 1955, 185). Nine months later, Roosevelt signed the bill that created 682,000-acre Olympic National Park, with provisions that he or a future president could add an additional 300,000 acres simply by proclamation.

From the beginning, the park was designed to be a different kind of national park. There is no grand residential lodge situated in a scenic location like there is in Yosemite or Mount Rainier National Park. Also there is no grand drive like there is in Yellowstone. Early national parks, such as Yellowstone or Yosemite, were developed with accessibility and the new-fangled automobile in mind. Olympic National Park was designated from the start as our nation's first wilderness park. Harold Ickes wrote (www.nps.gov/history/history/online_books/olym/hrs/chap4.htm) in 1938:

"When a national park is established, the insistent demand is to build roads everywhere, to build broad easy trails, to build air fields, to make it possible for everybody to go everywhere—without effort. . . . But let us preserve a still larger representative area in its primitive condition for all time by excluding roads. Limit the roads. Make the trails safe but not too easy, and you will preserve the beauty of the parks for untold generations. Yield to the thoughtless demand for easy travel, and in time the few wilderness areas that are left to us will be nothing but the back yards of filling stations. . . . It is our intention to build overnight trail shelters for hikers and horseback parties, but those who want all the comforts of home, including facilities for reading while taking a bath, will have to look for them in the communities that encircle this park at the base of the mountains."

Even with Secretary Ickes's opposition, clamor for a transpark road was heard but met with little support from Washington, D.C. Today the longest road in the park is Hurricane Ridge Road (and its dirt extension, Obstruction Peak Road). The Hurricane Ridge Road was connected to the Whiskey Bend Road from the Elwha River but that has since been abandoned. (It is now the Wolf Creek trail, which drops from the ridge just west of the visitor center in the parking lot.) It has taken many a decade for local citizens and politicians to get their minds wrapped around the idea of a national park designed for the wilderness and not the automobile or future development.

National Park Lodges

Even without a grand lodge, Olympic National Park still has various legacy locations where you can spend the night in a room rather than a tent. **Lake Quinault Lodge**, where President Franklin Delano Roosevelt had lunch, most closely resembles what one might expect of a classic national park lodge. The other lodges include **Kalaloch Lodge** on the Pacific beach, **Lake Crescent Lodge** and the **Log Cabin Resort** on Lake Crescent, and the **Sol Duc Hot Springs Resort.**

In 1940 President Roosevelt added the Queets River bottom and the coastal unit, increasing the size of the park by 187,000 acres. The president also added another 20,600 acres just south of Port Angeles in 1943 to protect the city's water supply. This new acreage included Glines Canyon Dam, on the Elwha River. President Harry Truman in 1953 added the last large chunk, including portions of the Bogachiel River and increasing the coastal unit. Other additions over the years have increased the size of the park to its present size of 922,650 acres, or 1442 square miles.

How Does Olympic National Park Measure Up?

Olympic National Park is now the fifth-largest national park in the Lower 48 states, behind Death Valley National Park (3.3 million acres), Everglades National Park (1.4 million acres), Grand Canyon National Park (1.2 million acres), and Glacier National Park (1 million acres). The other national parks in Washington State are Mount Rainier (0.236 million acres) and North Cascades (0.504 million acres). Olympic National Park also is the sixth most popular national park, with almost 3 million visitors per year. Mount Rainier has just over 1 million visitors; North Cascades, only 20,000.

In 1976 UNESCO nominated Olympic National Park as a Biosphere Reserve. This designation is given to areas that are committed to sustainability and are of a special or unique ecosystem. There are forty-seven Biosphere Reserves in the United States. In 1982 UNESCO also nominated the park as a World Heritage Site. The nomination indicates a special cultural or physical significance. There are twenty-one World Heritage Sites in the United States, ranging from Yellowstone National Park to Monticello and the Statue of Liberty.

The Washington Wilderness Act passed by Congress in 1984 created five new wilderness areas on the Peninsula: starting with the Buckhorn Wilderness (just west of Quilcene) and going clockwise, next is the Brothers Wilderness (up the Dosewallips and Duckabush rivers), then Mount Skokomish Wilderness and Wonder Mountain Wilderness (north and west of Lake Cushman), and finally Colonel Bob Wilderness (bordering Lake Quinault). These wilderness areas total more than 87,000 acres.

Elwha Dam in 1914. Photography by Asahel Curtis.

In 1988 Congress designated 95 percent of the national park as wilderness, which essentially locks the park up in perpetuity as being both a wild and an intact ecosystem.

Dams

Construction of the Elwha Dam was started in 1910. When it was completed in 1912 and Lake Aldwell behind it began to fill, the dam blew out at its base. The builders threw everything they could get their hands on into the breach. Eventually they "plugged" it and it came on line in 1913, producing electricity for Port Angeles. But it was never secured to the bedrock and never certified as safe. You could see the water leaking out of the base even in modern times. The Glines Canyon Dam, 12 miles upstream from the Elwha Dam, was completed in 1927 and created Lake Mills behind it.

The two dams closed off 170,000 acres (about 17 percent of the park) of salmon habitat. Prior to completion of the dam, historical estimates place the Elwha salmon runs at more than 400,000 fish every year in ten different annual salmon runs. The 38-mile-long river was the largest salmon-producing river south of Alaska and it included the famed 100-pound chinooks. By the end of the twentieth century, the river produced about 1 percent of its historic averages in its remaining 5 miles of free-flowing river.

The Lower Elwha Klallam Indians, prior to the dam, had never gone hungry due to lack of fish. They had draped nets across the river's mouth so when the fish arrived they were corralled into smaller and smaller spaces. All the tribe had to do was to easily spear whatever they needed. And if the tribe didn't want salmon for dinner, the river estuary and beach produced copious amounts of clams and oysters. But by the end of the twentieth century, there weren't any shellfish in the area. The historic beach ecosystem required new sediment brought down by the river every year to replenish what was washed away. The dams above trapped all the sediment and the beach quickly became nothing but cobblestones.

In the 1980s a new regulatory and licensing commission was established by Congress, the Federal Energy Regulatory Commission (FERC). Its mission, besides ensuring the safety of dams, was also to consider all the other stakeholders of dams, including fish and wildlife, when issuing a license. The Elwha Dam had never been licensed, and the Glines Canyon Dam's license had expired in the 1970s. By the 1980s and 1990s, the Indians began to ask for the restoration of their fishing heritage and environmentalists asked for restoration of the river valley to align with the National Park Service's mission statement. It was then that the unthinkable was broached: tearing down the dams.

The two dams had been instrumental in the growth of Port Angeles, but public opinion was swinging away from economic development to

The beach at the mouth of the Elwah River.

recovery and preservation of ecosystems. This fight was propelled forward by the spotted owl fight (see Old-Growth and Owls in this chapter). The Peninsula and its bounty were just in the middle of a bruising battle over old-growth forests and the Northern Spotted Owl. Now the whole nation knew not only where to find the Olympic Peninsula on a map but also how special and unique it is.

In 1992 President George H. W. Bush signed the Elwha River Ecosystem and Fisheries Restoration Act, which called for the removal of the dams. The U.S. government eventually purchased the dams for $29 million, and plans were developed for their removal (see chapter 7, The 21st Century and the Future).

Logging Sitka Spruce

Sitka spruce (*Picea sitchensis*) grows from northern California to southern Alaska; here on the Peninsula, it grows to enormous heights. It is a rather unique tree since it has one of the highest strength-to-weight ratios of any tree and so makes excellent aircraft parts. The Wright brothers used Sitka spruce to build the world's first powered aircraft, *The Flyer,* flown at Kitty Hawk, North Carolina, in 1903.

World War I brought incredible demand for this wood as armies were creating new air forces for the conflict. In 1917 the U.S. War Department established the Spruce Production Division with Lieutenant Colonel Brice Disque as its commander. (The hamlet of Disque, just west of Joyce and Port Angeles, is named for him.) The idea was to punch numerous rail lines into Olympic National Forest to harvest the spruce to aid the war effort. At the peak of all the construction, 100,000 private contractors were joined by 30,000 soldiers throughout the Pacific Northwest. Thirteen rail lines were built, three on the Peninsula. A 5-mile line went south from Pysht, and another 5-mile stretch entered the Quinault valley.

The highest concentration of effort was spent on the 36-mile line that stretched south from Joyce and then west along the shoreline of Lake Crescent before terminating at Lake Pleasant near Beaver. The rail line was the fastest built and most expensive in the United States up to that time. And it never carried a single spruce log during the Great War. In November 1918, armistice was signed as the last rail was being laid, and the war was over. The Spruce Production Division also built a mill in Port Angeles that was to convert all the logs into usable lumber but it never opened. Sitka spruce again became important for the war effort in WWII, but demand was much less than in WWI and the logs were transported along logging roads with logging trucks, not railroads.

One thing the Spruce Production Division did was to stabilize fragile labor relations on the Peninsula. The military was required by law to provide much higher wages and better housing than the local logging operations did. This forced other loggers to do the same. Unfortunately, this labor peace didn't last. In 1917 the labor unions struck mill owners again in Aberdeen. Martial law was declared in the 1930s, with arrests of hundreds of striking mill and logging workers (see Milestone 8, Lake Quinault to Aberdeen).

The Lake Crescent rail line was acquired by private owners who eventually went into bankruptcy after WWII, though spruce logs were shipped on the line during the Second World War. About 5 miles of the line are inside the park and have been turned into a popular hiking and biking trail along the lakeshore. Trailheads can be found east of Fairholm and west of Piedmont along the north shore (see Milestone 6, Elwha to Forks).

Log Trucks and Chainsaws

The interior of the Peninsula and the national monument were protected from logging due to their rugged landscape and remoteness. But pressure built because of new harvesting technologies and the scarcity of timber. Grays Harbor production peaked in the 1920s. It was during the '20s that railroads were largely abandoned in favor of the mobile logging truck. The U.S. Forest Service (USFS) aided this

transformation by becoming the nation's largest road builder. Today it manages more than three times the miles of roads than our interstate highway system comprises.

The USFS also became a willing co-conspirator with the timber industry in attempting to maximize the cutting of everything. Clearcuts started to become the preferred harvesting technique for two reasons: (1) hemlock, which accounted for 40 percent of the forest, was now in

demand for pulp; (2) high lead logging, assisted by the old steam donkeys, was a far more efficient way to remove the trees from the forests.

With high lead logging, a tall tree at the top of a hill was topped off by a high climber. This perilous task required scaling an enormous tree, cutting up to 80 feet off the top, and attaching a cable that went from the nearby steam donkey at one end and then down the hill to the newly cut logs at the other end. The harvested timber was dumped into a neat pile that the newly introduced logging trucks could quickly load. Between the paper pulp industry and high lead logging, the loggers were encouraged to and could penetrate deeper into the forest.

Logging didn't subside until the 1980s. During the second half of the twentieth century, loggers were aided and also replaced by chainsaws as labor productivity soared. And as productivity increased, so did the amount of timber cut down. In spite of sustainability efforts, in such places as Shelton, the last old-growth tree that could be cut down was coming into view at about this time.

Old-Growth and Owls

As the ancient forests were being cut down and replaced with tree farms or clearcuts, several basic "truths" were or became popular. One was that the ancient forests were biological deserts, void of any meaningful wildlife. This idea was promoted by the state's Fish and Game Department, whose mission at the time was to manage and increase hunting opportunities. The Indians knew that wide-open spaces promoted hunting of deer and elk, which is why they tried to keep the Forks prairie a prairie by burning it periodically.

The second "truth" was that old-growth forests are the worst way to maintain a sustainable forest. Foresters and university researchers prescribed cutting the ancient forest down and planting *tree farms* as the way to maximize the land's potential. Another "truth" was the attitude that loggers deserved the trees growing on government land and that nothing should get in the way of the tree going to the mill.

Another "truth" was that an intact ecosystem had value all by itself even if the value couldn't be determined. And it was this last truth that was to become a lightning rod for the 1980s and 1990s.

At first it was all about a diminutive, friendly, cute owl that requires lots and lots of old-growth habitat. In the end, the Northern Spotted Owl fight was transformed into a fight for ancient forests. The owl became the surrogate species for the bigger fight of saving the oldest forests in the Lower 48. And the term "intact ecosystem" became the rallying cry.

The Northern Spotted Owl (*Strix occidentalis caurina*) is probably one of the most studied birds of recent years. But given its scarcity, it is not surprising that we know so little about them. The spotted owl ranges from northern Mexico to British Columbia and is split between two subspecies: the northern and the southern. Scientists have determined

Northern Spotted Owl

that it has a very low reproductive rate. And only two in ten birds survive one year; plus, they do not breed every year. (These numbers are only the scientist's best guess. The numbers vary dramatically based on latitude, elevation, and local climate.) Even if all forests in the Northwest were old-growth, it might take decades, if ever, for the Northern Spotted Owl to recover to its historical populations. The most startling detail was exposed when scientists determined that each nesting pair on the Peninsula required 10,000 acres for their range.

Scientists and environmental groups started pressuring the Forest Service to acknowledge that continued cutting of the old growth would put the spotted owl at risk. When confronted with lawsuits that forced the Forest Service to acknowledge the owl as an endangered species, the agency dragged its feet. Since its inception, the primary activity of the Forest Service was managing timber sales; now, they had to do actual hard science. Out on the Peninsula and especially in the West End, the area around Forks, the logging industry didn't appreciate any interference and was used to getting its way through its long (and often sordid) relationships with legislatures in both Washington State and Washington, D.C.

The clearcutting foes clearly outmatched the Forest Service and the logging industry through the use of scientific research, lawsuits, and public outreach. In 1991 a U.S. District Court judge in Seattle shut down 80 percent of logging in the old-growth areas, ruling that the lack of a coherent plan by the Forest Service to help the owl "exemplifies a deliberate and systematic refusal by the Forest Service and the (U.S.) Fish and Wildlife Service to comply with the laws protecting wildlife" (Dietrich 1992, 213). From the courts to the General Accounting Office in Washington, D.C., scorn was heaped on the Forest Service and other agencies regarding their foot dragging. And while the problem worked its way through legal courts and the courts of public opinion, up to 5 square miles of old-growth timber were cut down every week from northern

California to the Olympic Peninsula, all prime habitat for the Northern Spotted Owl.

Subsequent rulings virtually eliminated the cutting of old-growth forests, and logging economies such as that in Forks collapsed. Thousands of loggers did indeed lose their livelihood just as buffalo hunters had a century before. At one point in the early '90s, the largest source of income for the local citizens was government unemployment benefits and welfare.

But the economic hit to the state was just a fraction of what doomsayers, loggers, and the timber industry had predicted. The state had become, during and after the Second World War, more economically diversified. Building airplanes employed more people than did logging timber after WWII. In the 1980s, the timber industry was at the tail end of its glory years, and timber harvests had peaked. Productivity had increased so dramatically over the century that the timber companies could cut more and more timber with fewer and fewer loggers. The industry also was dramatically increasing log exports which in turn diminished the need for mill workers. The pulp and paper side of the forest industries became the dominant employer, with large plants in Port Angeles, Shelton and Port Townsend.

The *Seattle Times* published an editorial cartoon that showed a logger on one side and the unemployment office on the other. It offered two different paths: one directly to the unemployment office and the other through a clearcut.

The Northwest Forest Plan, aka the Clinton Forest Initiative, was introduced in 1994. As with many political compromises, it pleased no one completely. Harvest from public lands was dramatically reduced, but old-growth logging continued, as well as habitat degradation.

Our cute little spotted owl will probably never recover. Besides habitat destruction, the Barred Owl is the new scoundrel. The Barred Owl is just a little larger than the Northern Spotted Owl and looks very similar. Historically the Barred Owl was an eastern bird but it has migrated to the west and outcompeted the spotted owl. In the times of Lewis and Clark, the plains were a barrier between the east and the west that prohibited the Barred Owl from migrating. The Barred Owl is an arboreal species, and there was a complete lack of trees in central North America. Over the centuries, as development has occurred and trees have been planted across the continent, the Barred Owl has hopscotched across and has now set up residence in the Northwest. It is more aggressive than our spotted owl and even interbreeds. Other than "harvesting" Barred Owls, there might be no way to prevent the downfall of the Northern Spotted Owl.

Mining

Over the years, hundreds of mining claims were filed for the Peninsula. Irondale, south of Port Townsend, was convinced that it would become the next Pittsburgh because it was sitting on a seam of coal that stretched from the Strait of Juan de Fuca to Olympia. Copper was estimated to be more plentiful on the Peninsula than anywhere else in the world. Probably the only commercially viable mineral was manganese. Mines were dug primarily west of Lake Crescent and in the Lake Cushman drainage. These mines were briefly profitable just prior to and during WWII. The Park Service fought mining inside the boundaries of Olympic National Park despite the strategic importance of manganese in making steel for the war.

Placer gold is found in river and beach channels (unlike hard rock gold, which is found in tunnels where miners look for seams of it). Placer gold, because of its physical properties, will gravitate together when separated from the rest of the dirt by washing and rinsing. The gold rushes in California, the Canadian Klondike and Nome, Alaska, were all about placer gold. Knowing of these successes and seeing minute bits of "color" along the Northwest Coast beaches, dozens of miners set up sluice boxes on the beach from near Ozette south to Kalaloch. Unfortunately for the miners, no one was able to make it work. Some of this mining activity is still barely visible on the beach, though no one has been allowed to mine gold on the beach since the coastal unit was added to the park in 1953 by President Truman.

Oil has been located in numerous small seeps, primarily on the coast and in the southern part of the Peninsula. Natives used to call it "smell mud." The first serious drilling venture was near Third Beach, south of La Push, at the turn of the twentieth century. Standard Oil spent a year drilling but came up dry. Some of that equipment is still in the forest on the head between Second and Third beaches.

Ten years later, the Olympic Oil Company spent two years drilling for oil at the mouth of the Hoh River and again came up dry. But they did find time to plat a new town, named Oil City, and publish their own *Oil City News* (although for only three issues), mostly filled with stories about how wonderful it was going to be once the oil started gushing up, so buy more stock now.

There isn't any commercially viable oil in Washington State. When the idea of the coastal unit addition to the park was starting to gather steam many oilmen asked that drilling be allowed in the newest part of the park. Olympic National Park Superintendent Preston Macy, in a bit of clarity and common sense, noted that there were numerous areas on the Peninsula where oil wells had been drilled and later abandoned. "Within the past year there have been several oil prospect wells drilled on the Peninsula and all abandoned for lack of oil. . . . It would appear that with fifteen wells over the past thirty years being abandoned on the Peninsula that [sic] there is no justifiable claim on commercial oil fields which our area is preventing development of" (www.nps.gov/history/history/online_books/olym/hrs/chap3.htm).

Recreation

It wasn't all commercial development on the Peninsula. In the 1920s and '30s, the Forest Service and locals started to promote the area for recreation purposes. Tourism on the Peninsula slowly grew as news about the "Last Wilderness in the United States" spread. Railroads promoted the Peninsula as a way to build traffic on their lines and the Quinault area tried to get more visitors to the community's huts along the Quinault River up to Enchanted Valley.

Three hundred miles of trails were completed by 1930, with dozens of shelters and campsites. Roads were created up the Quinault River, to Lake Cushman and Lake Crescent, and to other prime recreation areas. A road was built up to the Olympic Hot Springs, above the Elwha River and Glines Canyon Dam. A lodge in the Enchanted Valley, up the Quinault River, was built. Primitive areas were also set aside to be never developed. The Forest Service, whose mission is multiple-use, planned to set aside 300,000 interior acres to be forever primitive. Planned but never built was a ski area at Deer Park and a road that would transect the current park by way of the Elwha and Quinault rivers.

The Depression-era Civilian Conservation Corps established five camps on the Peninsula, beginning in 1933 at Lake Quinault. The camp in Quilcene had about 1000 men and reported (Rooney 2007) the following accomplishments:

- 1 million trees planted

- 2500 man days fighting fires

- 4300 signs and markers, benches, and tables constructed

- 20 miles of trails constructed

- 24 bridges built

- 56 buildings erected

- 32 miles of telephone line strung

- 17 campgrounds developed

- 760 miles of road maintained

And this was just in their first four years. The CCC activity eventually wound down by the end of the decade as national employment increased.

The Peninsula's population grew steadily but slowly during the whole twentieth century. The cities that were most dependent on logging, such as Forks and Aberdeen, suffered population decreases in the 1990s. Port Angeles, whose employment was anchored by the large paper mill on Ediz Hook, grew just sparingly in the '90s. But Sequim enjoyed the distinction of being one of the fastest-growing towns in the state during this time due to its hospitable weather and influx of retirees (see Milestone 4, Discovery Bay to Elwha).

Glossary: The 20th Century

Barred Owl: an eastern bird a little larger than the Northern Spotted Owl that looks very similar; has migrated west and outcompeted the spotted owl; an arboreal species; more aggressive than the spotted owl and even interbreeds with it

Biosphere Reserve: area committed to sustainability of a special or unique ecosystem; forty-seven Biosphere Reserves in the United States

clearcuts: logged areas in which all trees are cut to the ground

color: minute bits of placer gold found in river and beach channels by washing and rinsing dirt to separate out the gold

Elk National Park: first national park on the Peninsula, proposed in 1904 but not successful

high lead logging: a high climber scales an enormous tree, cuts up to 80 feet off the top, and attaches a cable to it that goes from the nearby steam donkey at one end and then downhill to newly cut logs at the other end

Mount Olympus National Monument: created in 1909 by President Theodore Roosevelt to preserve elk

Northern Spotted Owl: *Strix occidentalis caurina;* ranges from northern Mexico to British Columbia; has a very low reproductive rate, with only two in ten birds surviving one year, and they do not breed every year; each nesting pair requires 10,000 acres for their range on the Peninsula

Olympic Forest Reserve: created in 1897; administration transferred by U.S. Congress from Department of the Interior to newly formed U.S. Forest Service under Department of Agriculture in 1905; a few years later name changed to Olympic National Forest

Sitka spruce: *Picea sitchensis*; grows from northern California to southern Alaska; grows to enormous heights on the Peninsula; has one of the highest strength-to-weight ratios of any tree, and so makes excellent aircraft parts

smell mud: natives' name for small oil seeps found primarily on the coast and in southern part of the Peninsula; first serious drilling venture was near Third Beach, south of La Push

tree farms: plantations of single-species trees advocated during the 20th century by foresters and university researchers

World Heritage Site: UNESCO designation for a place with special cultural or physical significance; the United States has twenty-one World Heritage Sites

7

THE 21ST CENTURY AND THE FUTURE

What issues face the Peninsula and Olympic National Park in our current century and beyond? Salmon protection and restoration is a significant enough concern that two dams within or near the park's boundaries are being removed and habitat restored. Cleanup of beached garbage brought by ocean currents continues with the added burden from Japan's 2011 tsunami which has already sent enormous wreckage to the Washington coast. Increasing ocean acidity is affecting oyster farming on the Peninsula.

Land Protections

In 2008 the Park Service completed a new General Management Plan for Olympic National Park. It called for additional land acquisitions, mostly to protect river and lake habitats to ensure salmon success. Of the twenty endangered species on the Peninsula, ten are salmon (see "The Rivers: Salmon" in chapter 2, Natural History).

Park administration suggested a new land purchase strategy called *willing seller*. The park will wait until the land becomes available for purchase and then buy it. In the past, if the park wanted the property enough, it could just seize it by powers of *eminent domain*. Under the new strategy, until the land is purchased, the owner is allowed to do whatever they want as no new regulations are imposed on the target property.

The most dramatic proposals of the 2008 plan call for the acquisition of the following:

- land along the north side of the Queets River to provide more elk habitat along with river improvements

- land along the north end of Lake Crescent in the Lyre River and Boundary Creek areas for protection of native trout spawning habitat

- the complete watershed of Ozette Lake to protect the endangered sockeye salmon

- a large chunk of the South Fork of the Hoh River that borders the current park boundaries

While the park administration conducts hearings and gets feedback from the public, the Wild Olympics Wilderness and Wild and Scenic Rivers Act of 2012 was introduced in both the U.S. House of Representatives and the U.S. Senate. The act would add 126,000 acres of new wilderness to the Peninsula and give nineteen rivers a Wild and Scenic designation. All proposed areas are contiguous to either the park or other current wilderness areas.

The bad news is that Congress did not have a single hearing on the bill in 2012. The other bad news is that the congressman who proposed the bill in the House has retired. He was a long-serving Representative who was popular on the Peninsula and powerful in the House. Current candidates trying to replace him talk about both increasing the annual timber harvest on the Peninsula and not locking up land with a wilderness designation.

There have been some recent victories for environmentalists. The Hoh River, the longest river flowing out of the park, was protected at

A Sea Change?

Recent polls taken on the Peninsula show a dramatic increase from decades ago in support of wilderness versus logging. This may be caused by two factors. One is the increase in the number of tourists wanting to see the big trees and the recognition of the money they leave behind. The second reason might be due to the inward migration of people who aren't tied to the timber industry and have moved to the Peninsula for quality of life.

its mouth as part of the coastal unit and Hoh Indian Reservation. It was also protected at its source inside the park proper. In 2010 the Hoh Land Trust finished acquiring riverfront property that connected current state conservation property with acreage that they obtained so that the entire river from Mount Olympus to the Pacific is now protected.

The Hoh Indian Tribe Safe Homelands Act signed in 2009 gave the tribe an additional 460 acres on the headland above the river plain. Their 1-square-mile reservation, granted in 1893, in the river's floodplain was slowly but inexorably being washed away by the river and they had only about 460 acres remaining of the original 640.

At the mouth of the Quillayute River, the Quileute Tribe faces similar problems. The Tsunami Protection Legislation was introduced in 2011 by the same congressman who supported the Wild Olympics legislation. Hearings were held, but as of this writing the bill is languishing in Congress. It would provide land for the Quileutes to move their village to higher ground. The reservation is completely surrounded by the park, so they need Congress's support.

Fish Farms

As wild salmon runs improve along the Hoh and the Elwha, plans are being made to build a fish farm in the Strait of Juan de Fuca which would almost double the amount of fish farms in Washington State. An

Oregon company wants to build twenty-four 125-foot-wide pens near the mouth of the Lyre River to grow an estimated 10 million pounds of fish per year.

But fish farms are fraught with peril. Fish farms breed the smaller Atlantic salmon stock which, when they inevitably escape into the wild, breed with the Northwest's larger wild stock. This dilutes the native genetic stock.

There is also the problem of the fish's waste products. With so many fish concentrated in one spot, scientists are still not sure of the long-term consequences.

Finally, there is the issue of disease. There is some evidence that wild salmon here in the Northwest have contracted a virus that has decimated fish farms all across the world (seattletimes.com/html/local-news/2016565085_fishfarms21m.html).

Tsunami Debris

On the coast, the most pressing issue is tsunami debris. The March 2011 tsunami disaster in Japan swept an unknown millions of tons of debris into the Pacific Ocean. Estimates vary from 1.5 million tons to 25 million tons that will eventually reach landfall on the North American Pacific coast (see "The Coast: Whales" in chapter 2, Natural History).

In 2012 debris has already shown up on the Peninsula's beaches in the form of everything from small plastic toy buckets to enormous wharfs, floating houses and fishing boats. The good news about the large pieces is that we can cut them down to size and dispose of them properly. The bad news is they might be carrying alien seaweed and marine life which shouldn't be introduced on our coasts.

The bulk of the debris will be smaller pieces of plastic. We will be able to pick that stuff up right off the beach. Unfortunately, much of this plastic will have already started to degrade and enter the ocean food chain.

The really bad news is that we could be overwhelmed by it all for the next decade. Currently, government has allocated only about 10 percent of what has been estimated necessary to clean it all up.

> **Dumpster for Tsunami Debris Only-**
> Campers Please Use Small Dumpsters Located East & West of this Location

Ocean Acidity

With increased carbon dioxide in our atmosphere, the oceans have absorbed more of it, turning the water more acidic. While climatologists' computer models forecast that the ocean's pH levels would change, the acidity is changing faster than predicted.

This is having disastrous consequences for sea life. Oysters are a large industry in the state of Washington, stretching from Willapa Bay along the state's southern coast up and into Puget Sound. Baby oysters are especially sensitive to pH levels and have been dying off at alarming levels, threatening the whole industry.

But it isn't just oysters. Seabird populations are declining and mussels on the coast have thinner shells and break off of the rocks easier. The full effects of the ocean's increased acidity are just starting to be felt and studied. However, the future doesn't look bright for the Peninsula's marine ecosystem.

Elwha Restoration

To help Olympic National Park become even wilder, Congress passed laws in 1992 allowing for the removal of the Glines Canyon Dam and the Elwha Dam, draining both Lake Mills (within the park) and Lake Aldwell downstream. It was slated to be the largest dam removal project ever attempted in North America.

It was only in the latter part of the twentieth century that dams had even been considered for removal, so there wasn't a lot of history regarding what steps needed to be taken.

One of the biggest issues was what to do with all the sediment that had been dumped into Lake Mills behind the Glines Canyon Dam for the past ninety-eight years. This sediment is both a blessing and a curse. It is required at the river mouth to replenish the beach and clam beds; salmon also need the right mix of sediment on the river bottom to build their nests, called *redds*. But there were 1–2 million dump-truck loads of it. The plan that finally was developed was to leave the sediment where it was and let the river wash it downstream over time.

But this approach would cause other problems. Planners knew that the huge surge of sediment during the first years after the dam removal would bury the lower Elwha salmon redds. The lower 5 miles of the El-wha and last remaining free-flowing section would have to be tempo-rarily sacrificed as a salmon nesting area.

Also, the initial sediment rushing down the river would be too fine. In a normal free-flowing river, sediment gets differentiated and sorted as it moves downstream. Salmon need a Goldilocks type of river bot-tom, with rocks and sediment that are not too coarse and not too fine. This mix will take years to develop after dam removal.

The last remaining Elwha River salmon are the genetic seed for the restoration of the whole river, but the question was how to avoid the sediment-caused kills. The solution adopted was to build a new fish hatchery. It was completed on the Lower Elwha Klallam Reservation in 2011, and immediately it set to work to breed the next generation of Elwha River salmon. The hatchlings will be planted all up and down the river to help jump-start the salmon runs, which are expected to take twenty to thirty years to reach the maximum population.

The Elwha hatchery is not without its critics, for all the same reasons that fish hatcheries everywhere face (see Fish Farms earlier in this chap-ter and "The Rivers: Salmon" in chapter 2, Natural History). Hatcheries dilute the wild fish's genetics, and if not managed prudently, hatchery-raised fish overwhelm the native salmon population.

Image taken in October of 2011

The sediment in Lake Mills was 60 feet deep, and the planners didn't want the river snaking left and right every season as it carved a new riverbed through the soft sediment. This would have created an unnatural-looking landscape, inhibited reforestation, and sent surges of new sediment down the river for years. A large channel was dug, starting at the upriver end of Lake Mills in the general vicinity of the historic riverbed, to guide the newly released river downstream.

To jump-start the reforestation and to get ahead of invasive species, a large greenhouse was built years ago in which native plants were grown for the express purpose of reforesting the newly exposed lake bottom. Immediately as the lake was drained, volunteers rushed in and planted native plants. And will continue to do so for years to come.

Just shy of twenty years after the first President Bush signed the Elwha River Ecosystem and Fisheries Restoration Act, work began to demolish the dams. The lower Elwha Dam removal was completed about a year later in 2012. The Glines Canyon Dam removal is scheduled to be complete sometime in late 2013; the $320 million project should be finished about a year sooner than expected and under budget. All that will remain of the dams will be a few historic structures marking the dams' former locations.

Debris from upstream continues to get deposited and sorted on the beach.

On the beach at the mouth of the Elwha, the sediment is being closely monitored. The sediment will be sorted by gravity and the river current. The vast majority of it will go right into the Strait but some of it will remain on the beach and slowly start to fill all the spaces between the cobbles. It may take ten years, but eventually the beach will once again provide habitat for clams and the river will resemble what it looked like a hundred years ago, running clear and cold all the way from the Olympic Mountain glaciers to the Strait of Juan de Fuca.

As of this writing, with the Elwha Dam removed and Lake Aldwell completely drained the river has burst out with life. The Lower Elwha Klallam Tribe has planted hundreds of ready-to-spawn salmon above the old dam site but hundreds more have come past the lower dam on their own, fresh from the sea. And the beach is becoming restored much faster than was predicted.

Glossary: The 21st Century and the Future

Elwha Dam: lower of two dams on the Elwha River, forming Lake Aldwell; dam removed and lake drained in 2012 to restore salmon runs

eminent domain: power allowing a government or its agency to take possession of private land it requires for authorized purposes; compare *willing seller*

Glines Canyon Dam: higher of two dams on the Elwha River, forming Lake Mills, both within Olympic National Park; dam removal and draining of the lake for salmon restoration slated for completion in late 2013

Lake Aldwell: reservoir created by the Elwha Dam on the Elwha River; drained in 2012 for salmon restoration

Lake Mills: reservoir created by the Glines Canyon Dam on the Elwha River; slated for draining in 2013 for salmon restoration

pH levels: measurement of acidity versus alkalinity, with neutral in the middle of the range

redds: "nests" formed in stream- and riverbeds by salmon in which female salmon lay eggs that are later fertilized by male salmon; female salmon create a redd by swishing their tail in soft sediment and fine gravel, so if a riverbed is scoured of those finer materials, salmon can't build their redds and spawn

tsunami: extremely large tidal wave that occurs after a very large earthquake

Wild and Scenic Rivers: Wild Olympic Wilderness and Wild and Scenic Rivers Act: proposed in 2012 and, again, in 2014 to set aside over 126,000 acres on the Peninsula.

Wild Olympics Wilderness: Wild Olympic Wilderness and Wild and Scenic Rivers Act: proposed in 2012 and, again, in 2014 to set aside over 126,000 acres on the Peninsula.

willing seller: private property owner who chooses to sell property to a government or its agency; until the target property is sold, no new regulations are imposed on the land; compare *eminent domain*

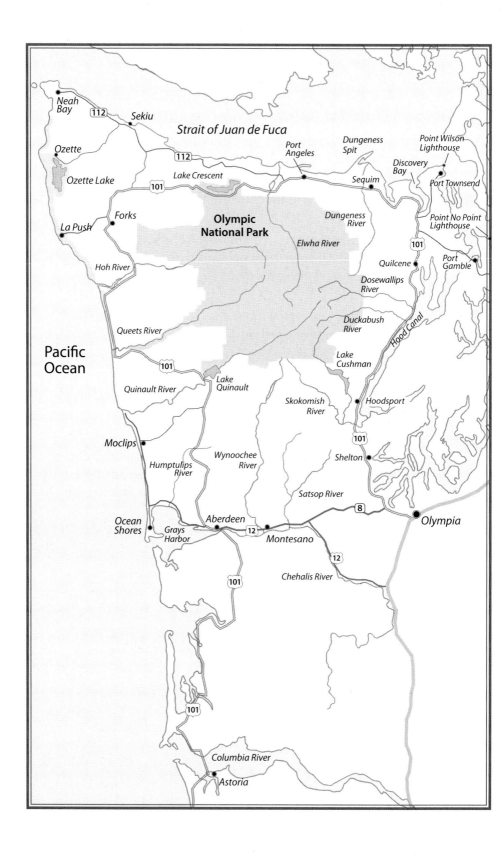

PART II.

OLYMPIC MILESTONE LOOP

In closing, I would state that while the country on the outer slope of these mountains is valuable, the interior is useless for all practical purposes. It would, however, serve admirably for a national park. There are numerous elk—that noble animal so fast disappearing from this country—that should be protected.

—Lieutenant Joseph P. O'Neil, 1896 report to U.S. Congress

MILESTONE INTRODUCTION

The following chapters, entitled Milestones, guide the traveler around the Peninsula in a counter-clockwise direction, starting in Olympia. Each chapter describes a leg of the loop around the Peninsula, with site-specific information on natural history, geology, history and more.

From Olympia the journey proceeds north and west up to Port Angeles, west and south to Forks, then to Aberdeen and then east back to Olympia. You can start on this circumnavigation at any point; each Milestone chapter stands on its own. You don't need to travel counter-clockwise, though it is easier to use this guide if you do.

The Milestone chapters guide you on four scenic byways, designated by the National Scenic Byways Program of the Federal Highway Administration or by the Washington State Department of Transportation. The majority of the Milestone loop route is on the Pacific Coast Scenic

Byway, a Washington State Scenic Byway that starts in Olympia and follows US Highway 101 north around the Peninsula and then south to the Columbia River. (The Milestones depart the Pacific Coast Scenic Byway in Aberdeen.)

There are three side-trip Milestones on other scenic highways. Washington highways 19 and 20 explore the Quimper Peninsula in Milestone 3. The Strait of Juan de Fuca Byway is a national designation for the 61 miles from Port Angeles west to Neah Bay, and the Cape Flattery Tribal Scenic Byway extends that byway another 12 miles west to Cape Flattery. These two byways are covered in Milestone 5, Port Angeles to Neah Bay, along with back roads to remote Ozette Lake. And, finally, the state-designated Hidden Coast Scenic Byway travels from US 101 south of Lake Quinault to Taholah on the Quinault Indian Reservation and south to Ocean Shores. I cover this in Milestone 9, North Beach.

A few Milestones also include short side trips off the highway to visit interesting spots along river and mountain roads. All of these side trips, long or short, as well as my suggested stops are of course optional, but they will enrich your understanding of the Olympic Peninsula's scenery, animals, plants, geology, and lengthy history.

Along with this book, get a good road map. A GPS device is also helpful; it should indicate shortcuts that will exempt you from having to go back and forth on some of the "side" trips. A good example of this is the Joyce cutoff to Lake Crescent in Milestone 5 and the Quilcene–to–Port Gamble shortcut in Milestone 3.

Finally, understand that the mileages listed in this book are approximations. For additional guidance, Appendix C is a mileage chart that provides distances between key places on the Peninsula.

However you choose to drive the Olympic Milestone Loop, take time to explore and enjoy your journey around the Peninsula. It is an adventure like no other.

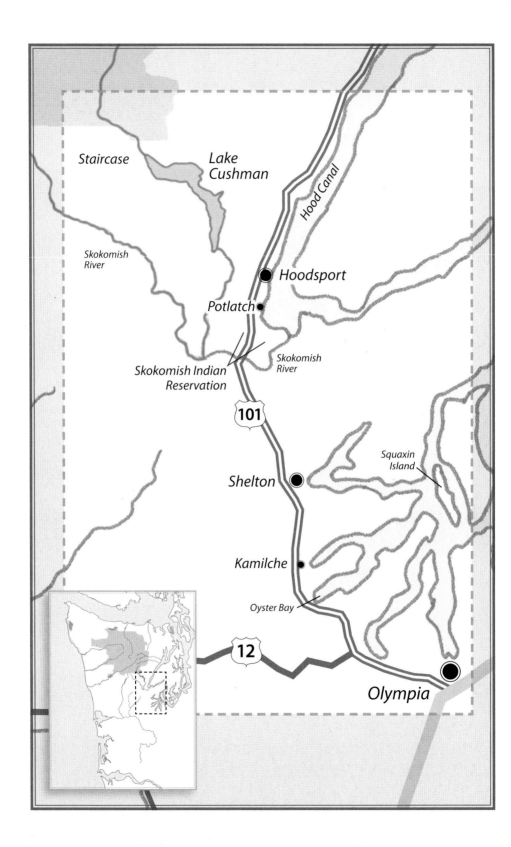

MILESTONE 1

OLYMPIA TO HOODSPORT

The Olympic Milestone Loop starts off of Interstate 5 at exit 104 in Olympia, which puts you on US Highway 101. This first Milestone, from Olympia north to Hoodsport, is about 37 miles. If you want to see Olympia before heading west on US 101, take the State Capitol exit, which is 1 mile north on I-5 at exit 105.

Exploring Olympia

The first place to start in Olympia is at the Visitors Center (www.ga.wa.gov/visitor) on Capitol Way. After a few hundred yards from the interstate off-ramp, go through a tunnel and take the first left onto Capitol Way, then take the first right. The Visitors Center is housed in an interesting-looking round building.

Olympia was covered with a glacier during the last ice age 13,000 years ago. To get a sense of the height of the glacier that scoured this area, find the tallest tree you can, then look up two or three times higher than that. Olympia was just north of the leading edge of the Vashon Lobe of the Cordilleran Ice Sheet that came down from Canada (see "Ice" in chapter 1, Geology). The area south of town, including Bush Prairie,

shows evidence of glacial till and melting. All the water from the Puget Sound drainage and the glacier flowed south into the Chehalis River and then west into the Pacific Ocean. You will see this broad Chehalis River valley on your way back to Olympia from Aberdeen, toward the end of the Olympic Milestone Loop.

Olympia was first seen by Europeans by Peter Puget on May 25, 1792, who was part of the George Vancouver Expedition (see chapter 4, Early Explorers). With Vancouver's ship *HMS Discovery* anchored off of Bainbridge Island, Puget sailed and rowed down Puget Sound. Puget found a village with about sixty individuals at the head of Budd Inlet who were both generous and friendly. Puget named the bay Friendly Inlet. The name didn't last, as Budd Inlet was renamed by the Wilkes Expedition for one of its crewmen when they came through in 1841 (see "U.S. Exploring Expedition" in chapter 5, The 19th Century).

At the time of the first settlement, Washington was still a part of the Oregon Country, whose ownership was in dispute between Britain and the United States. Two of the first pioneers in the Olympia region were Michael Simmons and George Washington Bush who reached Tumwater, just south of Olympia, in 1845. George Bush, a successful Missouri farmer of mixed racial heritage, moved west to avoid the slavery issue and to settle in the Willamette Valley. However, the Oregon Territorial government still allowed overt restrictions on people of color, so George moved north across the Columbia River to avoid most of the harassments. His migration hastened the time when settlers entered the Washington territory and legitimized the United States' claim to Washington. If it hadn't been for the Oregon Territory's position, Simmons and Bush might not have entered Washington, but since they did, the U.S. government used their presence to claim the territory from Britain.

The Bush family became pillars of the young community, befriending both pioneers and Indians. One of Bush's sons was named after a Nisqually Indian chief. Just south of Tumwater is Bush Prairie, named for the family. As a black man, Bush was unable to own land; it took a special act of Congress to grant him title to his property near what is now Tumwater.

Olympia proper was first settled by Edmund Sylvester and Levi Smith in 1846, who became the first Americans to live on Puget Sound. Smith cleared about two acres on the small peninsula that was to become Olympia, while Sylvester took as his new farm an area just to the east in the present town of Lacey. Smith, on his way to his first session as a legislator in the Oregon Territorial government, drowned in a boating accident. His land was then transferred to his partner, Sylvester, who was fresh from a brief stint in the goldfields of California.

In 1850 the town was christened Smithfield by Sylvester, in memory of the earliest pioneer. The name was soon changed to Olympia to acknowledge the nearby Olympic Mountains. Sylvester built the first building in town, a 16-square-foot cabin, out of a single cedar tree. The territory's first post office was established in Olympia in 1850, and a year later, the U.S. government named Olympia the site of the Customs House for Puget Sound. And in 1852, the first newspaper in Washington, the *Columbian*, proclaimed: "Citizens of northern Oregon! It behooves you to bestir yourselves, and proclaim your independence of the territorial authority exerted over you by the Willamette Valley." Was this the start of the heated rivalry between the University of Oregon Ducks and the University of Washington Huskies?

If you want to see what Olympia might have looked like back in the 1850s, drive up the East Bay Drive a few miles north to Priest Point Park. The park was named for Catholic missionaries who established their settlement in 1848. The forest was harvested more than 150 years ago right on the water. Imagine the trees being three to four times their current size, and you will have an idea of what Sylvester and Smith had to deal with to carve out their new community.

In downtown Olympia, Sylvester, a Mainer, laid out a town square, a common New England feature. During the Indian Wars of 1855–56, a blockhouse was constructed in the square that was large enough to protect all of the Olympian citizens. The town square has since been home to numerous presidential addresses and is still a center of goings-on with summer concerts and other activities.

Olympia has continued to thrive due to its government economic base. Situated on Puget Sound between Mount Rainier and Olympic National Parks and an hour east of the Pacific Ocean, Olympia boasts unlimited recreational opportunities. Evergreen State College, home of the Geoducks, was opened in 1971 and has been consistently rated as one of the top five liberal arts colleges in the country. It is nestled in the forest west of downtown. Olympia was recently noted as one of the "hottest" college towns in the country.

Oyster Bay

From Olympia, head west on US 101, and in about 4.5 miles from I-5, you will cross a bridge over Mud Bay, the southernmost portion of Puget Sound. At low tide, you'll see how it got its name. At about 6 miles from I-5, follow the signs to stay on US 101 north toward Shelton

The Shaker Church

In 1880, after numerous near-death experiences, Squaxin Island Indian John Slocum founded the Shaker Church. It is a combination of Native American Twana and Catholic traditions, using many of the same instruments as Catholicism such as candles, crosses, and vestments. The name, which comes from the motion the parishioners make during services, is not related to the eastern American religion of the same name.

When the Shaker Church was founded, the local Indian agent tried to ban it. The tribe had to go to court to be allowed to continue worshiping as they wish. The Shaker Church is still active today, with members spreading from British Columbia to California.

To find the modest church, from the intersection of WR 8 and US 101, continue west on WR 8/US Highway 12 toward Aberdeen, then take the first right after the US 101 exit, onto Shaker Church Road. The church is about a

quarter mile from WA 8/US 12. (You can continue east and north on this road and rejoin US 101 to continue the Olympic Milestone Loop.)

(the other highway, Washington Highway 8, is your return leg from Aberdeen in Milestone 10). To visit the Shaker Church (see sidebar), take a left here onto WA 8/US Highway 12. Otherwise, continue on US 101 as it follows the shore of Eld Inlet.

At 11 miles from I-5, you will pass Oyster Bay at the end of Totten Inlet just to the east of you. Pull over to the right at the first opportunity just after passing the tip of the bay, onto the Old Olympic Highway, and immediately turn into the parking lot on the right with a reader board. You will possibly see oystermen out in the bay. This is one of the prime oyster-growing areas in Puget Sound. Much of the land in the bay and along the northern shore is part of the Kennedy Creek Natural Area Preserve (NAP), a Washington State Department of Natural Resources protected area. Venture about a hundred yards north on the Old Olympic Highway to a reader board that explains why this area is so valuable. Across the highway, also on Old Olympic Highway, is an area along Kennedy Creek where it empties into Oyster Bay. It is designated a prime salmon habitat.

Natural Area Preserves

One state and three federal agencies have designated twenty-five sites for preservation, education and/or research over and above the wilderness designations that the Peninsula has. Though these sites are all "open to the public" only a small handful are accessible. The Kennedy Creek NAP is perhaps the most accessible. The Chehalis River Surge Plain NAP just south of Montesano is also developed for visitors. (The Natural Resource Conservation Area program is a subset of the NAP program; NRCA sites often include other features such as scenic or historic value.) The mission of the Natural Areas Program is "conserving Washington's native species and ecosystems, today and for future generations."

Puget Sound and Washington's southern coast are some of the best oyster- and shellfish-growing regions in the world. In fact, Washington State is the largest grower of shellfish in the country, producing more than 80 percent of all West Coast shellfish. The shellfish industry is the second-largest employer in Mason County.

Peninsula Counties

Mason County, named for the state's first territorial secretary in 1854, is the smallest, by both geographic and population standards, of the four Peninsula counties. The town of Potlatch is near the geographic center of Mason County. The other three counties are Jefferson (which spans the central part of the Peninsula), Clallam (borders the Strait of Juan de Fuca), and Grays Harbor.

The only native oyster in Puget Sound is called the Olympia (*Ostrea conchaphila),* a dollar-sized mollusk that was a staple for the Native tribes. Olympia oysters were first shipped to California to feed all the Forty-Niners in the goldfields. This native oyster became a victim of overharvesting, pollution, habitat destruction and intentional introduction of nonnative species, primarily the Pacific oyster (*Crassostrea gigas*). With the decline of the Olympia oyster, oyster farmers imported the Pacific oyster from Japan during the first half of the twentieth century. The most popular oyster in the world, it is well suited for the cold waters of Puget Sound, growing three times as fast as the little Olympia.

Loving It to Death?

Are we loving our little piece of paradise to death? With the ever-present demands of development in the Puget Sound watershed, we have witnessed the steady decline in the quality of the whole Sound ecosystem. Even though Puget Sound has a natural flushing action with every tide, the system now is completely overwhelmed by the amount of pollution that currently exists in this National Estuary Program site designated by the federal Environmental Protection Agency.

Because we have cut down the forests and replaced trees with pavement and homes, the ground cannot absorb and clean the water fast enough. This leads to our toxins washing directly into the Sound. These toxin sources numbering in the thousands, if not millions, range from large industrial complexes surrounding our waterways in Tacoma and Seattle to residents who wash their cars in their driveways and over apply pesticides and herbicides in their yards. Toxins also come from the many vessels that ply the waters of the Sound, from large container ships to thousands of small boats. Toxins also come from sewage systems overwhelmed by floods, which are due in no small part because the forests have been cut down, and toxins also come from septic systems that drain directly into Hood Canal.

The embattled Olympia oyster is making modest comebacks. Many oystermen still propagate the Olympia because it fetches such a premium price. The Nature Conservancy recently started a program in Woodard Bay, just north of Olympia, by "seeding" the bay with Olympia oyster shells in hopes of reintroducing the Olympia. That area is a Washington State Natural Resource Conservation Area with very specific protections against any development. (See "Natural Area Preserves" sidebar in this chapter.)

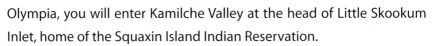

Kamilche Valley and Squaxin Island Indians

At about 14 miles from Olympia, you will enter Kamilche Valley at the head of Little Skookum Inlet, home of the Squaxin Island Indian Reservation.

On December 26, 1854, the nine tribes of southern Puget Sound gathered near the Nisqually River Delta on Medicine Creek (now called McAllister Creek) to sign the Treaty of Medicine Creek (see sidebar), negotiated by Isaac Stevens, the territorial governor of Washington. The treaty was negotiated in the Chinook Jargon, the common trading language of the Northwest Indians. Sixty-two Indian leaders signed by leaving their mark, and more than 600 natives attended the signing ceremony despite the driving rain and bad weather. The natives, in consideration of giving up more than 4000 square miles, or 2.56 million acres, in the Puget Sound region, received $32,500 and a few reservations where they were forced to settle. They also received "the right of taking fish, at all usual accustomed grounds and stations . . . " This last phrase would be rediscovered 120 years later and greatly benefit the Indians, much to the displeasure of nonnatives (see "Treaty Fishing Heritage and the Boldt Decision" in chapter 3, Original Inhabitants).

Treaty Of Medicine Creek—1854

Between the United States and the Nisqually, Puyallup, Steilacoom, Squaxin, Samamish, Stechass, T'Peeksin, Squiatl, and Sahehwamish Tribes

Article 1. The said tribes and bands of Indians hereby cede, relinquish, and convey to the United States, all their right, title, and interest in and to Wit: Commencing on the eastern side of Admiralty Inlet known as Point Pully, about midway between Commencement and Elliott Bays; thence southerly, along the summit of said range, to a point opposite the main source of the Skookum Chuck Creek; thence to and down said creek, to the coal mine; thence northwesterly, to the summit of the Black Hills thence northerly, to the upper forks of the Satsop River; thence north-easterly, through the portage known as Wilkes's Portage, to the Point Southworth, on the western side of Admiralty Inlet; thence around the foot of Vashon's Island, easterly and southeasterly, to the place of beginning.

Article 3. The right of taking fish, at all usual accustomed grounds and stations, is further secured to said Indians in common with all citizens of the Territory, and of erecting temporary houses for the purpose of curing, together with the privilege of hunting, gathering roots and berries, and pasturing their horses on open and unclaimed lands . . .

Once you're in Kamilche, turn right on Old Olympic Highway and travel a short mile to the Squaxin Island Tribe's Museum Library and Research Center. This educational and entertaining museum covers all aspects of the Squaxin Island Indians and southern Puget Sound Native history. Just the architecture of the building is worth leaving the highway to see. The building was designed to resemble a Thunderbird, a powerful symbol in native culture.

According to the Squaxin Island Indians, "We are the Noo-Seh-Chatl of Henderson Inlet, Steh Chass of Budd Inlet, Squi-Aitl of Eld Inlet, Sawamish/T'Peeksin of Totten Inlet, Sa-Heh-Wa-Mish of Hammersley Inlet, Squawksin of Case Inlet, and S'Hotle-Ma-Mish of Carr Inlet. We also belong to the surrounding watersheds. We are the People of the Water." The total tribal population from the 2000 census was 405.

Their designated reservation from the Medicine Creek Treaty was Squaxin Island, which is about 9 miles northeast of Kamilche near the mouths of Totten, Eld and Budd Inlets. The unpopulated island has no

Squaxin Island Tribe's Museum Library and Research Center

running water and the last resident left in 1959. Today the tribe owns various properties and off-reservation trust lands around the Kamilche area totaling 1700 acres, 1400 of which are on the island. Squaxin Island is off-limits to nontribal people. There used to be a boat-only state park, but the land was returned to the tribe when the state acquired Hope Island, just to the west of Squaxin Island, for another park.

Back on US Highway 101 in Kamilche, travel north just over 6 miles toward the town of Shelton.

Shelton Side Trip

To visit Shelton, take Washington Highway 3 northeast about 2 miles into downtown. This is the town that David Shelton plotted, Sol Simpson and Alfred Anderson put on the map, and Mark Reed made prosperous—the town where big timber meets access to the markets meets men with big ideas.

Hugh Goldsborough and Michael Simmons, from Olympia, built one of the first water-powered sawmills in the country on the south shore of Oakland Bay in 1853 on a donation land claim. David Shelton settled this area in the mid-1853 on another donation land claim at the mouth of what is now called Goldsborough Creek. His cabin was on the site of the current Public Safety Building.

Overlooking Shelton with the Olympic Mountains in the background

SITE OF
DAVID SHELTON
FIRST CABIN
1854

DEDICATED
BICENTENNIAL YEAR 1976
BY THE
FRED B. WIVELL POST No.31
AMERICAN LEGION

Donation Land Claim Act

The Donation Land Claim Act of 1850–55 was designed by Congress to encourage settlers in the Oregon Territory, now the states of Oregon, Washington and Idaho. This watershed law allowed women and Native Americans to acquire land.

In 1854 Shelton served at the first session of the Washington Territorial Legislature. He proposed that a new county be formed called Sawamish County, named after the original residents of the area. The name was eventually changed to Mason County to honor the Territorial Secretary of State and Acting Governor, Charles Mason. Isaac Stevens, then governor, was typically absent from Olympia as the "Negotiator" parleying with the Native Americans (see "The Tribes" in chapter 3,

Original Inhabitants). Shelton eventually plotted his holdings to establish the town named after him. He generously donated plots for four different churches and served as its first mayor in 1889 after the town became incorporated.

Logging was initiated to clear land for agriculture. With California's extensive demand for lumber, logging became the sole driver of the Shelton economy for many decades, if not a century. Initially, only logs that could be dropped or dragged into Puget Sound were cut. Oxen and horses were later employed to drag the logs over skid roads. The animal power was limited to about a mile from the shoreline. Logging really took off in the late nineteenth century due to mechanizations in the form of railroads and steam donkeys (see "Birth of the Timber Industry" in chapter 5, The 19th Century). Sol Simpson took advantage of all the resources and founded Simpson Timber in 1887. Simpson Timber, the end result of almost fifty years of bankruptcies and reorganizations of competitors, eventually became the state's largest employer and second-largest private real estate holder.

Shelton's pride in its logging and railroad heritage can be seen right on the main street, named, appropriately, West Railroad Avenue. You can see a railroad engine, a caboose, and a load of logs. The caboose is the current home of the Chamber of Commerce.

At the east end of West Railroad Avenue is the Rayonier paper mill. Oakland Bay and Hammersley Inlet on the far side of the plant were once one of the premier oyster-growing areas in Washington State. However, as the mill grew its effluent killed off more and more of the oysters until the oyster farmers sued and closed the factory down. This resulted in massive unemployment since virtually everyone in Shelton worked either directly or indirectly for the mill. The town rallied and passed the hat, generating $166,000, which was used to buy out the oyster farmers and restart the plant.

The biggest donor to the oyster buyout plan was Mark Reed, then the current owner of Simpson Timber. Reed married into the Simpson family and eventually was given complete control. Mr. Reed is widely crediting with successfully taking the lumber company through the 1910s and 1920s. He also continued David Shelton's tradition of philanthropy by donating monies for many of the civic improvements in the city. He went on to serve as Shelton's mayor and in the Washington State Legislature. While in the legislature, he promoted new laws that benefited workers, public ownerships of utilities and funds for reforestation (Mason County—Thumbnail History, 2009).

To return to the highway, go west on West Railroad Avenue, following the signs for US 101 North, which you reach in about a mile.

Creeks and Bridges

Once you're back on US 101, the airport that you pass in about 2 miles is on Scott's Prairie, named for an 1854 pioneer, John Tucker Scott.

In about 3 miles north of the entrance to the airport, you will see East Brockdale Road enter the highway from the east. You have just

Mark Reed's family home

crossed over an ancient stream bed that flowed from the northwest to the southeast, fed by a retreating glacier some 12,000 years ago (Alt and Hyndman 1994). The stream bed now is occupied by Johns Creek, which empties into Oakland Bay, just north of downtown Shelton. This creek is fed by Johns Lake, which is a glacial kettle, as possibly are Island Lake and Rex Lake nearby (see "Ice" in chapter 1, Geology).

The highway proceeds down Purdy Canyon, along the creek of the same name. This canyon and the Skokomish River Valley were possibly carved from water running underneath the glacier. After the glaciers re-treated, the land rebounded at the head of the canyon and cut off the source of Purdy Creek. The ice sheets were not static but waxed and waned over the course of thousands of years, shaping and reshaping the landscape.

If high bridges listed on the National Register of Historic Places in-terest you, take a short side trip to check out the Vance Creek Bridge (347 feet high) or the High Steel Bridge upstream on the South Fork of the Skokomish. Both these bridges helped open up vast new swaths of land for timber cutting. The High Steel Bridge, built in 1929, is highest

South Fork of the Skokomish River and Vincent Creek as seen from the High Steel Bridge deck.

railway arch bridge ever built in the country at 365 feet high. To view it, turn west on West Skokomish Valley Road (follow the signs to the fish hatchery) a few yards before you actually cross the Skokomish River. Travel west on the Skokomish Valley Road for approximately 5 miles to Forest Service Road 23, where the road forks; take the right fork. Continue on the FS road for a little less than 2.5 miles to FS 2340. Another 2.5 miles or so on this road brings you to the High Steel Bridge. After your explorations, return 10 miles to US 101. It is hard and dangerous to see the bridge structure but the views from the bridge deck are quite dramatic. The drive on the Forest Service roads traverses an area of industrial logging which alternates between second growth and clearcuts.

Skokomish Indians

Continuing north along US 101 and across the Skokomish River, the largest river feeding into Hood Canal, you enter the Skokomish Indian Reservation, the only reservation on Hood Canal. The reservation, about 5000 acres, straddles the highway. In 2000 the population was 730.

The Skokomish Indians, aboriginally called the Twana, were first encountered by Europeans in 1792 during the Vancouver Expedition (see chapter 4, Early Explorers). At the time, the Twana lived up and down Hood Canal in nine or more separate groups, subsisting on the local seafood, plants, salmon and hunting in the Olympic Mountains to the west (Skokomish Tribe 2010). Vancouver's crew members gave them smallpox which decimated the tribe. They gave up all their original homelands by signing the Point No Point treaty of 1855 negotiated, again, by Isaac Stevens (see "The Peninsula Tribes" in chapter 3, Original Inhabitants).

At the turn of the twentieth century, a businessman from Tacoma had purchased and then diked tidelands in the Skokomish River delta. This wetland had been used by the tribe for millennia for hunting and harvesting of sweetgrass, a necessary component in their wonderful woven baskets. The state of Washington then rewrote the laws regarding tidelands, opening up development and restricting Indian shellfish harvest on all the state's tidelands. In addition, the City of Tacoma built dams along the North Fork of the Skokomish River in the 1920s.

All these actions significantly reduced the tribe's ability to live off their land. The tribe settled for $374,000 in 1965, which they used to purchase a fish processing plant along with other tribal improvements (according to Skokomish Indian Tribe). Currently, the tribal members earn their living with commercial fishing and logging. The Lucky Dog casino, near Potlatch north of the reservation, also provides employment.

In the 5 miles north of West Skokomish Valley Road, on the way to the hamlet of Potlatch, you will pass Potlatch State Park. This was a site of historic potlatch ceremonies that was carved out of the original reservation in 1960 by the state for this park. This was the final indignation the tribe suffered before going to court to seek retribution.

Skokomish River

Unfortunately, the Skokomish River remains one of the most flood-prone rivers in Washington State. All the logging upstream diminished the watershed's ability to absorb the rain. Also, the logging has dramatically increased the flushing of massive amounts of sediment into the lower, flatter sections of the river, reducing the carrying capacity of the river.

Soon after you pass Potlatch State Park, the Tacoma Lake Cushman Powerhouse appears on the west side of the highway. The powerhouse, the tallest building on Hood Canal, is an amazing building that looks completely out of place, which it is. The building, along with its two upstream dams, is listed on the National Register of Historic Places. And it is part of the system that gifts the City of Tacoma with some of the cheapest electricity in the country.

There are two dams up the North Fork Skokomish River. One is at Lake Cushman and another just over 2 miles downstream at Lake Kokanee.

Lake Kokanee was created with the building of the Cushman Dam No. 2. Electricity is generated at the dam No. 1. Water is pulled from Lake Kokanee and sent to the powerhouse on US 101 through the large penstocks behind the building. The whole system eliminated about 80 percent of the Lake Cushman and North Fork of the Skokomish River salmon run when it was completed in 1930. Building the dams and powerhouse was an enormous undertaking requiring that housing be provided for 550 men.

Potlatch and Hoodsport

On US 101, you will arrive in the hamlet of Potlatch in about a half mile after the powerhouse. If cemeteries are of interest, there is a modest but well-maintained one on the east side of the highway right next to the Lucky Dog casino. It contains graves that are 130 years old.

Potlatch was also the location of a native graveyard. Indians put the bodies, canoes and other personal belongings up in the trees, some-

Cushman Dam No. 1

times covering the burial with cedar shakes. The remains were moved when a logging camp moved in at the turn of the twentieth century (Dalby 2000).

Two miles north on US 101 is Hoodsport. In 1792, the Vancouver party found five native families living along Finch Creek, in what is now downtown Hoodsport (Bearden 1994). Hoodsport was founded in 1880 by Captain Robbins, a seafarer from Maine. The town eventually became a logging community, then evolved to a fishing center and later turned to tourism. It is the largest town on Hood Canal, with a population of about 2000.

Lake Cushman and Staircase Side Trip

In downtown Hoodsport, if you turn west on Washington Highway 119, you can access Lake Cushman and the Staircase area of Olympic National Park. Lake Cushman is the third-largest lake on the Peninsula, behind Ozette Lake and Lake Crescent near Port Angeles.

Lake Cushman is a glacially carved lake with a terminal moraine (see "Ice" in chapter 1, Geology) at its outlet (Tabor 1975). The moraine is now under water due to the Tacoma power project, which raised the level of the lake 180 feet and increased the lake's size threefold (Bearden 1994). The lake was named for Orrington Cushman, one of Isaac Stevens's interpreters. It was Cushman who suggested that all Northwest Indians be placed on a gigantic reservation on Hood Canal.

Directly east of Lake Cushman is the rounded hill of Saddle Mountain, reaching an elevation of 1800 feet. Dow Mountain, just to the south, more than 2500 feet high, is much less rounded. The comparison of these two hills indicates that the ice lobe coming south from Canada had a height of somewhere between the elevations of these mountains.

Lake Cushman has always been a tourist draw, especially when trophy-sized trout were discovered in the lake. Today Lake Cushman Resort, at the mouth of Big Creek, about 7 miles from US 101, provides lake access and a boat launch. A bit farther north on the road is Big Creek forest campground.

Big Creek flows south and crosses the road at the intersection with Forest Road 24, about 9 miles from US 101, before flowing into the lake. Archaeological finds show that this area was settled as long as 7000 years ago. Lake Cushman saw its first European settlers in 1888, including Alfred Rose. Mr. Rose died of smallpox and his home burned down. Mount Rose, 4000 feet high, at the north end of the lake was named after him.

WA 119 terminates inside Olympic National Park in the Staircase campground area, about 11 miles from US 101. This is one of the major jump-off spots for hiking in the park. The campground here is open year-round, with many sites directly on the river.

A Staircase Hike

If you have the time and inclination, wander up the Staircase Trail upriver from the campground as far as your legs will take you, strolling the nearly level path along the North Fork of the Skokomish River. It is one of the most accessible places to see big trees on the east side of the Peninsula. Imagine Lieutenant O'Neil with his expedition of mules, men, and equipment hacking the same way up the river in 1890.

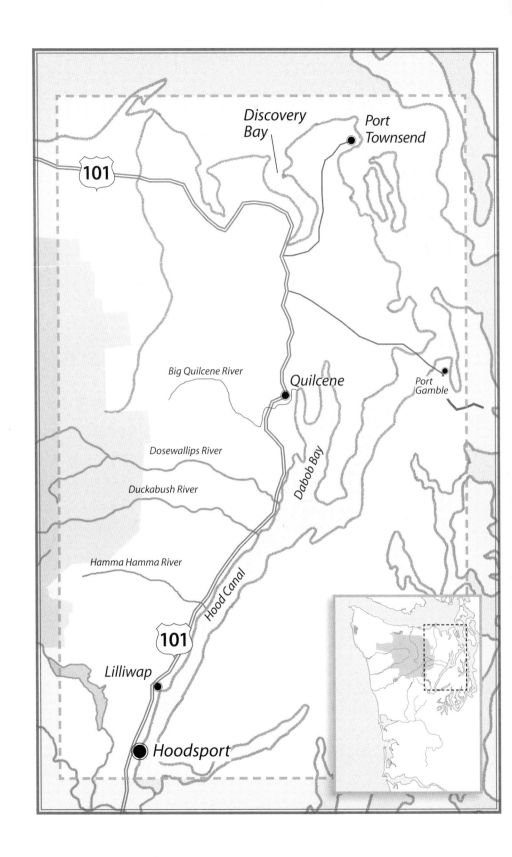

MILESTONE 2

HOODSPORT TO DISCOVERY BAY

Continuing on US Highway 101 north from Hoodsport to Discovery Bay, Milestone 2 is about 48 miles. The first thing you'll encounter, in just over 4 miles from Hoodsport, is Lilliwaup, one of the oldest communities on Hood Canal.

Lilliwaup

Named for the Indian word for "inlet," Lilliwaup is situated on a small bay where Lilliwaup Creek empties into the canal. The creek is home to one of the most spectacular waterfalls but it is, unfortunately, on private land and not accessible.

First homesteaded in 1860 by Captain McNair, Lilliwaup was Lieutenant O'Neil's starting point for the first east-to-west trans-Peninsula expedition which terminated at Lake Quinault. O'Neil would have been better served to start west from Hoodsport, not Lilliwaup. It was very difficult to move all the men, animals and supplies through the waterfall area (see "Exploring the Mountains" in chapter 5, The 19th Century).

The lieutenant's progress can be judged by his campsites past the Staircase Ranger Station (see "Lake Cushman and Staircase Side Trip" in

Lilliwaup from across Lilliwaup Bay

Milestone 1, Olympia to Hoodsport). At about 2 miles past Staircase is Stream Four and another 1.5 miles is Stream Five, representing O'Neil's fourth and fifth camp spots. Staircase Ranger Station is about 12 "trail" miles from Lilliwaup, so the expedition was going only about 3 miles per day just to reach Staircase. This is not hard to believe when you consider how difficult it must have been to travel through virgin forest where many of the trees were dozens of feet in diameter.

Lilliwaup had high hopes, built a hotel and was considered as a site for a state college (Fredson 1993). It was looking toward a bright future when the bottom fell out during the Panic of 1893 and plans for a railroad were cancelled. Today, it has a population of only a few hundred. A privately owned salmon hatchery here promotes plenty of fishing opportunities.

More Creeks and Bridges

Just under 6 miles north of Lilliwaup, Jorsted Creek empties into Hood Canal. It was here in the mid-1700s that a brutal battle took place

between the local Twana (Skokomish) and tribes from the north. Word had reached the Twana in this area that a raiding party was headed down the canal. They tricked the marauders by leaving the women and children at camp. When the attack began, the women and children rushed up the creek, drawing the attackers into the trap that had been laid. The Twana swept out of their hiding places and it was complete annihilation. The victorious Indians just abandoned their camp and the bodies that littered the ground. Early Europeans even noticed what remained of the corpses.

The bridges that cross the Hamma Hamma River a couple miles north of Jorsted Creek are listed in the National Register of Historic Places. They were built in 1924 using a novel construction technique of substituting concrete for steel. They are two of only five bridges in the state built this way. Their engineering removed any need for enormous foundations and abutments.

Up ahead, notice all the pilings just offshore in the canal. These are remnants of the logging industry. Logs were brought down to the water

and collected into large rafts waiting to be moved to the mills, primarily in Shelton and Port Gamble. The pilings were used to secure the log rafts prior to their being towed away; these pilings were used up to the 1970s.

Just over 1.4 miles north of the North Hamma Hamma Bridge, Waketickeh Creek empties into Hood Canal. Virtually all the streams and rivers that flow into the canal are rich with salmon, but Waketickeh Creek does not support salmon. Native Twana stories tell of one of its members stubbing his toe in the creek and cursing it. Through a fluke of geology, the stream bed does not have the necessary gravel beds for salmon redds, the nest that female salmon create to hold their fertilized eggs (see "Elwha Restoration" in chapter 7, The 21st Century and the Future).

Hamma Hamma River Side Trip

If you want a short diversion, just north of Waketickeh Creek turn west off US 101 onto Hamma Hamma Road and travel about 3 miles. Just north of here for the next 2 miles is the state Department of Natural Resources' (DNR) 900-acre Hamma Hamma Balds Natural Area Preserve. The Hamma Hamma Balds NAP was created to maintain an ecosystem that supports up to a half dozen rare and endangered plant species. There is no reader board or any other visible designation of where exactly the NAP is. That is intentional, as this is a very sensitive area that is not conducive to unguided visitors.

Department of Natural Resources

The DNR, the largest landowner on the Peninsula, manages 5.6 million acres across the state for the primary purpose of generating revenue for

Washington's public schools. The agency's mission, in part, reads: "To provide professional, forward-looking stewardship of our state lands, natural resources, and environment. To provide leadership in creating a sustainable future for the Trusts and all." Some of the land that DNR manages are wild areas such as the Hamma Hamma Balds Natural Area Preserve.

Farther up the Hamma Hamma Road, you will come to Hamma Hamma Cabin, an old Forest Service ranger station. This cabin built in 1937 by the Civilian Conservation Corps has been nominated to be listed on the National Register of Historic Places. Its location puts you smack in the middle of Olympic National Forest with easy access to the Brothers Wilderness, Mount Skokomish Wilderness and Olympic National Park. The cabin, which sleeps six, can be rented. (Contact www.reservation.gov.) There are two other ex-Forest Service cabins for rent on the Peninsula, both on the east side.

After your explorations, return 6 miles back to the junction of the Hamma Hamma Road and US 101 where there is a retail establishment and processing center, indicative of the rich shellfish beds in this area.

Interrorem cabin

Duckabush River

Just shy of 8 miles north on US 101 is the hamlet of Duckabush, on the river and road of the same name. "Duckabush" is Indian for "reddish face," which refers to the supposed color of the cliffs nearby. The bridge across the Duckabush River, also on the National Register of Historic Places, was completed in 1934 with the same novel concrete construction techniques as the Hamma Hamma bridges to the south.

Interrorem Guard Station Side Trip

For a short jaunt into the foothills, go up the Duckabush River Road 3.5 miles to the Interrorem Guard Station. The building, available for rent (like the Hamma Hamma cabin), was built in 1907 as the original Forest Service administrative site for the Olympic National Forest. Listed on the National Register of Historic Places, it is the oldest building in Olympic National Forest. If you have a chance to get inside, look at the old photos on the walls. When the photos were taken, it appears that the cabin was built in a meadow since so much logging had been done. A short stroll on the path adjacent to the property indicates otherwise. The enormous stumps reveal what the earliest pioneers had to deal with when they settled.

The remnants of the original old-growth forest can be found less than 100 yards from the cabin.

The peninsula to the east of US 101 is Black Point. At the tip of Black Point is Quatsap Point, which is Indian for "Cougar Point." Indian legend tells the story of the cougar that backed up into a campfire, forever giving him a black-tipped tail (Lund and Smyth 1999).

About 1 mile north of the Duckabush River Road, primitive Pleasant Harbor State Park (no services) is on the right of US 101. A Canadian development company is trying to move ahead with plans for a $300 million 890-unit complex on 250 acres of Black Point and Pleasant Harbor, improving the marina and building a golf course. Many local residents are doing their best to stop it (Chew 2008).

Dosewallips River

About 3 miles north of Pleasant Harbor is the small town of Brinnon, population of about 1000, and the Dosewallips River. This was the southern reach of the north coast Klallam Indians, who spent summers camped out on the bank of the Dosewallips. The name Dosewallips is native for "place of thieves, selfish people, people who'll take it away from you."

Brinnon was first platted in 1875 by Ewell Brinnon. Mr. Brinnon married a Skokomish woman and adopted two Indian children. He gave an acre of land for the first school, and by 1890 there were thirty-three students. The community finally received electricity in 1949 with the help of the federal Rural Electrification Administration (Bailey 1997). Today Dosewallips State Park, at the mouth of the river just south of Brinnon, offers camping, picnicking and beach access.

The first bridge across the Dosewallips cost $888 in 1888. Another new bridge in 1890 cost $1300. Another bridge was built in 1894, and others in 1902, 1909, and 1910. The current bridge was completed in 1923 for $50,000.

Dosewallips River Side Trip

If you turn left (west) onto the Dosewallips Road, in 3 miles you'll reach Rocky Brook Falls This 120-foot-high waterfall is only about 200 feet from the road beyond the diminutive concrete power station. The power station pulls water from above the falls.

About 10 miles west of the highway, the Dosewallips River washed away the road in 2002. This stranded Elkhorn Campground, a Forest Service campground about a mile from the washout and an Olympic National Park campground farther up the road. From the washout, you can climb up the steep hill and descend to the original road on the other side of the washout. Wandering around the campground is very eerie. It is a beautiful camping location right on the river. But nothing has changed since the washout, even the notices of ranger talks scheduled for long-past evenings. Everything is left in place, and all that is missing are the campers.

There are plans to repair the road, and an environmental impact statement has been finalized. The Forest Service has estimated that it will take $2.75 million to 3.5 million to reroute a new road. The issue has pitted the local residents wanting the road repaired against environmental groups wanting to return what's left of the road beyond the washout to a trail.

Back on US 101, in another short mile north you will pass Seal Rock Campground. This lovely spot is right on Hood Canal. It is also the only

Rocky Brook Falls

place where Olympic National Forest touches salt water. In about 1.5 miles, the highway turns inland, away from the shore of the canal.

Mount Walker Side Trip

Six miles north of Brinnon is the turnoff on the right for 2800-foot Mount Walker. The road leads 1.4 miles to the top, affording dramatic 360-degree views of everything from Seattle to the east to Olympic National Park to the west. Come here in late May and early June for one of the best wild rhododendron shows on the Peninsula.

Quilcene and Dabob Bay

Continuing north on US 101, 5 miles from the Mount Walker turnoff is the town of Quilcene, population 600, home to the world's largest oyster hatchery. Founded in 1860 by a Mainer, Quilcene has gone through numerous reinventions. First it was a lumber town, then a railroad and mining center and finally an oyster town (with a little floral industry thrown in). It is also the home of the Olympic National Forest district headquarters.

The town's location on Dabob Bay was the northernmost reach of the Twana people, but the last of the Quilcene natives died in the 1920s. The Quinault on the west side of the Peninsula and the Quilcene natives had a trading relationship that spanned the area that is now the national park. Unfortunately, in the early 1800s warfare broke out and all but eliminated the Quilcenes.

As you continue north on US 101, in 12 miles you reach Discovery Bay. If you want to go to see Port Gamble and then on to the Quimper Peninsula and Port Townsend (Milestone 3), turn east on Center Road just north of Quilcene's modest downtown. You will save a couple of miles and hook up with Washington Highway 104, which crosses Hood Canal about 8 miles from Quilcene.

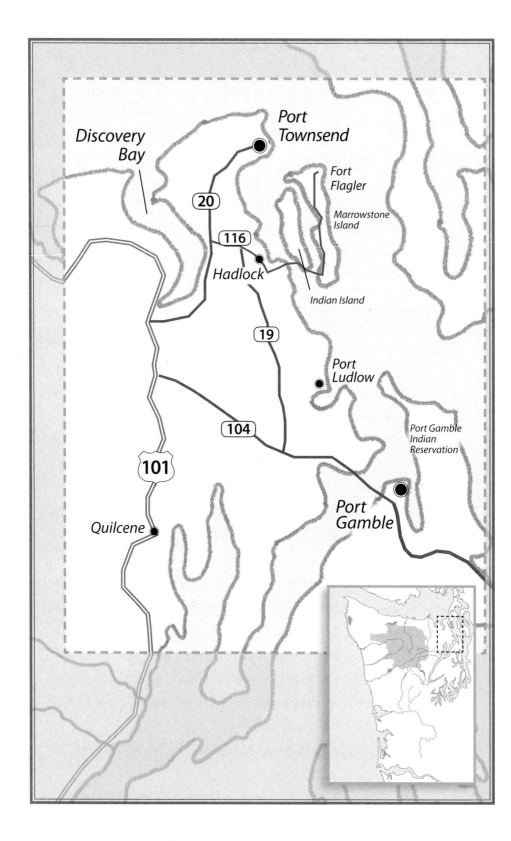

MILESTONE 3

QUIMPER PENINSULA

This 28-mile loop around the Quimper Peninsula visits a town where the whole community is on the National Register of Historic Places, then goes to another where fifty-eight locations are listed either on the National Historic or Washington State Registries—or both. In between are islands and naval stations, lighthouses and forts.

To start this loop, on US Highway 101 about 2 miles south of Discovery Bay (about 10 miles north of Quilcene), turn east on Washington Highway 104 for about 11 miles to WA 19. Here you have a choice: continue east on WA 104 to visit Port Gamble or turn north on WA 19 to start the loop of the Quimper Peninsula.

Port Gamble Side Trip

Port Gamble, one of the more interesting cultural artifacts in the state, is not on the Olympic but the Kitsap Peninsula. But its uniqueness, its historic ties to the west, and the fact that it is right on one of the main arteries onto the Peninsula invites its inclusion here.

To reach Port Gamble from the intersection of WA 104 and WA 19, continue east on WA 104 for another 5 miles, crossing the 1.5-mile-long

*The Tea Room at Port Gamble is an excellent example of the architecture
and history of the town.*

Hood Canal Bridge; across the canal, stay left and in about a mile you'll
reach Port Gamble.

Hood Canal Bridge

The famous Hood Canal Bridge is the longest floating bridge over salt
water in the world and the third largest overall. Initially built in 1961 amid much
concern over its feasibility, it stayed afloat for eighteen years before a storm of
hurricane forces sank much of it in 1979. In 1982 the rebuilding was complete
and it reopened. The Hood Canal Bridge is a draw span to allow submarines
passage; occasionally, when the bridge is closed to let a submarine through you
can see one cruising in or out of Hood Canal.

Port Gamble, the best-maintained company town in the state, with
its white picket fences and beautiful homes, looks as though it's right
out of a Norman Rockwell painting. Like virtually every other location
on the Olympic Peninsula, Port Gamble had been occupied by Indians.

Looking west from Point Julia to Port Gamble

A tribe related to the Elwha River S'Klallam and Jonestown S'Klallam Tribe was camped on this northernmost tip of the Kitsap Peninsula when, in 1853, a Mainer, William Talbot, came ashore. Talbot used trinkets and gifts to convince the Indians to move across the bay of Port Gamble to Point Julia. He soon set up a sawmill. The Indians now occupy the Port Gamble Indian Reservation at the same location they moved to in 1853 (see "The Peninsula Tribes" in chapter 3, Original Inhabitants).

The Pope and Talbot operations quickly grew into one of the largest on the Peninsula. To entice workers to what was then a wilderness called the Washington Territory, they recruited men from their home state of Maine. And in order for the workers to feel more at home, the mill owners built the community of Port Gamble to resemble a New England town.

The Pope and Talbot company has gone through numerous changes, including selling the operation prior to WWII and then foreclosing

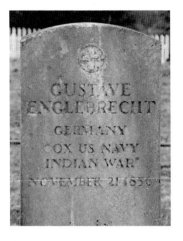

and gaining control again. The mill finally shut down in 1995, making it one of the longest-running mills in the nation.

The first U.S. Navy sailor, Gustave Englebrecht, to die in the Pacific is buried in the cemetery just above town. He was killed near Port Gamble during a Haida Indian raid from Canada in the Indian War of 1855–56 (see chapter 3, Original Inhabitants).

Bangor Naval Submarine Base

Twelve miles south of the eastern end of the Hood Canal Bridge (via WA 3) is the Bangor Naval Submarine Base. Initially it was an ammunition depot for WWII, but its role changed dramatically when it became a submarine base. Currently, eleven submarines operate out of the base. It is the third-largest depository for nuclear weapons in the country, with more than 1700 nuclear warheads stored onshore or onboard the submarines. Employment on the Kitsap Peninsula is driven by the military: Bangor has more than 11,000 employees while the Puget Sound Naval Shipyard in Bremerton employs thousands more.

Once you've finished exploring the east side of Hood Canal, re-cross the Hood Canal Bridge heading west on WA 104, and in 8 miles east of Port Gamble turn north on WA 19 to continue the Quimper Peninsula loop.

Port Ludlow

From WA 104, turn north on WA 19, then east on Oak Bay Road to reach the affluent community of Port Ludlow, now a retirement, golf resort and vacation home village, in 4 miles.

Settled one year earlier than Port Gamble, Port Ludlow's mill operated independently until 1878 when Pope and Talbot purchased it at auction. The mill opened and closed for the next sixty years before being disassembled. Many of the old pilings for the log rafts are still visible in the bay of Port Ludlow.

As you head north from Port Ludlow along Oak Bay Road, in just over 7 miles is the turnoff on the right (WA 116) to Indian Island Naval Reservation and Marrowstone Island.

Indian and Marrowstone Islands Side Trip

To reach these two islands, turn right onto WA 116. After another mile, the entrance to the Naval Ordnance Center, Port Hadlock base, located on Indian Island is straight ahead. The 2700-acre Indian Island, completely owned by the U.S. Navy, has been used as a munitions depot since the 1940s. The Navy had a land dump at the north end of the island where it disposed of military-generated wastes, including heavy metals and PCBs. These wastes eventually made it into Puget Sound, forcing the closure of the beaches and bays on the north end of both Marrowstone and Indian Islands. The site has recently been removed from the Environmental Protection Agency's Superfund list but remains toxic.

Indian Island is also home of the Peninsula's tallest structure. In 1999 a 280-foot-high crane was installed to handle munitions-filled containers. To see this crane, you need either a boat or a view from Port Townsend.

Almost 2 miles farther east on WA 116, you will reach Marrowstone Island, home to about 1000 people. When George Vancouver viewed the cliffs of this island, he was reminded of the "Marrow-stone" cliffs of his native England. Just shy of 8 miles long, the island's largest community, Nordland, is situated halfway up the island on the eastern shore. Nearby is Mystery Bay State Park. At the northern tip of the island is Fort Flagler State Park, one the three points of the "Triangle of Fire" (see sidebar). Fort Flagler has been designated an important birding area (IBA).

Marrowstone Island Lighthouse with Mt. Baker in the distance

The Triangle of Fire

Fort Flagler joins Fort Worden, north of Port Townsend, and Fort Casey, on Whidbey Island, as one of the three forts straddling Admiralty Inlet at the entrance to Puget Sound. Designed to defend Puget Sound from any water-based attack, the three forts were built around the turn of the twentieth century, providing a great boost to the local economy as the area was just recovering from the Panic of '93. No shot from the dozens of artillery at each fort was ever shot in anger; the forts were mainly used as training areas for the military. Decommissioned and sold to Washington State in the 1950s, all three forts offer camping, conference facilities and opportunities to see the old fortresses, as well as terrific views, lighthouses and beachcombing. The three are also on the National Historical Register.

Marrowstone Lighthouse is on the northeast corner of the island, where WA 116 ends; the lighthouse has been operational since 1888. The buildings house a marine research station operated by the U.S. Geological Survey.

When you've completed your explorations, return 11 miles to WA 116 and turn right.

Chimacum Valley

Once off the islands, you are now on the Quimper Peninsula proper, named for the Spaniard Manuel Quimper who, in 1790, sailed these waters two years prior to George Vancouver. Quimper was also the first European to land at Neah Bay (see chapter 2, Early Explorers).

Going north on WA 116, you are entering the Tri-Area of the little burgs of Chimacum, Port Hadlock and Irondale. Chimacum is known for its farms and as being the home of Ma and Pa Kettle, famous fictitious rural bumpkins of the 1940s from the best-selling book *The Egg and I* and the movies based on the book. (It is a slight detour, 2 miles to the left, at WA 19.)

Port Hadlock, a sawmill town on WA 116, enjoyed the same successes and downfall that every other sawmill town of the Peninsula enjoyed. It is located at the southern end of Port Townsend bay, with a view of Indian Island.

Irondale is just beyond, near the northern junction of WA 116 with WA 19. Puget Sound Iron Company started creating steel in Irondale in 1879, thinking that it sat upon an ocean of coal. It closed ten years later, only to reopen as Western Steel a few years hence. The *Seattle Post-Intelligencer* declared in 1910 that Irondale had the potential "of becoming the largest and most important manufacturing city in Western America." Dramatically, Western Steel declared bankruptcy one year later, and Irondale has never recovered.

Continuing north, WA 116 merges into WA 19 which then joins WA 20 in about 2.5 miles. A left turn takes you back to Discovery Bay at US 101, but to continue exploring the Quimper Peninsula, turn right.

Less than a half mile on WA 20 is the turnoff on the right for Old Fort Townsend State Park. The fort was established to provide protection for the Indian Wars of 1855–56. Not many had faith that it would provide any help in case of attack. It was too far south of the town of Port Townsend

Port Townsend in 1890

and lacked adequate water supplies. The fort was opened and closed over the next forty years before it finally burned down in 1895. It was revived during WWII when the Navy used it to defuse torpedoes.

The state purchased the fort in the 1950s, and it remains the best example of old-growth forest on the whole Quimper Peninsula. Camping, short hiking trails through the forest and a small beach are available. From the park turnoff, head north on WA 20 about 4 miles to reach downtown Port Townsend.

Port Townsend

Originally settled in 1851, Port Townsend is "the Town that Time Forgot." Originally named Port Townshend by George Vancouver for his fellow soldier and friend, the Marquis of Townshend, the new city's future looked bright. It quickly became the economic hub of all Puget Sound because of its central location and its excellent harbor.

In 1854 the U.S. Point of Entry and Customs House were moved from Olympia to Port Townsend, forcing all ships entering Washington

Former Customs House, now the town's post office

State waters to stop there. It was quite a battle with Port Angeles for the right of the Customs House (see Milestone 5, Port Angeles to Neah Bay). Often Port Townsend was the ships' first port of call in a long time and the sailors, needing a place to burn off steam, were greeted by one of the most robust and ribald wharf areas on the West Coast.

The end of Port Townsend's boom was caused by the Panic of '93 when railroad investors decided to abandon the idea of making Port Townsend the westernmost terminus of the Union Pacific Railroad up from Tacoma. Also at that time, steamships started to just bypass the port because of the vessels' speed and dependability. Seattle was named the location of the Customs House in 1913 and Port Townsend was soon forgotten.

The city's population plummeted from 7000 when the railroad hysteria was at its peak to less than 2000 ten years later. It is now only about 10,000. The railroad never went farther south than Quilcene. The city did receive economic bumps from the Klondike Gold Rush in 1897 and from Fort Worden, 1 mile north of downtown, and Fort Flagler on Marrowstone Island.

Point Wilson Lighthouse

The good news is that Port Townsend's economic downfall is now our gain. The whole downtown, along with numerous other buildings, has been listed on the National and Washington Historical Registers. Residents take great pride in their city's architecture and Port Townsend has become the unofficial bed-and-breakfast capital of the state. The large paper mill on the south end of the city has provided a stable employment base but the city is growing due to tourism.

Another look into Port Townsend's past can be gained from Fort Worden and Point Wilson Lighthouse just north of downtown. The point was first landed on by Quimper in 1790 and then Vancouver in 1792. Vancouver walked the beach for a few hours while waiting for the fog to lift so that he could sail into Admiralty Inlet. The first lighthouse at the point came on in 1879. The current lighthouse was built in 1913 and has been automated since 1977.

At Fort Worden, beautifully maintained as a state park, you can rent some of the former military housing for vacations or just camp on the beach. The fort also does a robust conference business, hosting arts festivals, musical gatherings and more. Trails connect the conference buildings with bluff top views and the beach below.

To conclude this circuit of the Quimper Peninsula, return south on WA 20 out of Port Townsend, in 4.5 miles passing the junction with WA 19, and in another 8.5 miles returning to US 101 at Discovery Bay. The last few miles on WA 20 have stunning views of the bay and, on a clear day, the Olympic Mountains to the southwest.

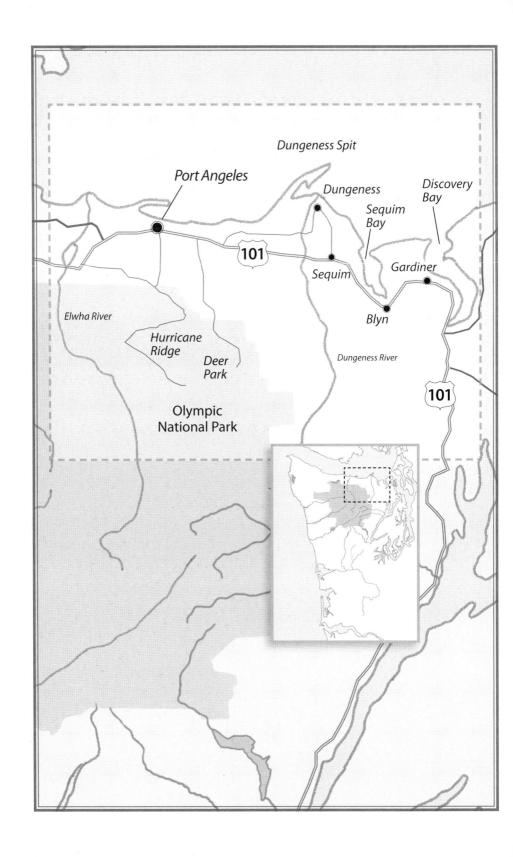

MILESTONE 4

DISCOVERY BAY TO ELWHA

At the intersection of US Highway 101 and Washington Highway 20, the Quimper Peninsula connects to the Olympic Peninsula at Discovery Bay. This Milestone travels 43 miles from the bay to just past the town of Port Angeles.

Discovery Bay

In May 1792, George Vancouver sailed his two ships, the HMS *Chatham* and the larger HMS *Discovery,* into this bay, naming the bay after his flagship. Vancouver was not the first European to enter these waters, however. The bay was discovered two years before and named Bahía de Bodega y Quadra by the Spanish.

In July 1790, the Spanish ship *Princesa Real* sailed into Bahía de Bodega y Quadra under the direction of Manuel Quimper and Gonzalo López de Haro. Quimper and de Haro named much of the northern portions of Puget Sound: Haro Strait, which separates Vancouver Island and the San Juan Islands; Lopez Island, the third largest of the San Juan Islands; and the Quimper Peninsula (Milestone 3), to the east of Discovery Bay.

Protection Island

The *Princesa Real* was originally a British merchant vessel. It arrived on the Pacific Northwest coast in 1787 searching for sea otter furs for the Chinese market. In 1789 the Spanish captured it as part of the Spanish strategy to lay claim to the region, which precipitated the Nootka Crisis (see chapter 4, Early Explorers). Quimper used the ship until he could return it to the English as part of the first Nootka Convention. The Spanish eventually sailed the ship to the Philippines in 1791, where it was returned to the British.

For Vancouver, Discovery Bay was the ideal location to drop anchor, repair his vessels after weeks and weeks at sea, and start his exploration of Puget Sound. The bay is 10 miles long and 1.5 miles wide at its mouth. The location is deep enough for ships and has a large island at the mouth to protect the bay. The island is the current Protection Island National Wildlife Refuge.

The location near where Vancouver settled for his repair work at Contractors Creek is marked on US 101, halfway up west shore of the bay from the from the US 101 and WA 20 intersection. It was from this anchorage that Vancouver, Peter Puget and Lieutenant Baker began their historic tour of Puget Sound.

Vancouver and his shipmates were used to encountering natives who had never seen a European before. But upon sailing through the Strait of Juan de Fuca, they were surprised that the natives barely looked up from the beach as they sailed by. Vancouver was ignorant at the time that the Spanish had preceded his voyage by two years.

Discovery Bay was also home to one of the Peninsula's first homesteaders. John Tukey, a sailor, jumped ship in 1850 from one of the numerous vessels that were plying the surrounding waters in search of lumber for California. Tukey first set up home deep in the woods south of the bay but eventually settled on the east coast of Discovery Bay.

Just under a mile west of the intersection of US 101 and WA 20 is the almost abandoned hamlet of Maynard, from the days when Discovery Bay was a hub of the lumber industry. Timber was felled and dragged into the bay, where it was gathered and processed by two local mills. From there, the lumber was shipped down the coast, primarily to California.

Gardiner

As you travel "north" on US 101 from Discovery Bay, you are actually traveling almost due west as the highway makes a bend through Gardiner in another 5 miles on the way toward Sequim. To the attentive eye, you can notice a distinct change in the flora here. You are entering the Sequim Prairie region (see Rain Shadow sidebar below).

Troll Haven

To catch a glimpse of the absurd, turn right (east) on Gardiner Beach Road and follow the signs to the boat ramp. Turn left at the water and navigate a third of a mile to the intersection of Gardiner Beach Road and Rondelay Road. There you will find Troll Haven, with dozens of enormous carvings right alongside the road. The 150-acre estate is privately owned, but many of the facilities are available for rent for weddings and such. To top it off, I've seen a buffalo herd on the property.

Near Gardiner, you can view Protection Island by turning right off US 101 just past Gardiner onto on Diamond Point Road and driving 3.3 miles north to Diamond Point. The westernmost tip of Diamond Point is George Vancouver's first landing spot in Washington State.

Miller Peninsula

Heading west on US 101, 5 miles past Gardiner you cross the Miller Peninsula and reach the head of Sequim Bay, the hamlet of Blyn and the Jamestown S'Kallam Indian Reservation. This small reservation is one of three S'Kallam reservations. The others are the Port Gamble and the Lower Elwha (see "The Peninsula Tribes" in chapter 3, Original Inhabitants). Sequim is the native word for "quiet waters," which is indeed true for Sequim Bay due to the overlapping sand spits at its junction with the Strait of Juan de Fuca.

Four miles past Blyn you will pass the turnoff to John Wayne Marina. Yes, the marina is named after the Duke. He had spent many days in this part of the world cruising in his yacht and donated the twenty acres for the marina. In the main building, a few mementoes honor Mr. Wayne. The marina and surrounding area have been designated an important birding area (IBA). A little before the turnoff for the marina is Sequim Bay State Park on the right, with camping in a deep forest high above the beach.

Sequim Prairie

Up ahead on the highway is a large sign warning of elk. If the sign is flashing, please slow down and keep an eye out for them. The Sequim Prairie is prime elk habitat, especially during the winter. Some of the elk in the herd have radio collars that will trigger the flashing lights and warn of their proximity. You do not want to approach these wild animals, nor do you want to hit one with your car—they weigh many hundred pounds, and running into one can total a small car. The herd consists of about a hundred individuals.

First visited by Europeans in the late eighteenth century, the Sequim Prairie area was inhabited by natives from the S'Klallam tribes. Because of the dry climate, it was open prairie with a few Garry oaks and pine trees.

Rain Shadow

Just over forty miles away from Sequim is the Hoh Rain Forest which receives over 140 inches of rain per year. Sequim, on the other hand, gets under 20. The weather and winds on the Peninsula tend to come from the west and southwest. The storms slam into the Olympic Mountains, dumping all that Pacific moisture on the western slope and drying out before they drift toward Sequim. The top of the mountains receive an estimated 200 inches of moisture per year at their summits.

Sequim

In another 4 miles you reach Sequim, the "Lavender Capital of North America." (Note that the "e" is silent: it is pronounced "skwim.") Sequim is the fastest-growing town on the Peninsula. The weather is fabulous compared to other parts of the Northwest; the recreational opportunities are vast; and, the housing prices are somewhat moderate for Puget Sound. It is the

third-largest city on the North Peninsula, behind Port Angeles and Port Townsend. It is also becoming the retirement capital of the state. However, it is quickly losing its small-town feel as development and big-box stores have moved in. The population has increased more than 40 percent since 2000.

Initially development took place along the Dungeness River, but in the 1890s the river was diverted for irrigation. In 1895 the Sequim Prairie Ditch Company was formed. One year later, water flowed in the newly constructed canals. The first canal was 2 miles long, irrigating 2000 acres. Now there are 97 miles of canals irrigating 11,000 acres, including farms and lawns. This is celebrated with the Irrigation Festival, held every May.

This irrigation project is another example of "death by a thousand cuts" for the salmon. The Dungeness watershed, close to 100,000 acres, was a prime Peninsula source for salmon, and now, in spite of the hatchery 10 miles upstream from the coast, the river salmon production is just a shadow of its aboriginal self. Spring chinook salmon, the biggest of the salmon family, has declined to about 2 percent of its aboriginal numbers and is now a threatened species. (The chinook is now either threatened or endangered in virtually its entire habitat in the Lower 48 states.) The pink salmon, a fish unique to Puget Sound, is down to about 6 percent of its historic levels in the Dungeness River (Goin 1998).

Dungeness Side Trip

The first town in this area was Dungeness, north of Sequim on the strait at the mouth of the Dungeness River. The Spaniard Manuel Quimper stopped at the Dungeness River in 1790, and George Vancouver named it in 1792 after a region in his native England: "The low sandy point of land, which from its great resemblance to Dungeness in the British Channel, I called New Dungeness." This locale was home to the West Coast's first commercial fishery, which started in 1848. The fishery primarily harvested the Dungeness crab, which was named for this area.

Dungeness Spit

New Dungeness was also the county seat of Clallam County, created in 1854 by the state legislature. In 1890 a posse of Port Angelenos moved all the county records by force to Port Angeles; subsequently, New Dungeness lost a three-way election with Port Angeles and Port Crescent for the honor. Port Crescent is now a tiny community 13 miles east of Port Angeles, just north of Joyce (see Milestone 5, Port Angeles to Neah Bay). The vote was 7 for New Dungeness, 687 for Port Angeles, and 293 for Port Crescent.

No trip to the Sequim area would be complete without visiting the Dungeness National Wildlife Refuge. Just follow the signs north of US 101 for 5 miles or so. This refuge, established in 1915, consists of more than 600 acres of tidelands, forest area, and one of the largest natural sand spits in the world. At the end of the 5-mile-long spit is a lighthouse, originally turned on in 1857 and now, though it's automated, enthusiastic volunteers are just itching to give you a tour of the facility. Come in the spring or autumn and view all the migratory birds; the spit and surrounding park have been designated an IBA.

Dungeness Spit is a remnant of the last ice age. During that time, the ice was more than 4000 feet high above the strait. When it melted, it created this landform, perhaps as a lateral moraine (see "Glaciers" in

View from Deer Park

chapter 1, Geology). When the glaciers receded from the northern peninsula during 13,000 years ago, flora and fauna moved in.

One particular species of fauna appears to have been killed by another 12,000 years ago in the Sequim Prairie. A mastodon skeleton was unearthed in 1977 by a local farmer. The mastodon had a bone projectile lodged in one of its bones. Did a hardy group of hunters take down this enormous animal? Also at this site, caribou and bison bones were discovered. Plant remnants from the dig suggest that this area was so arid that it supported cactuses. Conifers wouldn't move in for another 1000 years. The skeleton can be viewed at the Museum and Arts Center in downtown Sequim.

The 16-mile stretch of US 101 west from Sequim to Port Angeles is pretty uneventful. Remnants of the big old forests are interspersed with small farms and hamlets that gradually grow larger and closer together as you approach one of the Peninsula's largest cities. A replica of George Washington's Mount Vernon, on the north side of the highway roughly halfway between Port Angeles and Sequim, is open for guests.

Deer Park Side Trip

One of the most spectacular camping spots in Washington State is Deer Park. It provides timberline views of Olympic National Park but,

compared to nearby Hurricane Ridge and its amenities, Deer Park gives you a huge sense of being in the wilderness. It is a primitive camping site with pit toilets but no running water.

To reach it, from US 101 about 11 miles west of Sequim (4.7 miles east of downtown Port Angeles), turn south off the highway adjacent to the Toyota dealership onto Deer Park Road. Travel south 20 miles to the end of the road, where you'll find the campground and numerous trailheads into the national park. The narrow road, which climbs 5000 feet, is a narrow dirt road and is not appropriate for RVs or trailers. There is no fee for entering the national park at this location. Numerous easy trails in and around the area all offer spectacular 360-degree views.

Port Angeles

Continuing west on US 101, you reach Port Angeles. It is the commercial hub of the North Peninsula: the largest town on the Peninsula, with a large paper mill; an active port with ferries to Victoria, British Columbia, just 17 miles north across the Strait of Juan de Fuca; headquarters for Olympic National Park; and, site of one of the largest Indian graveyards in the country. Port Angeles is also one of three cities in the

Clallam County Courthouse.

country to be designed by the federal government (the others are Washington, D.C., and Anchorage, Alaska).

Originally this site was named Puerto de Nuestra Señora de los Angeles in 1791 by Francisco de Eliza y Reventa during his pre-Vancouver Spanish expedition. Eliza y Reventa's ship reached north into the Strait of Georgia, which separates Vancouver Island from the BC mainland, before returning to his base at Nootka Sound. He noticed the large bay of the Fraser River and thought if the Northwest Passage was anywhere, it was probably there. He also correctly surmised that Vancouver Island really was an island.

Port Angeles from Ediz Hook

Port Angeles's first pioneer was sea captain Alexander Sampson in 1856. After brief difficulties when he tried to homestead the Indian cemetery at the base of Ediz Hook, he went on to be the Tatoosh Island Lighthouse keeper until he died on the island in 1893.

The Customs House Rivalry

Port Angeles's real "father" was Vincent Smith, a newspaper editor and good friend of fellow Ohioan Salmon Chase, President Lincoln's Secretary of the Treasury. In 1861 Smith was appointed the customs collector for the Puget Sound region. The customs collector had the power to stop all incoming maritime traffic and inspect the vessels. Wherever the Customs House was located, money flowed into the local economy.

At the time of Smith's appointment, Port Townsend—more developed and an older town than Port Angeles—was the home of the

Customs House. Smith had control of significant Port Angeles real estate holdings and could only benefit if the Customs House were relocated to his town. He personally lobbied Secretary Chase and Congress, until finally President Lincoln signed a bill in 1861 creating the town of Port Angeles as a military reserve. The Coast Guard station at the end of Ediz Hook is all that is left from the reserve (Morgan 1955). The rest was sold off to homesteaders and pioneers.

Also, Congress formally moved the Customs House to Port Angeles in 1862. While Smith was in Washington, D.C., the books were audited at the Customs House and it was revealed that $15,000 was missing. Port Townsenders, convinced that Smith was a criminal, resisted moving the Customs House. Upon Smith's return to the Peninsula, he commandeered a federal gunboat and forcibly seized all the records, moving the Customs Office to Port Angeles into a building that he owned and rented to the federal government.

When Smith landed in Port Angeles with the customs records, his family and entourage had doubled the population of the town to about twenty. Soon thereafter, he was promoted to chief of all customs houses on the West Coast. Vincent Smith was eventually indicted of embezzlement, though never convicted. Smith died in a shipwreck off the coast of northern California in 1865. Port Townsend got the Customs House back in 1886.

After the Customs House affair, Port Angeles grew only modestly in the subsequent two decades, to about 400 residents. In 1887 the population doubled as the Puget Sound Co-operative Colony moved into town alongside Ennis Creek in an attempt to form a utopian community. It lasted only a few years, but in that brief time the settlers built Port Angeles's first sawmill, office buildings and an opera house.

Ediz Hook

The primary reason for Port Angeles being such a great harbor is Ediz Hook, a large spit formed by coastal erosion west of the spit and by

Nippon Paper is on the left, Tse-whit-zen is just off to the lower right and the Coast Guard Station is in the upper right at the end of the hook.

accumulation of Elwha River sediment. Ediz Hook has been designated an IBA. It has a U.S. Coast Guard station, with an airstrip, at its tip and a large paper mill at its base.

Nippon Paper Industries produces 470 tons of paper per day; much of the source pulp is recycled newspapers and telephone books. The mill has been in production since 1920 and until recently derived about of a third of its power needs from electricity generated by the dams on the Elwha River. It is one of the smallest of Washington State's eleven paper mills and only one-half the size of the Port Townsend Paper Company.

Tse-whit-zen

The Port Angeles area has been home to the Lower Elwha S'Klallam and related Indian tribes for thousands of years. In 2003, the state began construction of a dry dock that was to be used in the rebuilding of the pontoons for the Hood Canal Bridge. Immediately, the excavation work began to turn up artifacts of a native village, Tse-whit-zen. Soon after, bones were discovered. Over time, the construction ceased and the Lower Elwha S'Klallam Tribe and archaeologists took over.

Tse-whit-zen

More than 330 skeletons were unearthed, including more than a dozen skulls with holes in the top, thought to be displayed as a warning to other tribes. It was soon determined to be the largest native village ever discovered in Washington State. The thousands of artifacts (along with trade goods from Russia and China) and the condition of the remains indicate that the site had been occupied for 2700 years. The number and condition of the graves, along with radiocarbon dating, also indicate that the site was possibly a victim of the smallpox pandemic that swept through the Pacific Northwest in the late eighteenth and early nineteenth centuries. The industrial-looking site is at the base of Ediz Hook. Plans are to create a museum and memorial on the site when funds become available.

Hurricane Ridge and Obstruction Point Side Trips

The crown jewel of scenery for Olympic National Park and the Olympic Peninsula is Hurricane Ridge. Located 17 miles south of Port Angeles up a twisty road, it is one of the largest of the park's facilities. The most popular destination inside the park, it includes a snack bar, a gift shop and a ski area with a day-use lodge.

Like Deer Park, Hurricane Ridge is right at timberline, with magnificent views of the Olympic Mountains to the south and the

View from Hurricane Ridge

Strait of Juan de Fuca to the north. Deer and other wildlife are often seen casually walking among the visitors.

To reach Hurricane Ridge from Port Angeles, follow the signs to the Olympic National Park Visitor Center off of US 101 on Race Street. The Hurricane Ridge Road heads due south to the visitor center near the park's popular Heart of the Hills campground before climbing up to the facilities on Hurricane Ridge.

Obstruction Point Road

Hurricane Ridge Hikes

Numerous hikes are possible from Hurricane Ridge. Some are just walks on paved footpaths and others are a bit more strenuous. One of the most popular, accessed from the end of the road, leads to Hurricane Hill, west of the visitor center. This trail can take you straight down to the Elwha River. A car shuttle is quite appropriate here, as you drop 4000 feet in just over 4 miles.

Indicates the turn off from the Hurricane Ridge Road right before the parking lot.

If you have a chance in the summer, take the Obstruction Point Road, the dirt road that travels southeast just before you reach the parking lot at Hurricane Ridge. The 8-mile-long road winds through meadows and forests to Obstruction Point, at 6100 feet, with more great scenery. This is a prime location to see the Olympic marmot, an endemic species of the Peninsula (see "The Mountains" in chapter 2, Natural History).

Elwha River

From Port Angeles, US 101 winds west through town—follow the signs toward Lake Crescent. Just over 6 miles west of downtown is the turnoff for Washington Highway 112, which leads west to what's left of the 108-foot Elwha Dam, then on to Clallam Bay, Sekiu, and Cape Flattery (see Milestone 5, Port Angeles to Neah Bay). About 3 miles past the intersection with WA 112, US 101 crosses the Elwha River, the endpoint of this Milestone.

Upper Elwha River Side Trip

Just before you cross the Elwha River, turn south from US 101 onto Olympic Hot Springs Road and follow signs into Olympic National Park to visit the upper Elwha River Valley. Madison Falls, a pleasant and easily accessed scenic spot immediately prior to the park entrance, is 40 feet high and only 200 feet from the parking lot; the flat trail is ADA accessible. Beyond is Elwha Campground and the Elwha Ranger Station (a road to the right leads to Altair Campground and the trailhead to Olympic Hot Springs). Just under 5.5 miles from the highway, the main road leads to 210-foot Glines Dam, slated for removal in late 2014, and the Whiskey Bend trailhead.

Whiskey Bend Trailhead

A short drive beyond the Elwha Ranger Station, the Whiskey Bend trailhead provides immediate access to the park's interior. From here you can hike all the

Lake Mills with the Glines Canyon Dam at the far end of the lake.
Final demolition is scheduled for 2014

way up the Elwha to its headwaters at Low Divide, then down the North Fork Quinault River to Lake Quinault. For the first 40 miles, the trail follows the Elwha River and thus is relatively flat, taking you right down the middle of the wildest part of the Peninsula.

The upper Elwha River valley was a glacially dammed lake during the ice ages. Evidence for this is found 20 miles beyond the Whiskey Bend trailhead, near Godkin Creek. It is surmised that the Canadian rock found here was transported from Canada on a glacier that crossed the Strait of Juan de Fuca. There the glacier may have calved off an iceberg from its leading edge that then floated south on Glacial Lake Elwha to come to rest at Godkin Creek.

If going straight up is your thing, from the Whiskey Bend trailhead you can catch the Hurricane Hill trail, which leads you 4000 feet up to the visitor center at Hurricane Ridge.

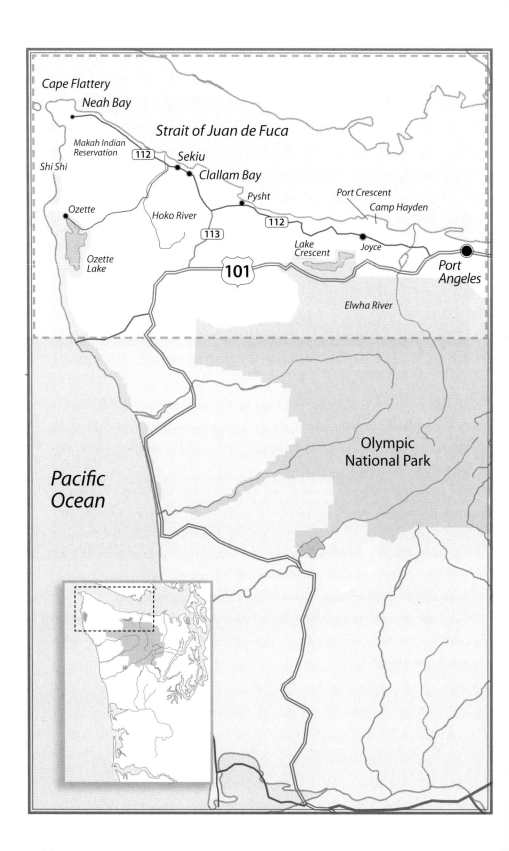

PORT ANGELES TO NEAH BAY

The 73-mile drive out to Neah Bay and Cape Flattery parallels the Strait of Juan de Fuca on the federally designated Strait of Juan de Fuca Byway and the state of Washington–designated Cape Flattery Tribal Scenic Byway. The highway ends at Cape Flattery, so this Milestone is an out-and-back (you could loop down to US Highway 101 at Sappho rather than retracing your route to Port Angeles, but then you'd miss Lake Crescent, which you really shouldn't). Also, from this drive you can take a side trip to Ozette Lake, which adds 42 miles round-trip in an unforgettable visit to a wilderness lake in the national park and access to ocean trails and beaches.

Lower Elwha River

From downtown Port Angeles, take US 101 west just over 5 miles to Washington Highway 112 and turn right onto it.

Elwha Dam

Less than 1 mile from US 101, turn left onto Lower Dam Road to see the remains of the lower dam on the Elwha River, about a third of a mile from the highway (see "Elwha Restoration" in chapter 7, The 21st Century and the Future).

The Elwha Dam is gone, Lake Aldwell has been drained, and the river is in the process of returning to its natural state. The dam site is changing rapidly and will soon be open for up-close viewing. As of this writing, a short, level path gives a good scenic view of the site.

WA 112 continues west, crossing the lower Elwha River.

Mouth of the Elwha

To see the Elwha River's mouth and beach, from WA 112 turn north on Place Road and proceed just under 2 miles to the beach parking lot. It is a 200-yard, level walk to the beach. The beach has already begun to resume its natural state, with sand and silt from the river covering the formerly cobbled beach. The Elwha River estuary has been designated an important birding area (IBA).

Camp Hayden and Port Crescent

In 6.5 miles from US 101, you reach the turnoff to Camp Hayden Road. True, you can continue due west on WA 112, but instead take this scenic detour via Camp Hayden Road, which reaches Salt Creek County Park in about 3.5 miles. This area has a campground, an old military installation and some of the best tide pools in the state. The park has been designated an IBA.

Fort Hayden, staffed by 3000 soldiers during WWII, had two guns. One, 45 feet long, was the largest ever produced in the United States; it could fire a one-ton projectile 28 miles, twice the distance to the opposite shore, in Canada. From the campground, walk west out to Tongue Point at low tide and marvel at all the marine life.

When you leave the recreation area, instead of retracing your route to return to WA 112, instead head west on Crescent Beach Road to travel past Port Crescent, on the point at the west end of Crescent Bay. Port Crescent, home to a sawmill and a minor village, challenged Port Angeles and Dungeness for the county seat in 1890. The Port Crescent city fathers had such faith in the town's future that they laid out 160 city

Top : Lower Elwha Dam holding back Lake Aldwell. Both are gone now.
Bottom: Tongue Point, low tide is the best time to go.

blocks. It lost badly in the county seat election, and the town was abandoned during the Panic of 1893. It is now home to a smattering of vacation homes at the end of a beautiful stretch of beach.

The road leaves the scenic beach and goes due south to rejoin WA 112. Once you hit the highway, take the time to backtrack east for a few blocks to visit the hamlet of Joyce.

Joyce

The general store building in Joyce is one of the only surviving buildings from the town of Port Crescent. This isn't your typical minimart. It has everything you could ever want and much that you don't. Just wander the aisles. Also check out the town museum just down the street. That building was erected in 1915 as a railroad station for the Milwaukee Railroad.

The Spruce Railroad, built toward the end of WWI, followed this road and turned left just a mile or so west of Joyce down the Joyce

Crescent Bay

Piedmont Road, then south to Lake Crescent (see "Logging" in chapter 6, The 20th Century).

Joyce to Pysht

Continue west from Joyce on US 101, past a turnoff on the right to the Lyre River campground and through the tiny hamlets of Shadow and Twin. At the latter, 12 miles west of Joyce, the road hugs the strait and follows it for another 10 miles, sometimes right on the water. This is a spectacular drive when the weather is clear, a nerve-racking one when it's foggy.

As the highway turns south, you enter the community of Pysht. The name Pysht is an Indian term meaning "land where the wind blows from everywhere." It was first settled by Europeans in 1880, and for forty years it was accessible only by boat. The first road connecting Pysht went to Clallam Bay to the west and then south to Forks. Eventually a road connected the town to Fairholm (at the west end of Lake Crescent), where

Sekiu at west end of Clallam Bay with the Strait of Juan de Fuca and Vancouver Island in the background.

travelers took a ferry to the east end of Lake Crescent and then a road to Port Angeles.

In Pysht, visit the Pillar Point picnic ground for a dramatic view of Pillar Point and the Strait of Juan de Fuca.

WA 112 now leaves the coastline and winds its way southwest along the perennially flooded Pysht River to a junction with WA 113, where you stay right (WA 113 is the shortcut to Sappho and Forks on US 101). From the junction, WA 112 heads northwest, down the Clallam River to Clallam Bay.

Clallam Bay and Sekiu

Clallam Bay was the original gateway to the Peninsula's West End. Early pioneers could land in the bay and take the "road" south to Forks. It was the only way to reach the West End, other than through La Push (west of Forks). In 1892 the road-trail followed what is now WA 112 to WA 113 to Sappho, Beaver, and on to Forks. When it was "improved," the 28-mile route was a ten-hour wagon ride.

The town of Clallam Bay is at the bay's east end, and the village of Sekiu (pronounced "C-Q") is at the bay's west end, near Sekiu Point. Sekiu's first major industry was producing tanning liquor. Leather was used everywhere during those days, and the liquor was in much demand for the curing of hides. Local hemlock trees were stripped of their bark, which was cooked and distilled into tanning liquor. Sekiu produced the liquor and Clallam Bay provided the barrels to ship it in.

Now Sekiu and Clallam Bay are centers for sport fishing. On opening days of fishing, Sekiu gets crazy. Every piece of open dirt, every dock, and every campsite will be covered by boats or trailers.

Sekiu to Neah Bay

Continue west on WA 12 for 2 miles past Sekiu, to the junction with the Hoko-Ozette Road. After you visit Cape Flattery, you'll return to this junction, where you can follow this road south to Ozette Lake and the northern end of Olympic National Park's wilderness beaches (see Ozette Lake later in this chapter).

Beyond this junction, another 2 miles west on US 101 puts you right on the shores of the strait again for the next 10 miles. Try to catch this drive at a low tide. And stop often. At moderate to low tide, you can see some interesting geology. Notice that the fracture lines in the rocks parallel the beach. These are sedimentary layers deposited millions of years ago and tilted up, which shows each layer. What is more interesting is that these rocks are now perpendicular from the direction they were when they first slammed into the coast.

At the end of this waterfront drive, you will be in the Makah Indian Reservation, at Neah Bay. A small turnout at the top of the hill has won- derful views of Seal and Sail Rocks. Bring your binoculars, and you may even spot a gray whale. The best time to see them is in March and April. The whole coast is a great place to see whales as they migrate north for the summer (see "The Coast: Whales" in chapter 2, Natural History).

Makah Indians

Neah Bay is home to the Makah Indians. This reservation, established in 1855, encompasses 27,000 acres. Their ancient society is more closely related to the Indians across the strait in Canada than to other tribes on the Peninsula. Their language is spoken only on the reservation and in Canada.

If you have any interest in Indian culture, do not miss the Makah Cultural and Research Center Museum, a world-class museum. In times long past, the Makah Indians may have occupied up to a half dozen sites around Neah Bay, some permanent and some seasonal. Two sites have been excavated: Ozette Beach and Hoko River (both sites are closed to visitors). The Ozette site is about 15 miles due south on the Pacific Ocean near Cape Alava (see Ozette Lake later in this chapter); the Hoko River site is about 13 miles east between the highway and the strait. The Makah museum contains an amazingly large variety of artifacts retrieved mostly from the Ozette archaeology site.

In 1790 Manuel Quimper (the same Quimper who named the peninsula Port Townsend occupies) landed at Neah Bay and called it Bahía de Nunez Gaona. Two years later, from their base on Vancouver Island, the Spanish, anxious to establish and extend their "control" of the Pacific Northwest, sailed from Nootka Sound on Vancouver Island across the strait to Neah Bay and built a fort in May 1792. It was the first European settlement in Washington State, but it lasted only six months.

Neah Bay, before the breakwater was built, was not a very good harbor and a poor choice for the first settlement. [history]In 2007 a new memorial to the Spanish fort was erected on the same spot. It is straight ahead as you drive into Neah Bay on WA 112. It also serves as a veterans memorial.

Tatoosh Island

Cape Flattery

Make sure that you pick up your recreation pass, available at the minimart, before you proceed to west Cape Flattery. Follow the signs south out of town for the 6 miles to the cape. The 0.75-mile-long, almost flat trail from the parking lot has been recently renovated. It leads to spectacular vistas of the Pacific coast and Tatoosh Island (listed on the National Register of Historic Places). You will feel like you are at the end of the world.

Cape Flattery was named by James Cook in 1778 on his trip north to Alaska. He was also looking for the famous, though not confirmed, Strait of Juan de Fuca. "In this very latitude geographers have placed the pretended Strait of Juan de Fuca. But nothing of that kind presented itself to our view, nor is it probable that any such thing ever existed." It was a foggy day when he sailed by but was "flattered" that a harbor might present itself and so named the point.

Cape Flattery

Englishman John Meares first described Tatoosh Island in 1788 and named it for the local Makah chief. The island, long a fishing camp for the Makah, became the location for the United States' northwestern most lighthouse, in 1857. Currently it is automated, but until 1977 it remained one of the last staffed lighthouses in the country. Vincent Smith, the scoundrel from Port Angeles (see "The Customs House Rivalry" in Milestone 4, Discovery Bay to Elwha), appointed his father as one of the first lighthouse keepers. His father did such a horrible job that government inspectors called for the elder Smith's termination. Vincent then appointed his father to the lighthouse in Port Angeles.

Shi Shi and Point of Arches

If you drive a bit farther south, you reach the trailhead to the world-famous Shi Shi Beach and Point of Arches. It is a flat, but very muddy, 2-mile walk through the Makah reservation and then a steep drop down to this wilderness beach inside Olympic National Park. There are dramatic islands and rocks at both ends of the beach. Don't be surprised to see surfers out in the water. This is the northern terminus of the park's Coastal Unit.

From Shi Shi (pronounced "shy-shy"), you can backpack 30 miles south all the way to Rialto Beach, across the Quillayute River from La Push. Once on the southern side of the Quillayute River, you can backpack another 20 miles south to the Hoh River, all within the park. Both of these coastal stretches have no

Shi Shi Beach and Point of Arches

automobile access. This wildly scenic and isolated route is highly recommended for long-distance hikers.

From Neah Bay, backtrack on WA 112 to the Hoko-Ozette Road, approximately 15 miles east.

Ozette Lake Side Trip

To visit the westernmost community of any in the Lower 48 and to reenter the national park, turn south onto the Hoko-Ozette Road to travel 21 miles southwest.

The road to Ozette Lake wasn't finally completed until 1932, but during the 1890s, scores of Scandinavian farming pioneers settled in this area, totaling more than a hundred families. The lake has such geographic spots as Tivoli Island, Birkstol Point, Ericsons Bay, and Jersted Point, all named by the pioneers. Scores of them left when the area was included in the original Olympic Forest Reserve because farming wasn't allowed in a forest reserve. Later, politicians, with the help of powerful

logging interests, "rezoned" this area as agricultural, taking it out of the reserve and allowing the timber companies to come in and grab it.

What's in a Name?

Is it Lake Ozette or Ozette Lake? It all depends who you ask. Maps, which tend to have the correct answer, especially those drawn by governments, designate this as Ozette Lake. But a picture is worth a thousand words, and this image was taken right on the shore of the lake itself. Even the Park Service doesn't know what it should be called.

Eight-mile-long Ozette Lake, the third-largest natural lake in Washington State, is a remnant of the last ice age, dammed by a glacial moraine that indicates the southern

terminus of the glaciers (see "Ice" in chapter 1, Geology). The lake's surface is just a few feet above sea level, and its bottom is more than 300 feet deep. Birding during the migration seasons can be quite fruitful, as the lake is a designated important birding area (IBA).

If sunshine is your thing, you might want to avoid Ozette. It has been calculated that the Ozette area gets less sunshine than any other point in the United States. If it is not raining here, then the fog will step forward and block out the sun.

When you've finished exploring the Ozette Lake area, return northeast along the Hoko-Ozette Road to WA 112 just west of Clallam Bay, then turn right to follow WA 112 east back to Port Angeles to begin Milestone 6. Or from WA 112 at Joyce, you can follow the Joyce-Piedmont Road south 5 miles to the north shore of Lake Crescent, then take East Beach Road to pick up US 101 at the lake's eastern end.

Cape Alava Hike

If you have the time and inclination for an easy walk to the ocean, from the Ozette Ranger Station on the shore of Ozette Lake you can follow either of two trails that lead out to the Pacific coast on flat boardwalks, both just over 3 miles long. This is the only access to the Peninsula's north coast other than Shi Shi Beach from Neah Bay (see Shi Shi and Point of Arches sidebar in this chapter) and Rialto Beach near La Push (see Milestone 7, Forks to Quinault). You can also walk the beach between the two trails from Ozette to make a flat, 9-mile loop hike.

On the northern trail, in about 2 miles from Ozette Lake is Ahlstroms Prairie and the site of that family's homestead. There is nothing left standing to indicate where the buildings were located. You don't even want to step off the boardwalk since it seems to be a never-ending swamp. Imagine living out here in the 1890s. Once you reach the beach, if you walk just 1 mile north up the beach from the northern trail, you will find Cape Alava, the westernmost point in the contiguous United

States. It is just slightly farther west than Cape Flattery. Cape Alava is where the Ozette Beach camp was unearthed in 1969.

For hundreds, if not thousands, of years, the Makah Indians used the Cape Alava beach area as a summer camp. Then about 300 years ago, it was completely buried in a muddy landslide, possibly triggered by the 1700 earthquake (see "Gravity and Earthquakes" in chapter 1, Geology). In 1969 ocean storms cut into the bank, and out washed paddles, fish hooks, and numerous other artifacts. During the next decade, more than 55,000 objects were recovered from this site.

The original camp was more than a mile long along the beach and included many longhouses, some 2400 square feet in size. The recovered items are viewable at the Makah Cultural and Research Center in Neah Bay (see "Makah Indians" above). The Ozette site is listed on the National Register of Historic Places but is currently closed for public viewing.

The southern trail from Lake Ozette takes you to Sand Point. The beach walk between Sand Point and Cape Alava is about 3 miles, taking you past interesting petroglyphs known as the Wedding Rocks.

Whichever trail you take, return to Ozette Lake and your car to continue your journey back to US 101.

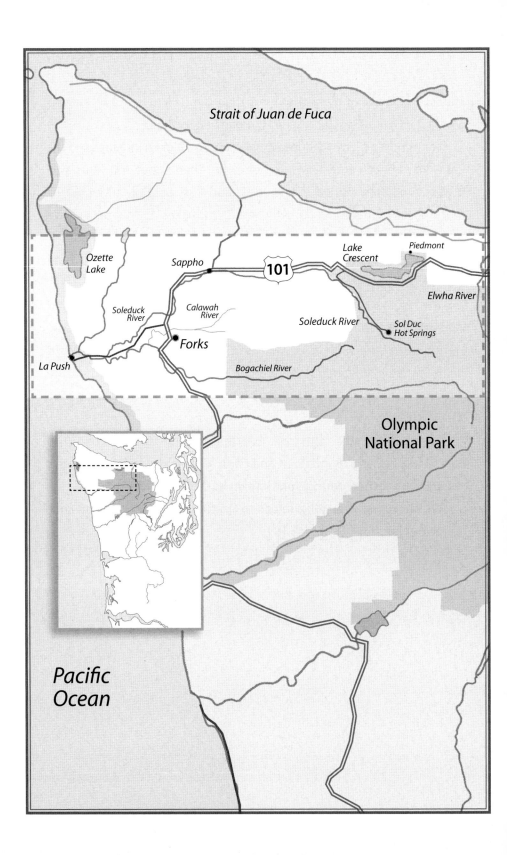

MILESTONE 6

ELWHA TO FORKS

This Milestone covers the 47 miles between the Elwha River at US Highway 101 and the town of Forks in the Peninsula's West End, taking you past Lake Crescent, the Soleduck area, and access to the ocean at La Push and Rialto Beach.

From US 101 at the Elwha River, continue west on the highway; in 6 miles is Lake Sutherland, privately owned and home to numerous residences and campgrounds. In the Elwha River watershed, the lake drains east along Indian Creek to the former Lake Aldwell on the Elwha (see Milestone 4).

Salmon species here have been isolated since the Elwha Dam was built. Sockeye salmon, as juveniles, use lakes to mature before their travels to the ocean. The sockeye isolated in Lake Sutherland used Lake Aldwell as their "ocean." Landlocked sockeye are called kokanee salmon. It is believed and hoped that these fish will resume their ocean travels now that the dam has been removed and Lake Aldwell drained (see "Elwha Restoration" in chapter 7, The 21st Century and the Future).

About a mile west on the highway after it leaves the shore of Lake Sutherland is East Beach Road, which borders Lake Crescent's northeast shore. This road connects US 101 to WA 112 at Joyce (see "Ozette Lake Side Trip" in Milestone 4, Port Angeles to Neah Bay).

A Tale of Two Lakes

Lake Sutherland and Lake Crescent are glacier-carved lakes that were once joined. Lake Crescent flowed into Lake Sutherland, which flowed into the Elwha River. Eight thousand years ago, an enormous landslide cut off the two lakes. Lake Crescent now flows due north down the Lyre River into the Strait of Juan de Fuca. The two lakes were originally "discovered" by Mr. Everett and Mr. Sutherland, Hudson Bay trappers from Canada, in 1850; Lake Everett was later renamed.

Lake Crescent North Shore Side Trip

To visit Lake Crescent's north shore, turn south onto East Beach Road and in about 3 miles you reach the small hamlet of Piedmont; the road continues on another mile to the start of the Spruce Railroad Trail, which follows the rest of the lake's north shore (see below). Piedmont, first settled in the 1890s, was one of the first settlements on Lake Crescent; it is at the headwaters for the Lyre River.

Just over a mile farther west from Piedmont is the Spruce Railroad Trail. The trail follows the lake's north shore for 4 miles until reaching the North Shore Road, near the lake's west end.

Community organizers are attempting to link the old Spruce Railroad grade (see "Logging" in chapter 6, The 20th Century) with other abandoned railroads to form the Olympic Discovery Trail (ODT). The ODT has been laid out to go from Port Townsend all the way to La Push, west

Storm King Ranger Station, just east of the Lake Crescent Lodge at Barnes Point. Listed in the Historic Register.

of Forks, and much of it has been paved. The Spruce Railroad Trail along Lake Crescent is on the national park's To-Do list to widen and pave.

After you've explored the north shore, retrace your route to US 101 and continue west along Lake Crescent's south shore. This narrow, winding road right at the water's edge demands slower speeds for safety and your enjoyment of the amazing lakeshore views.

Lake Crescent

Lake Crescent is the second-largest lake on the Peninsula and, at more than 600 feet deep, is one of the deepest lakes in Washington State. The bottom of the lake is below sea level. Lake Crescent's brilliant blue color is due to lack of nitrogen, which inhibits the growth of algae. The lake, while crescent shaped, was actually named because of its proximity to Crescent Bay (see Milestone 4) on the strait (Majors 1975, 15).

Lake Crescent has, as does the Olympic Peninsula in general, species and subspecies found nowhere else. Here's a tale about one of those species: In 1895 Clallam County invited the U.S. Pacific Fleet to Port Angeles to celebrate the local fair. Much to the community's surprise, the fleet accepted and started a tradition that lasted forty years. It may have been Lake Crescent that drew the fleet to Port Angeles for so many years, because Admiral Beardslee, the first admiral to bring the fleet north to Port Angeles, was a very enthusiastic fisherman. He fished at the lake so often that there is a trout named after him, the Beardslee trout, *Salmo gairdneri beardsleei*. This endemic fish spawns on the Lyre River.

The Lake Crescent cutthroat trout is also endemic. Scientists suggest that this fish is becoming less distinct since it is hybridizing with introduced rainbow trout. The largest fish caught in the lake was a Lake Crescent cutthroat trout that came in at a whopping 12 pounds and 32 inches long.

On US 101 just under 4 miles west of the East Beach Road turnoff is Barnes Point, home of the Lake Crescent Lodge, NatureBridge, and Storm King Ranger Station. This beautiful peninsula right on the lake is at the foot of Mount Storm King. The original lodge, built in 1916, maintains an "old lodge" feel with a wood interior and large fireplace. Prior to 1922, when the highway was completed, guests drove to the East Beach area and took a boat to the lodge. Take time to enjoy the sun room at the lodge.

The nearby NatureBridge is a nonprofit organization aimed at environmental education. The ranger station, built in 1905, is listed on the National Register of Historic Places. It has been moved from its original location, which was nearby. Just across the highway from these buildings is the 1-mile trail to 90-foot-high Marymere Falls.

About 6 miles farther west is Fairholm, at the west end of the lake; it had its own post office in 1891 and was the ferry terminal for those traveling from Port Angeles to Sol Duc Hot Springs or beyond to the West End of the Peninsula. The highway was eventually completed from Port Angeles to Fairholm in 1922. The town is now nothing more than a national park campground with a small seasonal store that carries tourist and fishing supplies.

Just under 2 miles west of Fairholm is the turnoff on the left for Sol Duc Hot Springs, and shortly after US 101 enters the Soleduck River valley.

Sol Duc Hot Springs Side Trip

You can travel 12 miles up the Soleduck River road to the Sol Duc Hot Springs Resort, which features rooms to rent and a couple very large hot spring pools. The lodge has been rebuilt several times since the original one burned down in 1916. A national park campground is also here. Both Sol Duc Hot Springs and Sol Duc Falls feed into the Soleduck River. The similar but differently spelled names are just a legacy of who named what when.

Shooting Fish

A couple of miles up the Soleduck River road from the highway, a turnoff allows you to view salmon migrating upriver. The best photographic light is not direct sun, as that will produce too much contrast between the wide cascades and the almost black fish. Use your flash to freeze the action, and be prepared to take dozens and dozens of images as you try to catch the fish navigating over the boulders.

At the end of the Soleduck River road, past the campground, is the trailhead for the 1-mile hike to Sol Duc Falls, worth any effort you will make to get there. It is the most dramatic of all the waterfalls on the Peninsula. The trail gains only about 250 feet as you stroll through a pristine old-growth forest. Plus you explore the CCC-built Canyon Creek Shelter that is on the National Register of Historic Places.

Shooting the Falls

Sol Duc Falls is a great place to practice your tripod and flash skills. As at the salmon migration spot mentioned in the Shooting Fish sidebar, lighting is critical here. In the shot shown above, I was able to catch sunlight streaming in from the right, highlighting some vine maple in the foreground. But I used a tripod and slowed the shutter speed down (1 second exposure) to give the falls a silky look and to capture a larger depth of field. If I wanted to have every drop of the falls in sharp focus, I would have lost a lot of the depth of field, and much of the image would have been too dark.

After exploring the Soleduck–Sol Duc area, retrace your way back to US 101. From the Sol Duc Hot Springs turnoff, US 101 now enters the Soleduck River valley and is incredibly straight for the next 15 miles until you get to the deserted town of Sappho.

Sappho

The Sappho town site is at the intersection of US 101 with WA 113, which goes north to WA 112 between Pysht and Clallam Bay (see Milestone 5, Port Angeles to Neah Bay).

Sappho was founded by Martin Van Buren Lamoreux, in the early 1890s. He brought his wife and eleven children west from Kansas, stopped briefly in Seattle, and then went on to a native settlement on the strait. After hiking 20 miles through the virgin rain forest up the Pysht River to reach the area, he named it after a favorite Greek poetess, Sappho.

Why did Mr. Lamoreux travel to Sappho? Who informed him that this was a good thing, with his eleven children? Why didn't he go another 3.5 miles to Lake Pleasant, also along the Soleduck River? Was Sappho in one of the prairies that Indians burned to keep it clear? The answers are missing, as is the town, today.

Near Sappho you are entering what the locals say is the Peninsula's West End. This designation describes the part of the Peninsula from here all the way south to Lake Quinault. It is not an official moniker but encompasses a region of rather uniform geography and weather. There is no "end" since there is no beginning. However, if you were a West End pioneer, it might occur to you that you were at the end of the country.

Soleduck River

In a third of a mile past the Sappho highway intersection is the turnoff for the Sol Duc Salmon Hatchery (to reach it, turn south on Clark Road, then immediately right on Pavel Road). This hatchery is another example of trying to improve on Mother Nature.

The Soleduck River has been producing thousands of salmon and steelhead every year forever. The river produces only what the river can accommodate, no more, no less. Now in our infinite wisdom, it was decided that we could increase the salmon production in the river by artificially "helping" with the use of a fish hatchery. This has resulted in wild stocks, which are perfectly designed for the Soleduck, being replaced by farmed fish. These farmed fish are a smaller and less robust type of salmon than the wild stock and are interbreeding with the wild stock, therefore diluting the wild stock's genetic library. Now the salmon are not perfectly tuned to the river but to the artificial conditions of a hatchery.

On US 101 3.5 miles farther west and then south are Beaver and Lake Pleasant, marked by a minimart. (Turn right on West Lake Pleasant Road if you want to access the lake, a couple blocks north.)

Continue south on US 101 for about 7 miles to cross the Soleduck River and then reach the junction with WA 110, the turnoff to the Pacific Ocean.

Pacific Ocean Side Trips

To visit La Push, Mora, and Rialto Beach, turn right onto WA 110. In 3 miles to the west is the modest community of Three Forks, which is close to where the Soleduck and Bogachiel (pronounced "BOGE-a-sheel") Rivers combine to form the Quillayute River. The numerous fishermen and the flotillas of boats attest that these are prime steelhead fishing waters. The Quillayute River is the second-largest river on the West End of the Peninsula, behind the Queets, which we visit farther south (see Milestone 7, Forks to Lake Quinault).

At Three Rivers Resort at the intersection of Mora Road and La Push Road, you have a choice: proceed west toward La Push on the south side of the Quillayute, or turn right to reach Mora and Rialto Beach on the north side of the river.

La Push Side Trip

Stay left on WA 110 to reach La Push, a Chinook Jargon word thought to be originated by French-Canadians as *La Bouche,* meaning "the mouth." In about 4 miles from the second fork is the trailhead to Third Beach, reached in an easy 1.5 miles of hiking, and in another 2 miles is the trailhead to Second Beach, an even shorter and easier hike. (If you choose one, choose the Third Beach trail. The sea stacks just offshore are simply amazing.) In about a mile you reach the end of the road at La Push and First Beach.

La Push is in the Quileute Indian Reservation, a square-mile coastal property that includes James Island right offshore and the mouth of the Quillayute River. This place name is spelled numerous ways: there is the Quileute Tribe, the Quillayute River (also sometimes spelled the Quillehute River or the Quillyhuyte River), and Quileut, the name attributed to the first tribal village. James Island is named for F. W. James, who ventured to Quileut to help salvage a ship that sank in 1855 at the mouth of the river. He is thought to be the first European to climb to the top of the island later named for him. There is a lighthouse and foghorn on the island but no public access.

La Push is also home to a substantial U.S. Coast Guard station. The coast north from here to Cape Flattery is the graveyard of dozens and dozens of shipwrecks, perhaps the most dangerous 30 miles of coast in the Lower 48 states.

The Quileutes signed the Treaty of Olympia in 1855, which required them to move south to Taholah, in the Quinault Indian Reservation. They never moved and were almost completely ignored because of their geographic isolation. They eventually were granted their own reservation in 1889 (see "The Peninsula Tribes" in chapter 3, Original Inhabitants).

The Quileute speak a language that is not spoken by any other tribe except the nearby Hoh. They were also one of three Washington tribes,

Rialto Beach

along with the Quinault and Makah, that hunted for whales. Their large cedar canoes could carry three tons.

Jacob, from the *Twilight* movies, is a Quileute Indian. He, along with the movie, has focused more attention on the tribe since its reservation was created in 1889.

Mora and Rialto Beach Side Trip

Across the river from La Push is Rialto Beach, which is accessible by turning right off of WA 110 in Three Rivers (3 miles west of US 101). At 2.5 miles from this second turnoff, you enter Olympic National Park. The entrance is quite noticeable, regardless of the sign, because there is an evident line where the forest has been logged and where it hasn't.

In just another 2 miles you arrive at the park's Mora Campground right at the Dickey River's confluence with the Quillauyute. A modest hotel, post office, and town site occupied this area during the turn of twentieth century. Nothing remains of it now.

Rialto Beach is just 1.5 miles farther west. The beach is the southern terminus of the 30-mile North Coast section of Olympic National Park's wilderness beach. Even if you don't plan to make that hike, take time to walk north along the beach, maybe as far as Hole in the Rock, for some beachcombing at low tide. Altogether, the park has 73 miles of coastline, the largest wilderness coastline in the Lower 48. [birding] With its sea stacks and bald eagles, the coast walk is one of the prizes of the Peninsula.

While the coast may be one of the crown jewels of the Peninsula, the coastal unit is especially messy due to its geography. The ocean currents and wind have the beaches in their crosshairs, resulting in a wilderness beach experience that can be disheartening. It is one of the areas hardest hit by marine-deposited debris and litter. Anything that can float seems to end up on these wilderness beaches. And what is floating is mostly plastic.

Plastic does not degrade; it persists forever. You can walk the beaches and see this "forever" garbage that has been generated by every nation in the North Pacific. Removing garbage from these beaches is hindered by their remoteness, since much of this part of the coast is accessible only by foot (see "Tsunami Debris" in chapter 7, The 21st Century and the Future).

Forks

On US 101 at the intersection with WA 110, continue south and soon cross the Calawah River; in just under 2 miles from the intersection is the town of Forks, the "Logging Capital of the World," with all the amenities you could ever want.

It is also home to 120 inches of rain per year and our favorite vampires, Bella and Edward. The movie series *Twilight,* based on Stephanie Meyer's teen vampire books, has gripped this town. It is everywhere. You can take tours and visit numerous gift shops. Even the large grocery store at the south end of town has a whole section dedicated to *Twilight* mania.

It wasn't always this way. Pioneered in 1878 by Luther Ford and others, Forks did not have a road to it until 1880, when a wagon road reached south from Clallam Bay. Forks is named for the three rivers that come together to form the Quillayute River: the Soleduck, Bogachiel and Calawah Rivers. Originally Forks was called Indian Prairie. Indians had burned this part of the Peninsula to enhance the elk population.

Indians historically burned much of the Americas for thousands of years to clear fields and maintain hunting grounds. An early 1852 exploration report of the West End mentions: "The country bordering on Cape Grenville to Cape Flattery, there is a large extent of country interspersed with prairies, which is entirely unoccupied, and well adapted to farming and grazing."

Early settlers survived on agriculture, but getting crops and livestock to market prevented any real success. Early livestock was driven on the beaches north to Clallam Bay before being loaded on steamships for market.

In 1921 a narrow road was finally completed connecting Forks to Fairholm at the west end of Lake Crescent. From there, a ferry sailed to the east end of the lake and a road that connected to Port Angeles.

It wasn't until 1931 that the Olympic Loop Highway connected Forks to both the north and the south. That was when Forks finally "took off." The vast tracts of old-growth timber were finally available for market, and it fired the Forks and West End economy until the 1980s (see "Logging" in chapter 6, The 20th Century).

On September 20, 1951, a few miles west of Lake Crescent a forest fire, previously thought extinguished, came to life again and began to burn all the way south to Forks. Driven by dry, gale-force winds, it traveled very quickly and almost burned Forks completely down. Many citizens of Forks lost their homes and businesses. The fire was turned away from Forks when the wind changed to the west, just in the nick of time. Soon rains returned and the fire was extinguished for good. But not until it had consumed about 33,000 acres and 600 million board feet of lumber, enough to build 37,500 homes (based on average requirements for a 2000-square-foot home, according to the National Association of Home Builders).

When the old-growth timber virtually vanished because of logging and the Northern Spotted Owl controversy reared its head, Forks' economy collapsed (see "Old-Growth and Owls" in chapter 6, The 20th Century). Lumber still is the largest employer, but tourism and harvesting of native plants for the floral industry have provided many of the new jobs. It doesn't hurt that vampires have been seen locally in the woods.

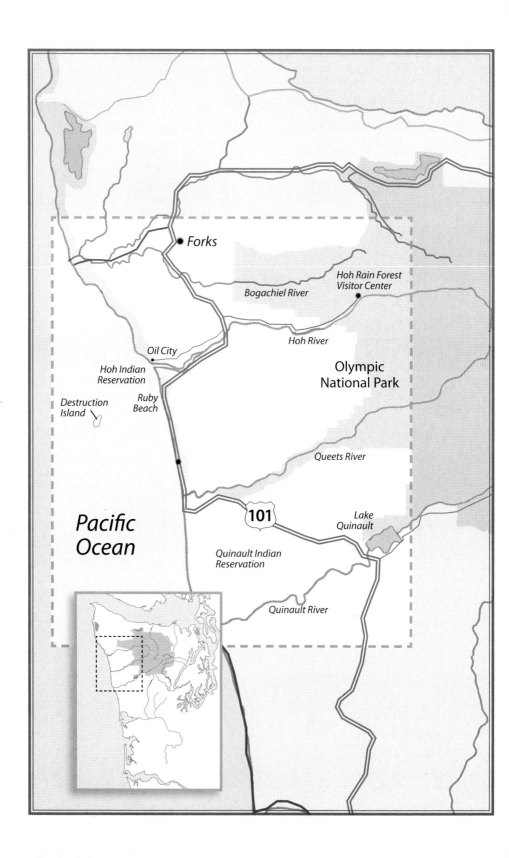

Forks

Hoh Rain Forest
Visitor Center

Bogachiel River

Hoh River

Oil City

Hoh Indian
Reservation

Destruction
Island

Ruby
Beach

Olympic
National Park

Queets River

Pacific
Ocean

Lake
Quinault

101

Quinault Indian
Reservation

Quinault River

FORKS TO LAKE QUINAULT

It rains in the West End. It rains 140 inches per year. Did I mention the rain? It rains 12 feet every year. It rains a lot! It is probably raining at the Hoh Rain Forest Visitor Center as you read this. This Milestone travels south some 64 miles through the West End, where the rivers meet the sea and the trees are enormous.

Bogachiel River

From Forks, follow US Highway 101 south and you'll be driving alongside the meandering Bogachiel River. At about 6 miles you cross the river at Bogachiel State Park, where camping and fishing are the primary activities.

Continue south as the highway climbs slightly, out of the Bogachiel drainage and into the Hoh watershed. In about 13 miles from Forks, you reach the Upper Hoh Road on the left.

Hoh Rain Forest Side Trip

Turn left onto the Upper Hoh Road and follow it east. The Hoh valley has seen glaciers that came all the way down close to the coast only 13,000 years ago. Evidence for these extended glaciers can be seen soon after you leave US 101 on the Upper Hoh River Road. Within a mile up the road, the surface rocks change to reveal a terminal moraine, indicating the end of a glacier. A semicircular arc of glacial debris extends from the hills in the north all the way to the south. It takes a trained eye to see the difference between the moraine and the river bottom. It all appears to be classic unsorted glacial till (see "Ice" in chapter 1, Geology).

Continue 18 miles east from the highway to the Hoh Rain Forest Visitor Center, another gem of Olympic National Park. This is the place to go to be completely immersed in the only temperate rain forest in the Lower 48 and one of only three in the world. [hiking]At the end of the road, a campground and lots of easy walks help you get a sense of what it is like to be in a place that averages almost a third of an inch of rain per day.

Don't be intimated by the rain if you travel in the summer. The vast majority of rain falls October through February. Summertime is remarkable for its lack of rainfall. But if it is not raining, there will be fog. In the summer, when it's "dry," fog from the Pacific Ocean rolls in and stays for days at a time. The fog provides the moisture equivalent of another 30 inches of rain a year.

The rain forest valleys here on the west side of the Peninsula have the most biomass per acre than anywhere else in the world, and the biggest instigator of the immense amount of flora is the combination of moisture, cloud cover, and cool temperatures. Plants have stomata, or pores, that allow them to breathe, taking in carbon dioxide and giving off oxygen. Water vapor also travels in both directions in a process called transpiration. The more the stomata are open, the more the plant can grow.

Forests in more arid regions grow only when it is cool enough for them to open their stomata and when there is moisture. If it gets too hot or too cold or the humidity gets too low, the stomata close to prevent too much water vapor leaving the leaves, terminating photosynthesis. The forests of the Rocky Mountains grow only in the spring, autumn, and summer mornings and evenings.

Here in the Hoh rain forest, because of our Goldilocks environment of just-right moderate temperatures and ample moisture, the trees keep their stomata open incessantly and grow year-round. One of the most prevalent local tree species, the Sitka spruce, is designed for this part of the world and nowhere else since its stomata lack the ability to close.

One of the marvels of this forest is its ability to absorb water. When it rains, not all the moisture reaches the forest floor immediately. The trees, especially the big-leaf maples with their large mats of moss hanging from them, capture the water and slowly drip it to the forest floor. The big-leaf maples can hold up to their weight in water in their canopies.

The Sound of Silence

While you're on one of the many short walks around the visitor center, pause and listen to the silence. If it isn't raining and/or blowing, you will recognize that this is one of the quietest places you have ever been to. It has been recognized as one of the ten quietest places on earth. Gordon Hempton, a local Emmy Award–winning acoustic ecologist, searched the whole country and declared that the Hoh is the quietest place in the country. You can learn more about him and his work by accessing his website, One Square Inch (onesquareinch.org/about/).

Bordering the visitor center grounds is the Hoh River, a typical glacial river system. Note the many braids and channels that the river has created. Some months the river goes one way through it all and the next month, it goes another. (This will also happen to the Elwha as it is freed.) The gravel has been deposited by the upstream glaciers and subsequently washed down by the river. The river drains numerous

One Square Inch. The small rock on the downed tree, more often missing than not, marks the designated spot. Don't get caught up in trying to find the exact place. Just walk the Hoh River trail about two miles from the ranger station and then a hundred yards away from the river.

glaciers, including three of the largest in the park: the Blue, the Hoh and the White Glaciers.

The Hoh valley is also one of the best places to see elk. The park was almost named Elk National Park. Elk are the park's groundskeepers; they have a huge impact on what the park looks like both at sea level and in the upper mountainous reaches. What they eat and what they don't eat determines what will not grow and what will grow. The Sitka spruce needles are rather sharp, and so elk avoid them. This is one reason the tree is so prevalent.

As you retrace your route back toward the highway, try to imagine what the whole West End of the Peninsula would have been like back when the pioneers first started chopping out a living in the forest that looked just like this. John Huelsdonk, aka the Iron Man of the Hoh, homesteaded on the south side of the Hoh River 8 miles west of where the visitor center is now, starting in 1890. He and his family lived there for thirty years before any road came near his farm, and that road was

Best time to see them is early morning or late afternoon.

US 101, about 10 miles downriver. Finally in 1942 he was able to drive to Forks and beyond.

Dora, his wife, gave birth to four daughters on the farm and didn't leave the homestead for seventeen years, until she took her daughters to see the Alaska-Yukon-Pacific Exposition in Seattle in 1909. Mr. Huelsdonk was a prodigious hunter, killing up to 200–300 cougars during his life. There is speculation that this amount of predator hunting allowed the elk population to suffer from overpopulation in the Hoh Valley.

When you reach US 101, turn left to rejoin the highway loop toward Lake Quinault.

Hoh River Pacific Beach Side Trip

In about a mile from the Upper Hoh Road, the turnoff for the Oil City Road is on the right; it leads about 12 miles west to Oil City, which is really just a trailhead for the southern entrance to the park's wilderness beach hike. You can enjoy a short, flat walk to the beach, where sometimes you'll see pelicans or seals fishing in the surf at the mouth of the Hoh.

Hoh Indians

Back on US 101 southbound, shortly you cross the Hoh River, and in about a mile or so you'll see the Hoh Ox Bow Campground, which lies right on top of the same glacial moraine you saw along the Hoh River on the Upper Hoh Road.

On US 101, 11 miles south of the Upper Hoh Road, you reach the turnoff onto Lower Hoh Road into the Hoh Indian Reservation. This is one of Washington State's smallest reservations. (It used to be bigger, but much has been washed away.)

It was established at about the same time as the Quileute Indian Reservation to the north. The Hoh Indians speak the same language as the Quileute but are suspected to be more closely related to the Quinaults. The Hoh were supposed to move from the Hoh River to the Quinault Indian Reservation to the south, by the Treaty of Olympia of 1855. They never did, and instead they were granted their own land. At the time of their receipt of their reservation, they numbered about 60 individuals. Today, they have about 150 members (see "The Peninsula Tribes" in chapter 3, Original Inhabitants).

Since the reservation was formed, the Hoh River has moved a half mile to the south, and now 90 percent of the reservation lies within a floodplain. In 2009, the tribe was granted another 460 acres on the high ground adjacent to the original reservation. Some of the land came from adjacent National Park Service property.

Ruby Beach

Continuing south on US 101, three miles south of the turn to Hoh Reservation, is the conspicuous turnoff to Ruby Beach. Turn right into the parking lot and stroll down to the beach. The large sea stack just

Ruby Beach and Abbey Island

offshore at the end of the parking lot is Abbey Island, named in 1866 supposedly for its shape.

For the next 12 miles, the highway parallels the beach. There are numerous pullouts along the highway to stop and get out of the car to admire the ocean views.

Destruction Island

Just over a mile south of Ruby Beach is the best vantage point of Destruction Island, the largest island off the Washington coast. Geologists estimate that this coast erodes at 3 inches per year. This would suggest that Destruction Island separated from the coast about 70,000 years ago. Inside of the Olympic Coast National Marine Sanctuary, the island is one of the largest seabird sanctuaries on the West Coast.

In 1775 the Spanish captains Bruno de Heceta and Juan Francisco de la Bodega y Quadra anchored their two ships near Destruction Island. After a couple of days trading with the local Quinault Indians, seven sailors were sent ashore for water and food. The Indians took that opportunity to completely massacre the mariners. Heceta named the spot Point of the Martyrs because of the deaths. It is now named Cape

Elizabeth. Bodega y Quadra named Destruction Island Island of Sorrow.

Twelve years later, Captain Charles Barkley dropped anchor and sent his men to the Hoh River to trade. They also were annihilated (see chapter 4, Early Explorers.) He named the river Destruction River. It took Captain Vancouver in 1792 to finalize the name of Destruction Island. The river's name returned to the native Indian name of Hoh.

Destruction Island lived up to its name: three ships crashed into it before a 94-foot-tall lighthouse was completed in 1891. It was staffed until 1968 when it was automated. The original Fresnel lens, now at the Westport Maritime Museum south of Grays Harbor, was removed in 1995. During WWII, it was staffed by Coast Guard sentries looking for enemy ships.

The lighthouse and island are now abandoned as part of the Quillayute Needles National Wildlife Refuge and Wilderness, inside the Olympic Coast National Marine Sanctuary. Perhaps the most interesting of the permanent islanders are rabbits, descendants of the lighthouse keeper's family pets.

Kalaloch

Just over 7 miles south of Ruby Beach is the Kalaloch Resort (pronounced "CLAY-lock"), first settled in 1895. The modest rooms provide a great place to experience the beach and ocean.

Kalaloch Beach, along with many other beaches on the coast, was used as the highway prior to the completion of the paved one in 1931. The Olympic Loop Highway reached Kalaloch from the south in the late 1920s just after the original resort was built. In 1931 Kalaloch hosted the celebration of the completion of the highway. Thousands attended the ceremony. During WWII, the Coast Guard used the resort buildings as a headquarters for the Coast Lookout System. Cabins, housing up to four men, were built all along the Olympic coast to keep a lookout for a Japanese invasion.

Quinault and Queets Indians

Soon past Kalaloch, you reach the park boundary and enter the Quinault Indian Reservation, then the small hamlet of Queets appears. The Queets Indians once had their own identity but are now considered part of the larger Quinault Tribe. They "signed" the same Treaty of Olympia in 1855 as did the Quinault, Hoh and Quileute Tribes.

A couple miles after you leave the park, the highway crosses the Queets River, then begins curving east. In 8 miles farther east, a turnoff on the left leads to the Queets River section of the park. (Continuing south on US 101, you are still within the Quinault Indian Reservation, and in 15 miles you reach the Lake Quinault area.)

Queets River Side Trip

The Queets River Road heads upriver 13 miles to the Queets Campground, but check with the park before you go, as the Queets River Road is prone to flooding and washouts. The campground area is another likely place to spot a herd of elk.

This part of the park is definitely a compromise, a slender peninsula that barely covers the river bottom. The park has proposed to acquire more river bottom property with a "willing seller" strategy (see "Land Protections" in chapter 7, The 21st Century and the Future).

One of the world's largest Douglas-firs is a few miles upriver from the campground, and it is well marked. The bad news is that you first have to ford the river. Since the river is just a few feet from the parking lot, don't bother with your hiking boots. Bring a good pair of river sandals for the crossing. In the summer, the river level is low, perhaps only up to your knees, and the water is slow moving. It is worth crossing the river since you immediately enter some of the loneliest rain forest on the Peninsula.

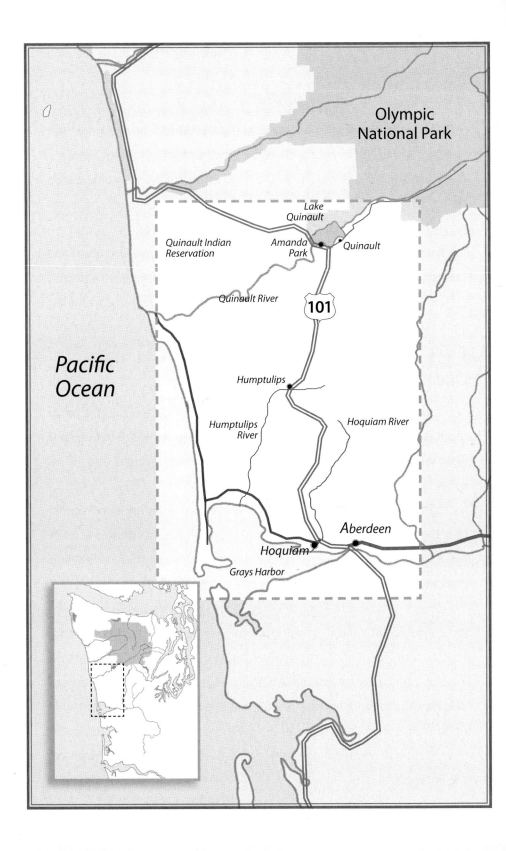

MILESTONE 8

LAKE QUINAULT TO ABERDEEN

Continuing south on US 101, this Milestone takes you through the Lake Quinault area south to Aberdeen in 43 miles.

Lake Quinault, located inside the Quinault Indian Reservation, is managed by the tribe. Fishing on the lake requires their permission. The Lake Quinault area was first pioneered in 1889. It took the settlers weeks to get here. They subsisted primarily by hunting, trapping and fishing, just like the Indians. In 1915 the road opened up from Hoquiam, which aided development, though it was still very modest. Lake Quinault was also the terminus for two historic cross-Peninsula treks: the Press Expedition (from Port Angeles) and the O'Neil Expedition (from Hoodsport), both in 1890.

In 15 miles after passing the Queets River Road, you reach the Quinault North Shore Road. This road, at first paved and then gravel, leads many miles up the lakeshore and then up the North Fork Quinault River, past several campgrounds, to remote trailheads that lead deep into Olympic National Park. It eventually loops back to the Lake Quinault Lodge, the South Shore Road and US 101.

The north side of the lake is in the national park; the south side, where the Lake Quinault Lodge sits, is inside of Olympic National Forest.

Most travelers stay on US 101 southbound another 3 miles, through the tiny community of Amanda Park, to the South Shore Road, the turnoff to Lake Quinault Lodge, on the left.

Lake Quinault Side Trip

Just 2 miles east on the South Shore Road are campgrounds and the fabled Lake Quinault Lodge, built in 1926. The lodge, styled after other great park lodges, is listed on the National Historic Registry. Its biggest claim to fame is the day in 1938 when FDR had lunch in what is now called the Roosevelt Dining Room. Nine months after his visit to the Peninsula, he created Olympic National Park. It is worth the stop just to look at the historic photographs in the lodge's lobby.

Check out the rain gauge on the front porch for a slight hint of the amount of rain that falls here. For a brief history lesson, visit the Lake Quinault Historical Society and Museum across the street.

The Quinault River valley has been characterized has having the most biomass per acre of any place on the planet, even ahead of

its neighbors, the Hoh and the Queets. And, of course, it grows big trees. The Quinault River valley is also called the "Valley of Giants." With its southwestern aspect and feet and feet of rain annually, it is the perfect environment for growing the world's largest trees.

Big Trees

The largest **Sitka spruce** in the world is just a mile east of the Lake Quinault Lodge, at the Rain Forest

Rain gauge on the front porch of the lodge

Resort. Estimated to be 1000 years old, it is the fourth-largest tree in the United States. The largest **Alaska yellow cedar** in the United States is located 7 miles off of the North Shore Road (see above). It is the nation's fifteenth-largest tree. The United States' largest **Douglas-fir** is located just south of the lodge, but it is not accessible by trail. It is the nation's fifth-largest tree. The largest **Western and mountain hemlocks** are up the East Fork of the Quinault River. Both are in the top 100 largest trees. And the largest tree in Washington State and the third-largest tree in the world is a **Western red cedar,** on a short trail off the North Shore Road. These trees have been crowned champions by the American Forests' National Big Tree Program, which annually publishes the National Register of Big Trees (see Appendix D, Resources).

Lake Quinault Hikes

There are numerous easy, well-marked hikes around the Lake Quinault Lodge. Some start right in front of the lodge on the lake side. Others are accessible just a short way back toward the highway.

Humptulips

Back on the highway, you soon enter the Quinault Research Natural Area (RNA). There are no signs, but you can tell when you leave the RNA because you immediately see evidence of logging. As the highway traverses this small 1500-acre parcel, imagine the pioneers traveling through here a century ago. Many complained that they rarely saw sunlight and it was always dark and gloomy. It is no wonder, if this stretch of the highway is any indication of what it looked like in the past.

Continuing south on US 101, in 6 miles south of Amanda Park and Lake Quinault is the Moclips Highway on the right. See Milestone 9, North Beach, for an interesting drive toward Hoquiam. It is 50 miles longer than following US 101 south, but there is much to see on the Moclips Highway.

In another 2 miles you pass from the Quinault River drainage, which flows into the Pacific, to the Humptulips River, which drains into Grays Harbor. Another 9 miles south is the modest community of Humptulips, along the Humptulips River. Humptulips is an Indian word meaning "hard to pole," probably because of the many snags in the meandering river.

This was also ground zero for the richest virgin Douglas-fir stand on the Peninsula. Stories tell of having to drop all the old-growth in the same direction since all the other directions were filled with other old-growth Doug firs. These logs were then transported down to mills in Grays Harbor.

Due south from Humptulips some 3 miles is the area called Axford Prairie, which was periodically burned by the natives. Now because of its glacial soil and repeated burnings, you can find stands of lodgepole pines (*Pinus contorta*), a tree that grows well in dry areas such as Eastern Washington and Oregon.

Hoquiam River

After passing the area south of Humptulips, the highway continues south down the Hoquiam River through forest that was first cut when logging appeared in the Grays Harbor area. The region was close to the tidelands, had gentle rolling hills and had enormous trees.

In 20 miles from Humptulips you reach the sister cities of Hoquiam and Aberdeen. You can tell you are getting close to Grays Harbor and downtown Hoquiam when you see the meandering Hoquiam River just east outside your car window. Note the tidal influences. The river barely drops 10 feet in 4 miles. Also note the pilings in the river, which were placed there during the great logging boom of the early twentieth century. The pilings helped keep the newly cut logs going in a straight line down to the harbor and were used to tie up the log rafts.

This land is about to be purchased by the Cascade Land Conservancy and Chehalis River Basin Land Trust because of its value as a unique natural area. The trust will encompass 1300 acres on both the main and the East Fork of the Hoquiam. The main river trust lands start at approximately river milepost 4 and go to river milepost 9, just where US 101 crosses the river.

Hoquiam River pilings

Grays Harbor

Continue south on US 101 into Hoquiam; just before the highway turns sharply east, you can turn west on Washington Highway 109 and follow it west for 1.5 miles to the turnoff for the airport and Grays Harbor National Wildlife Refuge, just west of the airport.

If you have the good fortune to visit the refuge from late April to early May, you will see the largest concentrations of shorebirds on the West Coast. Many of these birds are on their way from South America to the Arctic. They start returning in late June through October on their way south. The Grays Harbor NWR is designated an important birding area (IBA).

Grays Harbor is the largest bay north of the Columbia River: 95 square miles. It is fed by six rivers. The 60-mile-long Chehalis River, the largest on the Peninsula by a factor of two or three, drains an area as far away as the towns of Centralia and Chehalis on Interstate 5. From the north and the Olympic Mountains flow the Humptulips, the Hoquiam, and the Wishkah. From the south, the Johns and Elk Rivers fill the harbor.

Grays Harbor was named by George Vancouver for Robert Gray, the first American to circle the globe and the first to enter the harbor. He initially anchored about 7 miles due west from the wildlife refuge, two-thirds of the way to what is now Ocean Shores, on May 7, 1792. The explorers traded with the natives for a few days, killed a few of the natives who were deemed by Captain Gray to be too aggressive, and left on May 10. They were the first Europeans the natives had ever encountered.

The next day, Gray sailed into the Columbia River and named it for his boat, the *Columbia Rediviva*. This was Gray's second visit to this coast. Three years earlier, he had sailed right by Grays Harbor and the Columbia River aboard the *Lady Washington,* which accompanied the *Columbia* in 1789. A replica of the *Lady Washington* built in Grays Harbor in 1989 calls the harbor homeport. Perhaps Grays Harbor's most famous citizen, she has appeared in about a dozen movies, including all three of Disney's *Pirates of the Caribbean* films.

Chehalis Indians

The Chehalis Indians occupied the watershed of Grays Harbor and the Chehalis River. They probably numbered 1000 individuals in the whole area, scattered in numerous small villages and campsites, except for the main village, which was at Chehalis Point, now called Westport. In 1856 the tribe signed away its rights and slowly moved to their 4000-acre reservation in Oakville, near Chehalis.

Hoquiam and Aberdeen

Keep your navigational eye keen as you travel through the two merged towns of Hoquiam and Aberdeen—it's hard to tell where

Downtown Aberdeen in 1910.

one ends the other begins. US 101 goes south in Aberdeen, but you want to continue east on WA 12 to Olympia to complete the Olympic Milestone Loop.

Aberdeen and Hoquiam "should" be the largest cities in Washington State except for the fact that Grays Harbor is too shallow to handle any meaningful shipping. Add to that the fact that the railroad took so long in getting here. Seattle and Tacoma had excellent deep harbors and the railroads. The rest is history.

The first white man to settle in Grays Harbor was William O'Leary, in 1848. He eventually settled on the south shore and built himself a home not unlike what the Indians built. And, like the Indians, he survived on the native plants and animals, particularly salmon. His original homestead and the creek named after him are directly south of the airport, across the harbor on WA 105. Nothing remains there to mark the spot.

He stayed in the Grays Harbor area until his death and is buried in a small Catholic cemetery between Satsop and Elma on the old highway.

Hoquiam, the smaller of the two cities, was incorporated first. It enjoyed a small head start in the economic wars against Aberdeen with the first mills and canneries on the harbor, but Aberdeen got the railroad first. The rails took another four years to reach Hoquiam, farther west.

Aberdeen had a benevolent pioneer in the same fashion that Shelton enjoyed with David Shelton. Sam Benn arrived in 1859 and acquired most of the land that would become the city of Aberdeen. He provided most of the sites for the initial sawmills and canneries. Railroads were instrumental to any town's success; the Northern Pacific Railroad came close but veered south to Cosmopolis and Ocosta. Benn, forever the city promoter, gave a town lot to any volunteer who worked ten days on the railroad spur into Aberdeen. A city park, elementary school, high school gymnasium, disc golf course, and street are named after him. Benn, who lived to be 103, died in 1935.

Nicknamed the "Lumber Capital of the World," the two cities have economies that have been tied to that industry ever since their beginning. Both fish canning and lumber vied for initial supremacy, but with all those enormous trees, it was the lumber that prevailed. The heyday was in the early twentieth century. In 1900 the six mills in Aberdeen alone sawed up 250 million logs in one year.

All the logging and all those mills, and all those loggers and mill workers, created a long and storied history of labor unions. Logging

"The Workers", created by Tom Morandi, dedicated in 1996. It is located at the entrance of the Rotary Log Pavillion Park on the east end of town.

and mill working were neither well-paying nor safe. As the operations became larger, labor unrest developed and precipitated many strikes. One of the most famous was the 1912 strike by the radical Industrial Workers of the World union, aka the Wobblies. Martial law was declared during a strike in the early 1930s. The Armory Building was converted into a makeshift prison and surrounded by barbed wire and machine guns to house 300 strikers accused of violence.

Over time, the large swaths of uncut trees disappeared, logging and mill working became increasingly mechanized, and restrictions from environmental issues led, in the past three decades, to a significant decline of Grays Harbor's fortunes. Aberdeen and Hoquiam could be called the cities of the abandoned pilings: hundreds, if not thousands, line every waterway. Unemployment forced many residents to leave the county. The cities' combined population is 25 percent less than it was right before the Great Depression.

Only recently has the local economy started to grow modestly. The Quinault Tribe has built a large casino north of Ocean Shores, and tourism to the national park and ocean beaches has helped. Hoquiam thinks it has a boost with an $88 million biodiesel plant, the largest in the United States, built down on the waterfront. Politics and environmental issues are critical to the plant's success.

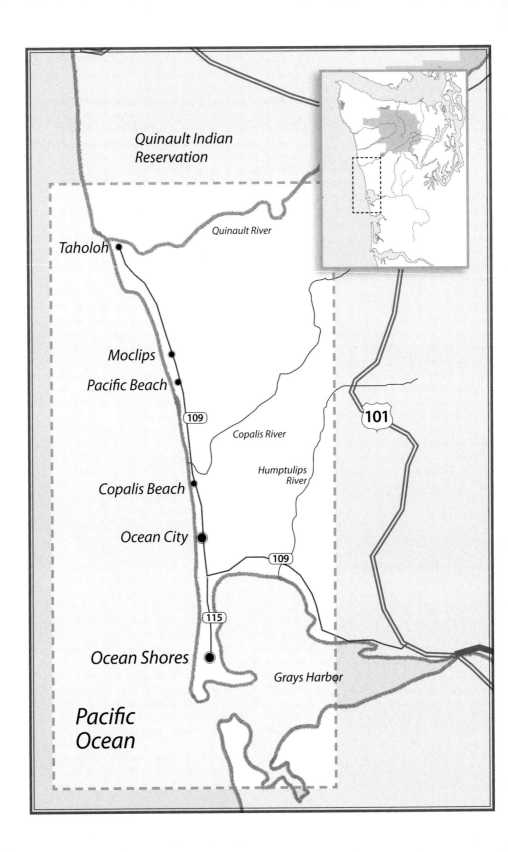

MILESTONE 9

NORTH BEACH

This 90-mile trip off of US Highway 101 leads you southwest to the coast, all the way south to Ocean Shores, and then east 22 miles to Hoquiam. It is the recommended way to go, since you won't be missing much by sidestepping US 101 between Lake Quinault and Hoquiam.

From US 101 about 6 miles south of Amanda Park and Lake Quinault, turn right onto the Moclips Highway. Follow it 20 miles southwest to the Pacific Ocean and the North Beach area. This highway roughly follows the southern border of the Quinault Indian Reservation until it gets to the coast at Moclips, where it ends at Washington Highway 109.

Taholoh Side Trip

At Moclips, turn right onto WA 109 to head north about 8 miles to Taholoh and the Quinault Indian Reservation. On the beach just north of Taholoh, across the Quinault River, is ground zero for the first encounters between Europeans and the indigenous people.

In 1775 the Spaniard Bruno de Heceta approached the Pacific coast with two ships. After two days of peaceful trading near Cape Elizabeth, the Indians attacked a shore party and killed them all, then hacked the

small launch to pieces. The onboard Spanish crews could do nothing but watch with horror.

Cape Elizabeth may also have been ground zero for the introduction of smallpox to the Peninsula (see chapter 3, Original Inhabitants). Heceta retreated to Destruction Island, which he named Island of Sorrows (see Milestone 8).

Taholoh is on the Quinault River roughly halfway between Cape Elizabeth to the north and Point Grenville to the south. As you return south to Moclips on WA 109, on your right you'll see Point Grenville (accessible only with tribal permission). The point was used during WWII as a lookout station and Coast Guard base. Many buildings still stand on the site. Point Grenville, a great place to see puffins, is designated as an important birding area (IBA).

Moclips

Moclips sits at the north end of a 25-mile expanse of sandy beach that stretches south uninterrupted to Point Brown at the south end of the Ocean Shores peninsula. This beach was the Olympic Peninsula's first "highway." Pioneers used the beach to move up and down the coast to the small villages of Moclips, Pacific Beach, Copalis Beach, Ocean City and Ocean Shores until the Northern Pacific Railroad came to Moclips in 1905. There are numerous opportunities to take your car down to drive on the beach all along the coast down to Ocean Shores.

Though Moclips was first settled in 1862, it was the railroad that brought a few years of prosperity. Initially billed as a perfect "healthy" getaway, the little town soon supported hotels, a theater, and schools. Thousands would disembark from the train every week to enjoy the fresh salt air and miles of perfect beach.

A BROKEN DREAM

In 1904, Jim Hill's Great Northern reached the Pacific at Moclips. For the first time people from population centers could reach these ocean beaches by rail. Recognizing a need, Dr. Edward Lycan opened The Moclips Beach Hotel in 1905. Over 5,000 people visited Moclips on weekends. The hotel burned down in its first year. In 1907, it was rebuilt with 270 rooms. In 1911, the new hotel fell victim to the sea in the biggest storm on record. Dr. Lycan's dream of a Moclips was washed away.

Disaster struck in the early twentieth century when the largest hotel, an enormous 150-room building, burned down. In 1907 the owners rebuilt it even larger, with 270 rooms, just 12 feet from the high tide line. By 1913, after a series of fierce storms, very little of it remained on the beach. A monument has been erected at the site near the beach on the north side of town.

Pacific Beach

During WWII, both Moclips and its sister city about 2 miles south down WA 109, Pacific Beach, were seized by the Air Force and Navy and all available lodging was converted to military use. After the war, the military all but disappeared except for a Navy recreation site still in Pacific Beach. Also in Pacific Beach is an oceanfront campground at the mouth of a creek.

New Urbanism

Just south across the creek south of Pacific Beach is Seabrook, "a New Beach Town." This development is designed unlike anything else in the state, with high-end homes clustered around public spaces. Bicycles and walking are the intended mode of transportation. The highly planned community is an example of New Urbanism, a development concept that supports tight-knit neighborhoods while spurning sprawl.

As you drive WA 109 south, you pass through little resort communities: Ocean Grove, Roosevelt Beach and Iron Springs.

Copalis Rock and Copalis Beach

Traders initially came to the Northwest Coast for sea otter pelts, and for about fifty years the system of being the middlemen between the Indians and China worked. The industry collapsed in the middle of the 1800s, because the sea otter was on its way to becoming extinct in Washington State.

However, the area from Point Grenville south to what is now Ocean Shores remained one of the last best hunting grounds for these beleaguered creatures. Continuing south on WA 109, in 5.5 miles south of Pacific Beach is Copalis Rock, just south of Iron Springs. On top of Copalis Rock, one of the first settlers built a shack and hunted sea otters from here.

Hunters used to build 20- to 30-foot-high derricks from which they would shoot sea otters offshore in the kelp, often at distances of hundreds of yards. The desired otter fur kept the dead animals afloat, enabling their bodies to reach shore on the next tide, hopefully. The hunters marked their bullets, like a brand, allowing them to claim the corpses when they washed ashore. The last otter was thought to have been killed in the early 1900s.

In another 2.5 miles you reach Copalis (pronounced "co-PAY-liss") Beach, historic home to copious razor clams. In fact this whole area is fa-

mous for its razor clams. This town supported numerous canneries until the resource was played out.

Ocean Shores

About 3 miles south of Copalis Beach is the little burg of Ocean City, and another 2 miles or so south of that, WA 109 heads east toward Hoquiam at the junction with WA 115. Continue straight ahead on WA 115 to finish exploring the coast here.

In another 2 miles (7 miles south of Copalis Beach) lies the community of Oyhut, at the north end of the Point Brown peninsula (2 miles south of the intersection with WA 109 and the region's largest casino, the Quinault Beach Resort and Casino). Oyhut used to be a natural gathering place for both Indians and pioneers who were traveling up and down the coast. Pioneers used to travel by boat to Oyhut, cross the peninsula, and board a wagon or horse for their journey up and down the beach.

A mile farther south is downtown Ocean Shores. Do you want to play miniature golf, go bowling, rent a moped, ride a horse on the beach, play the slots, fly a kite, watch movies, shop for antiques, ride go-karts, go clamming or just drive on the beach? It is all here. Ocean Shores is the Olympic Peninsula's most touristy destination.

The 6-mile-long strip of land that is the Ocean Shores peninsula, about 6000 acres, has been occupied for centuries by the Indians. The local tribes used permanent and seasonal camps on the peninsula as a common meeting ground and trading area.

The first pioneer, Matthew McGee, settled at the southern tip of Point Brown in 1860. He was soon joined by A. O. Damon, who eventually acquired the whole peninsula. Mr. Damon's grandson sold it all for a million dollars in 1960 to the Ocean Shores Investment Corporation. The development went through numerous boom and bust cycles, until the citizens finally wrested control of it all from the developers in the 1980s.

Point Brown at the southern tip of the peninsula offers superb birding; virtually all of the southern tip of the Ocean Shores peninsula is designated as an IBA. It's also a great spot for storm-watching. The Ocean Shores peninsula is different from the rest of the Olympic Peninsula because of the ocean influences. All the big trees have been chopped down, of course, but you can see shore pines, which are rare elsewhere.

It is obvious to the most casual observer that this peninsula is of a temporary nature. It was created by tidal and wave forces that have dumped all the "land" up out of the sea. Much of the land on the southern tip wasn't there in the late nineteenth century but has been added since by the sea, mostly due to the construction of the North Jetty at the tip of the peninsula.

The historic source of all this sand is the Columbia River. Now that the river doesn't discharge much sediment because it is dammed, any additions to the Ocean Shores peninsula are hard to come by. Recent storms have ravaged the southern tip, and the residents should expect things to get worse as sea levels rise and the intensity of the storms increase with global warming.

Also, any large earthquake will return the whole place to the sea. There isn't any solid ground, so the initial shaking will cause liquefaction and demolish all the buildings. A couple of moments later, the tsunami will crest over and wash everything into Grays Harbor.

Until that day arrives, you can enjoy the beach on both the ocean side and the Grays Harbor side, as well as Oyhut Wildlife Area and Duck

Lake, before returning north on WA 115 (which loops the Ocean Shores peninsula) to WA 109. Turn right on WA 109 to head east about 16 miles to rejoin US 101 in Hoquiam.

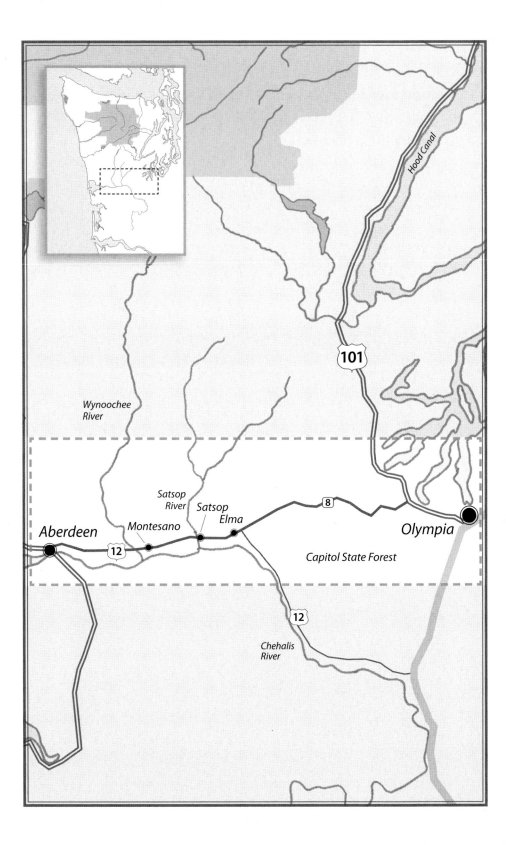

ABERDEEN TO OLYMPIA

From the junction of US Highway 101 and US 12/Washington Highway 8 in Aberdeen, follow the signs east out of Aberdeen toward Olympia, some 44 miles distant.

Montesano

In 10 miles you reach Montesano, the Grays Harbor County seat. Montesano was first pioneered in 1853 by a couple of Mainers, Isaiah and Lorinda Scammon. They settled on a donation land claim right on the Chehalis River about 1.5 miles south of the current downtown. He was known for his blacksmithing skills and hard work, and she was known for her religious nature. Their trading-post settlement was called Scammon's Landing. Their daughter, Eva, was the first pioneer child born in the new territory.

Though they settled there for the agricultural opportunity, the location was better suited for other purposes. It was close enough to Grays Harbor that ocean ships could dock there, and it was about midway between Aberdeen and civilization in Centralia, along the Chehalis River. Mr. Scammon operated a ferry and she a boardinghouse. When it came

time to create a real city, she wanted to call it Mount Zion. A compromise was reached, with the current name prevailing.

Montesano became the county seat in 1860 and for the next thirty years, county business was conducted in Lorinda Scammon's living room. The most spectacular building in Montesano, if not the whole county, is the County Courthouse that was built in 1911. It can be partially seen from the highway, but go into town to see inside during the week to view the murals and the dome. Montesano is also home to Washington State's oldest continuously published newspaper, the *Vidette*.

Courthouse Murals

The two large murals seen from virtually anywhere inside the courthouse were painted by artists who appear never to have visited Grays Harbor. One mural depicts the arrival of Robert Gray to the harbor. The other tries to re-create the scene of Governor Stevens negotiating a treaty at Cosmopolis. What do you notice is wrong? It appears that these two German-trained artists thought coastal Indians looked just like those of the northern plains. Also, no tribe on the Peninsula ever used tepees, wore headdresses or dear skin clothes.

AGRICULTURE, ABUNDANCE, DOMESTICITY.

Chehalis River Surge Plain
Natural Area Preserve

Chehalis River
Shoreline Access

Nature's Offerings

The very accessible Chehalis River Surge Plain Natural Area Preserve is about 3 miles from the river crossing on WA 107, south of Montesano. Just north of town is Lake Sylvia State Park, as well as Wynoochee Road, which heads north quite a distance to Wynoochee Lake in the southern reaches of Olympic National Forest. If you do go to Wynoochee Lake, bring your umbrella: it gets 150 inches of rain per year.

Satsop

Continue east on US 12/WA 8 another 6 miles to the town of Satsop, along the Satsop River. Not much has happened of note in Satsop with its population of 700—as long as you don't notice the two cooling towers on the southern horizon, looking like two enormous old-growth stumps.

Construction of two nuclear plants was started here in 1977 and terminated in 1983. Washington Public Power Supply System (WPPSS) was started in the 1950s as an organizing body to help manage the forecasted energy demand for the state. They eventually started construction on five nuclear plants across the state, including these two at Satsop.

The whole enterprise was way over the directors' heads since they had no idea what it took to build projects this large. Soon WPPSS was known as WHOOPS. The fiasco resulted in the largest municipal bond default in the nation's history. Only one of the five planned plants eventually came on line.

You probably will never get as close to a cooling tower as you will if you turn south off US 12/WA 8 onto Keys Road (the first southbound street after you cross the Satsop River) and visit the Satsop Development Park. There remains an amazing amount of infrastructure from the failed plant, but the now industrial park is doing quite well, employing about 400 in a variety of businesses occupying various buildings originally intended for the WPPSS plant.

Elma

In another 4 miles farther east on US 12/WA 8, you reach the town of Elma. Here, as you travel east of the little town, US 12 heads southeast, while you continue straight east on WA 8. Notice that the Chehalis River is also now bearing southeast. Also note how broad the valley is. The current Chehalis River is not large enough to create such a broad valley.

The base of one of the cooling towers

Some 13,000 years ago, during the last ice age the Puget Sound waters were blocked from entering the Pacific Ocean through the Strait of Juan de Fuca. All the water from melting glaciers and all the streams in the Puget Sound watershed flowed south over the top of Olympia, along the Black River drainage, and into the Chehalis River. Geologists estimate that the flow resembled the Columbia River's current flow over the Grand Coulee Dam. Back then, the Chehalis River was about a hundred times its current level and large enough to carve its current valley.

McCleary

In another 8 miles farther east on WA 8, McCleary is the home of one of the oldest mills on the Peninsula. Henry McCleary and his partner started their first mill nearby in 1897. The door mill was completed in 1912 and is still operating right in downtown McCleary. It was one of the most productive door plants in the country, at its height turning out 8000 doors per day.

The 1910s was the town's boom time, and its population doubled. But the late '20s brought the beginning of the decline as the lumber market dried up during the Great Depression and local timber became scarce. McCleary, both the company town and the industrial operations, were minimally maintained and McCleary, the man, wanted to retire in 1941.

Simpson Logging Company, from over the hill to the east in Shelton, had a long business relationship with McCleary, but all they wanted was the McCleary company's assets, mostly the mills. Simpson Logging eventually bought everything, including the town, and immediately went about convincing the townspeople that they needed to be a real town, which they did by incorporating in 1942. Simpson generously helped the new city fathers to create working utilities and sold the company homes for the price of eighteen months' rent. Mr. McCleary died six months after he retired.

The Black Hills

Continuing east on WA 8, in about 8 miles you can see to the south the Black Hills and the Capital State Forest, halfway between McCleary and Olympia. This is the first publicly owned forest in the country that practiced sustained logging techniques.

In another 4 miles or so, stay right to rejoin US 101—you have come full circle, and Olympia is another 4 miles or so to the east.

Appendix A. Timeline

13,000 to 15,000 BP The last ice age ends and the ice sheets melt, revealing the Strait of Juan de Fuca and Puget Sound.

12,000 BP Manis's mastodon dies in what is now Sequim.

1579 Sir Francis Drake may have sailed past the Pacific Northwest coast and entered the Strait of Juan de Fuca, though no definitive record exists of this accomplishment.

1775 Bruno de Heceta becomes the first European to land in what is now Washington State, near the Quinault River between Cape Elizabeth and Point Grenville. He is also the first to identify the Columbia River. (He thought that it might be the fabled Northwest Passage, aka the Strait of Anian.)

1778 The Great Navigator, British Captain James Cook, appears offshore in Oregon and sails north along the Pacific coast. He finally lands at Nootka Sound on Vancouver Island prior to sailing all the way to Alaska and the Bering Strait.

1792 British Captain George Vancouver and Peter Puget arrive and map Puget Sound for the first time. American Robert Gray enters Grays Harbor and the Columbia River; he names the harbor Bulfinch Harbor and the river after his ship, the *Columbia Rediviva*.

1824 A party of Hudson Bay Company trappers stationed at Fort Vancouver explores Grays Harbor.

1825 English botanist David Douglas, visiting the Pacific Northwest and staying at Fort Vancouver, travels north up the headwaters of the Chehalis River and proceeds downriver to Grays Harbor.

1833 Fort Nisqually founded by Hudson Bay Company as a station between Fort Vancouver and Fort Langley on the Fraser River.

1836 The first steamship appears, the *Beaver*.

1841 Charles Wilkes arrives with the U.S. Exploratory Expedition; they extensively map the Puget Sound region.

1845 George Washington Bush and Michael Simmons reach Tumwater and become the first nonnative settlers north of Oregon's side of the Columbia River.

1846 President Polk signs the Oregon Treaty with Great Britain, establishing the U.S. boundary line at the forty-ninth parallel, Washington's present northern boundary; this splits the jointly occupied Oregon Country in two.

1846–1847 British Captain Henry Kellett explores and surveys many parts of the Strait of Juan de Fuca, assigning names to Clallam Bay, Crescent Bay, Striped Peak, Freshwater Bay, Sek[i]u (applying it to a point of land on the north shore of the Peninsula) and Ediz Hook at Port Angeles

1848 The Oregon Territory is established by Congress; it includes Oregon, Washington, Idaho and western parts of Montana and Wyoming.

1850 Donation Land Claim Act passed; William O'Leary (1821–1901) enters Grays Harbor and settles near what is now Cosmopolis.

1851 First settlers arrive in Port Townsend.

1852 The first European trading post is established, in Neah Bay; smallpox follows, brought by a trading ship.

1853 Washington becomes its own territory, extending east to western Montana. Oregon also becomes a territory extending east to western Wyoming.

1855 All tribes on the Peninsula sign treaties relinquishing their claim to any lands. Eventually, they were all settled on reservations.

1859 Oregon becomes a state with its current borders.

1862 Homestead Act passed.

1880 Eldridge Morse describes an 1878 expedition into the southeastern section of the Olympics . . . but the trip might be fictitious.

1885 The O'Neil Expedition explores a sizable portion of the Peninsula from the north, via Port Angeles.

1889 Governor Elisha Ferry says, "Washington has her great unknown land like the interior of Africa"; John Muir visits the Peninsula; Washington becomes a state.

1890 Hoodsport incorporates; Lake Cushman and Hoodsport are connected by road (most travel on the West End is still on trails, as few roads exist); Mount

Olympus is climbed by members of O'Neil's second expedition; the Press Expedition is led by James Christie; Lieutenant Joseph O'Neil makes his second expedition into the interior.

1891 A post office is established at Boston at the confluence of the Dickey and Quillayute Rivers (the town is later renamed Mora); *Tacoma Press* publishes the idea of a national park.

1892 John Huelsdonk, Iron Man of the Hoh, arrives with his wife on the Peninsula; Olympic Hot Springs is discovered in the Elwha River drainage.

1893 Panic of 1893, a national financial depression, occurs.

1897 Olympic Forest Reserve is created with 2,188,800 acres.

1900 Frederic Weyerhaeuser purchases 900,000 acres of timberland from Northern Pacific Railroad, which initiates his company's presence in Washington State; the president reduces the size of Olympic Forest Reserve by 260,000 acres.

1901 Again, the president reduces Olympic Forest Reserve by an additional 450,000 acres.

1904 Congressman Francis Cushman introduces bills to create Elk National Park.

1905 The Peninsula's elk population reaches an estimated low of 2000; Washington State passes a ten-year moratorium on elk hunting on the Peninsula;

1908 Congressman Humphrey introduces his second bill to establish a national park.

1909 President Theodore Roosevelt creates Mount Olympus National Monument with 610,560 acres.

1911 Congressman Humphrey tries again, this time to establish Mount Olympus National Park.

1912 Forks is platted.

1915 President Wilson undoes President Roosevelt's creation and creates a smaller Olympic National Monument, at 328,000 acres.

1917 U.S. War Department establishes the Spruce Production Division.

1918 Work on Spruce Railroad is completed weeks before WWI ends.

1920 Washington Pulp and Paper plant is built on Ediz Hook to take advantage of power from Elwha dams and new technologies allowing hemlock to be converted into paper; the company pioneers the next stage of logging, moving from harvesting forests strictly for structural products (mostly Douglas-fir) to harvesting whole forests, including for cellulose for making paper.

1920s Mountain goats are introduced to the national monument.

1922 Wolves are essentially eliminated from the Peninsula, primarily by bounty hunters.

1926 Congressman Albert Johnson introduces a bill to establish Olympic National Park; the road between Clallam Bay and Swan Bay at the east side of Ozette Lake is completed.

1929 The Queets Valley Road, connecting the upper valley to US Highway 101, is completed.

1931 Work is completed connecting a road circumnavigating the Peninsula.

1935 Congressman Mon C. Wallgren of Washington State introduces a bill to establish Mount Olympus National Park; the bill fails.

1937 President Franklin D. Roosevelt visits the Peninsula.

1938 Congressman Wallgren submits successful bill to establish Olympic National Park, encompassing 680,000 acres; the bill gives authority to the president to increase the size of the park at his discretion in the future.

1940 FDR enlarges Olympic National Park with portions of the Queets River and the coastal unit from Queets to Cape Flattery.

1942 U.S. Army establishes Aircraft Warning System in all fire lookout towers on the Peninsula; Ozette Lake Coast Guard Station established 3 miles west of Ozette Lake with a tent camp.

1943 President Roosevelt helps protect Port Angeles' watershed by adding 20,000 along the Morse Creek, just south of town.

1945 John Huelsdonk, Iron Man of the Hoh, dies.

1946 Olympic National Park is finally dedicated at Lake Crescent; Governor Martin, who opposed the large park, says, "My conviction is that our government has done well to preserve this perpetual scenic memorial of the world's most remarkable scenic growth."

1953 President Harry Truman adds a section of the Bogachiel River valley to the park of about 47,000 acres.1960s The Ozette community gets electricity.

1961 Hood Canal Bridge opens.

1968 The Lower Elwha Klallam Reservation is created.

1970 An Ozette Indian village is unearthed on the coast south of the Makah Indian Reservation.

1976 Shi Shi, Point of Arches, and the east shoreline of Ozette Lake are added to the park; UNESCO selects Olympic National Park as part of the Biosphere Reserves.

1980s Big lumber peaks in production.

1981 The Jamestown S'Klallam Tribe gains federal recognition and establishes themselves in Blyn on Sequim Bay.

1982 Olympic National Park is selected by UNESCO as a World Heritage Site.

1984 The Washington Wilderness Act is passed, protecting current Buckhorn, Brothers, Mount Skokomish, Wonder Mountain, and Colonel Bob Wilderness Areas.

1988 Congress designates 95 percent of Olympic National Park as wilderness.

1992 Congress passes a law authorizing the removal of the two Elwha River dams.

1994 The Northwest Forest Plan is released, which attempts, among other things, to protect the Northern Spotted Owl.

1999 Makah Indians resume traditional whale hunting using traditional canoes and spears.

2011 Demolition of the Elwha River dams begins.

2012 The Elwha Dam is removed and Lake Aldwell is drained; Glines Canyon Dam is slated for removal, and Lake Mills to be drained, by late 2013.

Appendix B. Mileage

	Cape Flattery (Neah Bay)	Forks	Glines Canyon Dam (former site of upper Elwha Dam)	Hoh Rain Forest Visitor Center	Hurricane Ridge	Kalaloch	Lake Crescent (Barnes Point)	Quinault	Ocean Shores
Aberdeen	164	107	161	112	163	73	144	44	25
Cape Flattery (Neah Bay)		57	81	88	96	91	69	124	166
Forks			155	31	76	34	37	64	110
Glines Canyon Dam (former site of upper Elwha Dam)				84	26	88	18	120	163
Hoh Rain Forest Visitor Center					108	40	65	72	93
Hurricane Ridge						112	38	141	184
Kalaloch							67	33	76
Lake Crescent (Barnes Point)								104	146
Quinault									46
Ocean Shores									
Olympia									
Olympic National Park Visitor Center, Port Angeles									
Ozette Lake									
Port Townsend									
Rialto Beach									
Seattle (via ferry or bridge)									
Sol Duc Hot Springs									
Staircase (Lake Cushman)									

	Olympia	Olympic National Park Visitor Center, Port Angeles	Ozette Lake	Port Townsend	Rialto Beach	Seattle (via ferry or bridge)	Sol Duc Hot Springs	Staircase (Lake Cushman)
Aberdeen	49	130	162	122	122	109	147	76
Cape Flattery (Neah Bay)	213	78	45	125	68	172	72	177
Forks	157	56	54	103	14	138	40	155
Glines Canyon Dam (former site of upper Elwha Dam)	134	14	83	61	6	108	38	113
Hoh Rain Forest Visitor Center	162	88	85	135	45	156	72	191
Hurricane Ridge	138	18	94	66	86	89	57	117
Kalaloch	123	91	88	138	49	160	72	195
Lake Crescent (Barnes Point)	140	21	66	68	48	93	16	121
Quinault	93	124	121	166	82	153	107	120
Ocean Shores	75	166	164	148	124	134	149	101
Olympia		120	195	99	171	61	161	52
Olympic National Park Visitor Center, Port Angeles			76	48	68	94	41	99
Ozette Lake				123	65	169	70	174
Port Townsend					115	68	88	78
Rialto Beach						161	51	167
Seattle (via ferry or bridge)							114	110
Sol Duc Hot Springs								140
Staircase (Lake Cushman)								

Appendix C. Resources

Ranger Stations and Government Information Centers

Deer Park Ranger Station (NPS), Deer Park Campground

Eagle Ranger Station (NPS), Sol Duc Hot Springs

Elwha Ranger Station (NPS), 4 miles south of US 101 on Olympic Hot Springs Rd.

Forks NPS/USFS Recreation Information Center, 551 S. Forks Ave. (US 101), Forks, WA 98331

Hoh Rain Forest Visitor Center (NPS), Hoh Rain Forest, approximately 31 miles south of Forks, (360) 374-6925

Hurricane Ridge Visitor Center (NPS), Hurricane Ridge, about 17 miles south of Port Angeles

Kalaloch Ranger Station (NPS), Kalaloch

Mora Ranger Station (NPS), 1 mile east of Rialto Beach, 13 miles west of Forks on US 101

Olympic National Forest–Forks (USFS), 437 Tillicum Lane, Forks, WA 98331, (360) 374 6522

Olympic National Forest–Head Office (USFS), 1835 Black Lake Blvd. SW, Olympia WA 98512, (360) 956-2402, www.fs.usda.gov/olympic

Olympic National Forest–Hood Canal (USFS), 295142 US 101 S., Quilcene, WA 98376, (360) 765 2200

Olympic National Forest–Quinault (USFS), 353 South Shore Rd., Quinault, WA 98575, (360) 288 2525

Olympic National Park Visitor Center and Administration (NPS), 3002 Mount Angeles Rd., Port Angeles, 98362, (360) 565-3130, www.nps.gov/olym/index.htm

Ozette Ranger Station (NPS), north end of Ozette Lake

Quinault Rain Forest Information Station (NPS/USFS), Quinault

Quinault Rain Forest Ranger Station (NPS), 7 miles west on North Fork Rd. from Amanda Park, Lake Quinault

Staircase Ranger Station (NPS), near Staircase Campground, north end of Lake Cushman

Storm King Ranger Station (NPS), Lake Crescent, Barnes Point

Washington State Department of Natural Resources Headquarters (DNR), 1111 Washington St. SE, Olympia, WA 98504, (360) 902-1000, www.dnr.wa.gov/Pages/default.aspx

Washington State Department of Natural Resources (DNR), 411 Tillicum Lane, Forks, WA 98331, (360) 374-2800

Visitor Information

Clallam Bay–Sekiu Chamber of Commerce, www.sekiu.com

Enjoy Port Townsend, enjoypt.com

Explore Hood Canal, www.explorehoodcanal.com

Forks Chamber of Commerce, forkswa.com

Jefferson County Chamber of Commerce, jeffcountychamber.org

Neah Bay Chamber of Commerce, www.neahbaywa.com

North Hood Canal Chamber of Commerce, emeraldtowns.com

North Olympic Peninsula, northolympic.com

Olympia, Lacey, Tumwater Visitor and Convention Bureau, www.visitolympia.com

Olympia, Thurston County Chamber of Commerce, thurstonchamber.com

Olympic Peninsula Tourism Commission, www.olympicpeninsula.org

Port Angeles Chamber of Commerce, www.portangeles.org

Sequim Tourism, www.visitsunnysequim.com/index.aspx

Sequim Washington Chamber of Commerce, www.sequimchamber.com

Shelton Mason Country Chamber of Commerce, sheltonchamber.org

Campgrounds

Clallam County Campgrounds, www.clallam.net/Parks/OvernightFacilities.html

Olympic National Forest Campgrounds, www.forestcamping.com/dow/pacficnw/olymcmp.htm

Olympic National Park Campgrounds, www.nps.gov/olym/planyourvisit/camp-grounds.htm

Washington State DNR Campgrounds, www.dnr.wa.gov/RecreationEducation/Topics/OpenClosureNotices/Pages/amr_olympic_region_rec.aspx

Washington State Parks, www.parks.wa.gov/

Museums

Aberdeen Museum of History, 111 E. Third St., Aberdeen, (360) 533-1976, www.aberdeen-museum.org/

Chehalis Valley Historical Museum, 703 Pioneer Ave. W., Montesano, (360) 249-5800 www.montesano.us/index.aspx?NID=396

Clallam County Historical Society, The Museum at the Carnegie, 207 S. Lincoln St., Port Angeles, (360) 452-6779, clallamhistoricalsociety.com/

Coastal Interpretive Center, 1033 Catala Ave. SE, Ocean Shores, (360) 289-4617, interpretivecenter.org/

Coast Artillery Museum, Bldg. 201, Fort Worden State Park, Port Townsend, pscoastartillerymuseum.org/index.html

Commanding Officer's Quarters-Fort Worden State Park, 200 Battery Way, Port Townsend, (360) 385-1003, www.jchsmuseum.org/Sites/CommandingOfficersQuarters.html

Forks Timber Museum, US 101, Forks, (360-374-9663), forks-web.com/fg/timber-museum.htm

Grays Harbor Historical Seaport, PO Box 2019, Aberdeen, (360)532-8611, historicalseaport.org/

Jefferson County Historical Society Museum, 540 Water St., Port Townsend, (360-385-1003), jchsmuseum.org/

Lake Quinault Historical Society and Museum, 353 South Shore Rd., Quinault, (360) 288-2317 www.quinaultrainforest.com/Lake-Quinault/Lake-Quinault-museum.html

Makah Museum and Research Center, 1880 Bayview Ave., Neah Bay, (360) 645-2711 www.makah.com/mcrchome.html

Mason County Historical Society Museum, corner of Fifth St. and Railroad Ave., Shelton, (360) 426.1020 masoncountyhistoricalsociety.org/index.html

McCleary Museum at Carnell House, 314 S. Second St., McCleary, (360) 545-3026

Museum and Arts Center in Sequim-Dungeness Valley, 175 W. Cedar, Sequim, (360) 681-2257, macsequim.org/

Museum of the North Beach, 4658 WA 109, Moclips, (360) 276-4441, www.moclips.org/

Olympic Peninsula Community Museum (an online museum), www.community-museum.org

Polson Museum, 1611 Riverside Ave., Hoquiam, (360) 533-5862, www.polsonmuseum.org/

Port Townsend Marine Science Center, Fort Worden, Port Townsend, (360)385-5582, www.ptmsc.org/index.html

Quilcene Historical Museum, 151 Columbia St., Quilcene, (360) 765-4848, quilcenemuseum.org/

Quinault Cultural Center, 807 Fifth Ave., Ste. 1, Taholah, 360.276.4191, www.quinaultculturalcenter.org/

State Capital Museum and Outreach Center, 211 21st Ave. SW, Olympia, (360) 753-2580, www.washingtonhistory.org/visit/scm/

Environmental Advocacy and Information

American Forests' National Big Tree Program, www.americanforests.org/our-programs/bigtree/

Chehalis River Basin Land Trust, www.chehalislandtrust.org

Coast Savers, www.coastsavers.org

Dungeness River Management team, www.home.olympus.net/~dungenesswc/

Hood Canal Environmental Council, www.hoodcanalenvironmentalcouncil.org/index.php

Jefferson Land Trust, www.saveland.org

North Olympic Group of the Sierra Club, www.wa.sierraclub.org/northolympic/pages/NOG.html

North Olympic Salmon Coalition, www.nosc.org

Northwest Watershed Institute, www.nwwatershed.org

Olympic Coast National Marine Sanctuary, www.olympiccoast.noaa.gov/

Olympic Environmental Council, www.home.olympus.net/~oec/

Olympic Forest Coalition, www.olympicforest.org/index.html

Olympic Peninsula Environmental News, www.olyopen.net

Protect the Peninsula's Future, www.home.olympus.net/~oec/ppf.htm

Wild Olympics, www.wildolympics.org

Tribes

Chehalis Conferderated Tribes, www.chehalistribe.org/

Hoh Tribe, www.hohtribe.com/

Jamestown S'Klallam Tribe, www.jamestowntribe.org/

Lower Elwha Klallam Tribe, www.elwha.org/home.html

Makah Tribe, www.makah.com/

Port Gamble S'Klallam Tribe, www.pgst.nsn.us/

Quileute Tribe, www.quileutenation.org/

Quinault Nation, quinaultindiannation.com/

Skokomish Tribe, www.skokomish.org/

Squaxin Island Tribe, www.squaxinisland.org/

Appendix D. Birds and Birding

Birding (the act of looking for birds) sharpens your senses for the natural world and provides nothing more than another excuse to get outside. No special gear is required (binoculars help but are not mandatory). You can do it anywhere and for the rest of your life.

Birding is, literally, an activity that the whole family can enjoy. Just start walking where birds are and try to be aware of all the different species. It is a rare natural location where you won't see and/or hear at least a dozen different species in an hour.

Even though ardent birders (people who go birding) tend to be the ultimate list makers (listing every species they see, how many, etc., only to go home and add that list to other lists they have compiled, and so on), many others go on birding trips just to walk in the woods and enjoy the camaraderie. Some participants of organized birding trips spend more time identifying the plants than the birds.

There are numerous Audubon chapters on the Peninsula, in Puget Sound and the state. Their web addresses are listed below.

Admiralty Audubon Society, www.admiraltyaudubon.org/

Audubon Washington, www. wa.audubon.org/olympic-loop

Black Hills Audubon Society, www. blackhills-audubon.org/

Dungeness River Audubon Center, www.dungenessrivercenter.org/index.html

Grays Harbor Audubon Society, www. ghas.org/

Olympic Peninsula Audubon Society, www.olympicpeninsulaaudubon.org/

Seattle Audubon, www.birdweb.org/birdweb/ecoregion/sites/pacific_northwest_coast/site

Washington Ornithological Society, www. www.wos.org/WAList97.htm

They all offer birding trips around the Peninsula. Going birding with other birders is a great way to learn about birds and find the best birding spots. Birders tend to be as generous a group as there is and love to answer all questions. They will even encourage you to look through their expensive spotting scopes. And they love taking new birders out. Most trips are local, free, and open to all. Their web addresses are listed below.

Audubon Washington has put together a birding loop trip similar to my Milestone Guide. You can download it at wa.audubon.org/olympic-loop. It lists fifty-four birding spots, with complete driving directions, birds expected, and more. Of the fifty-four sites, twenty-six are noted as important bird areas

(IBAs). These locations are especially important for the long-term conservation of birds. IBAs are part of a global program managed in the United States by the National Audubon Society. The fact that the Peninsula has twenty-six IBAs is just another indication of how special the Peninsula is. I have indicated about dozen or so IBAs in the Milestone chapters.

Your First Bird List

The list below contains about a hundred of the most common birds on the Peninsula, as compiled by the Olympic Peninsula Audubon Society; the species are grouped by predetermined categories that you can investigate to expand your knowledge abo ut how birds are classified. (It is through their generosity that I publish this list. Visit their website to get a more complete listing of birds seen locally. Also, go on one of their many birding trips.)

One of the keys to birding is knowing what to expect in what season. Because the Peninsula is a major stopover along a major migratory flyway, some birds are superabundant (imagine thousands and thousands of just one species) in one season, only to vanish the next. The chart below tells you whether a bird is abundant, common, fairly common, unusual, or rare in the four basic seasons of spring, summer, fall, and winter (designated by months).

Another key to identifying birds is habitat recognition. The Peninsula is blessed with a variety of habitats, and so it has a variety of birds. Birds love their own preferred neighborhood and rarely venture to a different one. You won't see a Mew Gull at Hurricane Ridge, and you won't see a Northern Spotted Owl on Ediz Hook in Port Angeles. Each bird listing has one or more of the following abbreviations indicating its preferred habitat:

A = Alpine; high Olympic Mountains

B = Bays, estuaries, tidal flats

C = Coniferous forests

D = Deciduous-coniferous mixed forests

F = Fields, farmlands, prairies

H = Human habitats: towns, parks, yards, feeders

L = Coastal ocean, Strait of Juan de Fuca

M = Marshes, ponds

O = Overhead: aerial flyers, soarers

R = Rivers

S = Shorelines, beaches, spits, sea stacks

T = Brush lands, thickets, berry patches

Common Name / Group	Habi-tat	Mar–May	Jun–Jul	Aug–Oct	Nov–Feb
Geese & Ducks					
Canada Goose	FMS	Common	Common	Abundant	Abundant
Mallard	BFHMRS	Abundant	Common	Abundant	Abundant
Northern Shoveler	BMS	Common	Common	Common	Common
Northern Pintail	BMS	Common	Unusual	Common	Abundant
Green-winged Teal	MS	Common	Unusual	Common	Common
Harlequin Duck	BLRS	Common	Fairly Common	Common	Common
Surf Scoter	BL	Common	Fairly Common	Common	Abundant
White-winged Scoter	BL	Common	Fairly Common	Common	Abundant
Long-tailed Duck	BL	Fairly Common		Unusual	Common
Bufflehead	BLMR	Common	Rare	Unusual	Abundant
Common Goldeneye	BL	Fairly Common	Rare	Fairly Common	Common
Common Merganser	BR	Fairly Common	Fairly Common	Common	Fairly Common
Red-breasted Merganser	BL	Common	Unusual	Common	Abundant
Grouse & Quail					
California Quail	HT	Common	Common	Abundant	Common
Loons & Grebes					
Red-throated Loon	BL	Fairly Common	Unusual	Fairly Common	Common
Pacific Loon	BL	Common	Unusual	Common	Common
Common Loon	BL	Common	Fairly Common	Common	Common
Horned Grebe	BL	Fairly Common	Rare	Fairly Common	Common
Red-necked Grebe	BL	Fairly Common	Rare	Fairly Common	Common
Western Grebe	BL	Fairly Common	Rare	Fairly Common	Common
Pelicans, Cormorants & Herons:					
Double-crested Cormorant	BLM	Common	Fairly Common	Common	Common
Pelagic Cormorant	BL	Common	Common	Common	Common
Great Blue Heron	BMRS	Common	Fairly Common	Common	Common
Vultures					
Turkey Vulture	O	Common	Fairly Common	Common	Rare
Diurnal Raptors (Hawks, etc. & Falcons)					
Bald Eagle	BLMORS	Common	Common	Common	Common

Common Name / Group	Habi-tat	Mar–May	Jun–Jul	Aug–Oct	Nov–Feb
Northern Harrier	FM	Common	Fairly Common	Common	Common
Red-tailed Hawk	DFMOT	Fairly Common	Fairly Common	Fairly Common	Common

Rails & Cranes

Common Name / Group	Habi-tat	Mar–May	Jun–Jul	Aug–Oct	Nov–Feb
American Coot	BM	Common	Fairly Common	Common	Common

Shorebirds

Common Name / Group	Habi-tat	Mar–May	Jun–Jul	Aug–Oct	Nov–Feb
Semipalmated Plover	BMS	Common	Unusual	Common	Rare
Killdeer	BFMS	Common	Common	Common	Fairly Common
Greater Yellowlegs	BMS	Fairly Common	Unusual	Common	Unusual
Black Turnstone	BS	Common	Unusual	Common	Fairly Common
Sanderling	BS	Common	Unusual	Common	Common
Dunlin	S	Abundant		Common	Abundant
Short-billed Dowitcher	MS	Common	Unusual	Abundant	Rare
Long-billed Dowitcher	MS	Common		Common	Rare
Wilson's Snipe	FM	Fairly Common	Fairly Common	Common	Unusual
Red-necked Phalarope	BLP	Unusual		Common	Rare

Jaegers, Gulls & Terns

Common Name / Group	Habi-tat	Mar–May	Jun–Jul	Aug–Oct	Nov–Feb
Mew Gull	BFHLS	Fairly Common	Rare	Common	Abundant
Ring-billed Gull	BS	Unusual	Fairly Common	Common	Unusual
California Gull	BFHLS	Fairly Common	Common	Abundant	Unusual
Western Gull	BLS	Fairly Common	Unusual	Common	Common
Western x Glaucous-winged Gull	BLS	Abundant	Abundant	Abundant	Abundant
Glaucous-winged Gull	BFHLS	Abundant	Abundant	Abundant	Abundant
Caspian Tern	BL	Fairly Common	Fairly Common	Common	

Alcids (Auks, Murres & Puffins)

Common Name / Group	Habi-tat	Mar–May	Jun–Jul	Aug–Oct	Nov–Feb
Common Murre	BLP	Abundant	Abundant	Abundant	Common
Pigeon Guillemot	BL	Common	Common	Common	Fairly Common
Rhinoceros Auklet	BL	Abundant	Abundant	Common	Unusual

Pigeons & Doves

Common Name / Group	Habi-tat	Mar–May	Jun–Jul	Aug–Oct	Nov–Feb
Rock Pigeon	H	Common	Common	Common	Common

Goatsuckers, Swifts & Hummingbirds

Common Name / Group	Habi-tat	Mar–May	Jun–Jul	Aug–Oct	Nov–Feb
Vaux's Swift	O	Fairly Common	Fairly Common	Common	
Rufous Hummingbird	DHT	Common	Common	Fairly Common	Rare

Common Name / Group	Habi-tat	Mar–May	Jun–Jul	Aug–Oct	Nov–Feb
Kingfishers & Woodpeckers					
Belted Kingfisher	BRS	Common	Common	Common	Fairly Common
Lewis's Woodpecker	C	Common	Common	Common	Fairly Common
Downy Woodpecker	CDHT	Common	Common	Common	Common
Northern Flicker	CDHT	Fairly Common	Common	Common	Common
Flycatchers					
Willow Flycatcher	CDT	Unusual	Common	Fairly Common	
Pacific-slope Flycatcher	CD	Fairly Common	Common	Fairly Common	
Shrikes, Vireos & Corvids					
Warbling Vireo	D	Fairly Common	Common	Unusual	
Steller's Jay	CDH	Common	Common	Common	Common
American Crow	CDFHST	Abundant	Common	Abundant	Abundant
Common Raven	ACDFH	Common	Common	Common	Common
Larks & Swallows					
Tree Swallow	OH	Common	Common	Common	Rare
Violet-green Swallow	OH	Common	Abundant	Abundant	Rare
Cliff Swallow	OH	Common	Common	Common	
Barn Swallow	OH	Common	Abundant	Abundant	Rare
Chickadees, Nuthatches, Wrens, Etc.					
Black-capped Chickadee	DCHT	Common	Common	Common	Common
Chestnut-backed Chickadee	CDH	Common	Common	Common	Common
Bushtit	DT	Common	Common	Common	Fairly Common
Red-breasted Nuthatch	CDHA	Common	Common	Common	Common
Brown Creeper	DC	Common	Common	Fairly Common	Fairly Common
Bewick's Wren	TD	Common	Common	Common	Common
Pacific Wren	CDT	Common	Common	Common	Common
Marsh Wren	M	Common	Common	Common	Common
American Dipper	R	Fairly Common	Fairly Common	Fairly Common	Fairly Common
Kinglets & Thrushes					
Golden-crowned Kinglet	CDTH	Common	Common	Abundant	Abundant
Ruby-crowned Kinglet	DTHC	Common	Unusual	Fairly Common	Common

Common Name / Group	Habi-tat	Mar–May	Jun–Jul	Aug–Oct	Nov–Feb
Swainson's Thrush	DC	Fairly Common	Common	Fairly Common	
Hermit Thrush	CD	Fairly Common	Common	Fairly Common	Unusual
American Robin	DCHTF	Abundant	Common	Abundant	Abundant
Varied Thrush	CDH	Common	Common	Fairly Common	Fairly Common

Starlings, Pipits & Waxwings

Common Name / Group	Habi-tat	Mar–May	Jun–Jul	Aug–Oct	Nov–Feb
European Starling	HTFD	Abundant	Abundant	Abundant	Abundant
Cedar Waxwing	THD	Fairly Common	Common	Common	Rare

Warblers

Common Name / Group	Habi-tat	Mar–May	Jun–Jul	Aug–Oct	Nov–Feb
Orange-crowned Warbler	DT	Common	Common	Common	Rare
Yellow-rumped Warbler	CDTMH	Common	Fairly Common	Common	Unusual
Townsend's Warbler	CD	Common	Common	Fairly Common	Unusual
Common Yellowthroat	MRT	Common	Common	Fairly Common	Rare
Wilson's Warbler	CD	Common	Common	Common	Vagrant

Tanagers, Sparrows & Buntings

Common Name / Group	Habi-tat	Mar–May	Jun–Jul	Aug–Oct	Nov–Feb
Western Tanager	CD	Fairly Common	Common	Unusual	
Spotted Towhee	DHT	Common	Common	Common	Common
Savannah Sparrow	FMT	Common	Common	Abundant	Unusual
Fox Sparrow	MT	Fairly Common	Rare	Common	Common
Song Sparrow	CDFHMST	Common	Common	Common	Common
White-crowned Sparrow	FHT	Common	Common	Common	Fairly Common
Golden-crowned Sparrow	FHT	Common	Rare	Common	Common
Dark-eyed Junco	CDHT	Abundant	Common	Common	Abundant
Black-headed Grosbeak	CD	Fairly Common	Common	Unusual	

Icterids & Finches

Common Name / Group	Habi-tat	Mar–May	Jun–Jul	Aug–Oct	Nov–Feb
Red-winged Blackbird	FHMT	Common	Abundant	Abundant	Abundant
Brewer's Blackbird	FHMT	Common	Abundant	Abundant	Abundant
Brown-headed Cowbird	FDHT	Common	Common	Fairly Common	Unusual
House Finch	HT	Common	Common	Abundant	Abundant
Pine Siskin	CDH	Common	Common	Abundant	Abundant
American Goldfinch	DHT	Common	Common	Common	Unusual

Appendix E.
How to Get Your Best Photographic Images

One of the joys of experiencing the Peninsula is coming home with wonderful photos. By following just a few simple rules, you can create images that will tell the story of your travels far better, and their quality will be vastly improved over just pointing and shooting snapshots. Also, when you enter a landscape with a photographer's eye, the whole scene shifts. You become much more attuned to what's around you as you scan it for possible images.

First, slow down—and then slow down some more.

Then try to tell a story. Have a reason to take the shot. If you want an image of the beach or even Uncle Louie standing on the beach, ask yourself, "What story am I telling?" You probably did more than drive out to Ruby Beach, jump out of the car, snap the photo, and then drive off. Everyone knows what Uncle Louie looks like, so you don't need another bull's-eye shot of him. What did you do on the beach? Did Uncle Louie just sit there and stare out to sea? (That is a very worthy activity all by itself.) Take that shot, but put Uncle Louie to the side of the image and shoot it from behind him, showing what he is looking at or doing. See if you can include him, the ocean, and the sea stacks. Now the narrative has gone from "Here's Uncle Louie on the beach" to "Here's Uncle Louie staring out to sea on the beach. Finally getting him back into the car took some real effort on our part. It's so beautiful there, I didn't want to leave either."

Take lots of shots. Digital images are essentially free, so wander around and approach your subject from all angles. Take what you think is going to be your best shot first, then examine the subject from the left and the right.

Get close to your subject and shoot it with no context whatsoever. Get farther away and make your initial subject less prominent while showing it as part of a whole landscape. Put the subject really close in the foreground, then include a spectacular background. Does the foreground work? Does it draw the viewer deeper into the image? Or it just something they have to visually step over? Look through your viewfinder at all four corners of the image. What is included and what is excluded is very important. Frame the shot with foliage or anything else available.

If you plan on enhancing your image back home with Photoshop or something similar, know that it is a lot easier to get the shot correct in the field than to try to overcome the lack of correct composition when you are back home.

If animals are your subject, especially animals on the move such as birds, learn to lean on the shutter. There is a reason high-end cameras can take five or more shots per second. A lot can happen in that short amount of time. Also, get low and take the image of the deer or marmot at their eye level.

RTM (aka Read the Manual)! Unless you are using a camera phone (most of which have no adjustable elements except flash), learn all your camera's capabilities. RTM becomes even more important if your camera has more features. At a minimum, learn to use the various modes of landscape, people, etc., and use them the way they are designed. Learn one aspect of your capabilities at a time. Don't expect to read the manual on the drive over and be done with it. First learn about the different modes and experiment. Subsequently, after you've mastered one feature, tackle another one or two. Carry your manual with your camera. It doesn't do you any good when the manual is sitting back in the car, which might be a mile away down the trail or back at home.

If your camera has a flash, and most do, understand that it not just for nighttime use. Anytime your subject is lit from behind or the brightest part of the whole shot is not the subject, force the flash to fire. RTM to see if you can use fill-flash. Your images will thank you.

More and more cameras have the ability to show you on the back-of-camera LCD screen the distribution of the captured light in your image. This little chart is a histogram, and it displays the quantity of pixels across the spectrum of your camera's ability to capture both bright and dark light. This is called the dynamic range, and it is incredibly useful for determining if your shot is properly exposed. The professionals use this feature almost exclusively to review their images. You don't want the pixels to be butted up against either end of the histogram, which would suggest that you are losing part of the image, either as too bright or too dark.

And, finally, consider a tripod. If there is any piece of equipment that will force you to slow down and consider your motive for and composition of the picture, it is a tripod. That is reason enough to use one. In reviewing my favorite images, I found they were almost exclusively shot with a tripod. The tripod's stated use is to stabilize the camera for shots in which the shutter is open for longer than 1/(focal length) of a second. (For example: a 100mm lens requires a minimum of $1/100^{th}$ shutter speed for the image to be sharp.)

Before you balk at the price of a high-end tripod and head, consider that you might spend that same amount in less worthy tripods as you migrate to the one that works. First you buy a cheapo that looks like a tripod but doesn't quite hold the camera steady. Next you buy a more expensive one or two that hold the current camera and lens steady but aren't strong enough to stabilize a bigger lens and your camera nor durable enough to last during multiple seasons of field use. Then you eventually purchase a strong, bulky, heavy, awkward one that is built like a tank but works great. With the last purchase, your images will really start to improve.

Appendix F.
National and State Registered Historic Landmarks

Below is a list of all the Peninsula's locations that are on the National Historic Landmark (NHL) list, the Washington Heritage Register (WHR), and/or the National Register (NR) of Historic Places (all NHL sites are also listed on the National Register of Historic Places). Numerous locations on the Peninsula have restricted addresses; these are mostly Indian historic and archaeological sites that officials do not want to be visited. Washington also has an extensive Historic Barn listing, which is not included here. Note that the entire downtowns of Port Townsend and Port Gamble are on the National Historic Landmark list. DOE indicates sites that are in the process of being formally listed. County listings are indicated as follows:

- Clallam: CA

- Grays Harbor: GH

- Jefferson: JE

- Kitsap: KP

- Mason: MS

- Thurston: TN

To find out more about these registers, visit the following:

National Register of Historic Places: www.nps.gov/nr/
National Historic Landmarks Program: www.nps.gov/history/nhl/
Washington State's Department of Archaeology and Historic Preservation: www.dahp.wa.gov/

City	Register Name	Common Name	Listing Status	Street Address	Co
Aberdeen	Chehalis River Bridge	Bridge Number 101/115	WHR	WA 101 over the Chehalis River	GH
Aberdeen	Liberty Tavern		WHR	500 E. Schley	GH
Aberdeen	Sierra, MS		WHR/NR	1401 Sargent Blvd. (Chehalis River)	GH
Agnew	Aircraft Warning Service Observation Tower		WHR/NR	216 Spring Rd.	CA
Beaver	Beaver School		WHR/NR	US 101 N., west side	CA

City	Register Name	Common Name	Listing Status	Street Address	Co
Brinnon	Interrorem Guard Station		WHR	US Forest Service Rd. 2515, 4 miles west of junction of Duckabush Rd. and US 101	JE
Cape Flattery	Tatoosh Island Light Station		WHR/NR	Off Cape Flattery	CA
Chimacum	Bishop House and Office, Sen. William	Brown House	WHR/NR	Chimacum-Center Rd.	JE
Chimacum	Chimacum Post Office		WHR/NR	Chimacum-Center Rd.	JE
Chimacum	Kuhn Spit Archaeological Site	Kala Point	WHR/NR	Address Restricted	JE
Chimacum	Rover Homestead, Hanna	Nieminen House	WHR/NR	Chimacum-Center Rd.	JE
Chimacum	Van Trojen House	Ammeter House	WHR/NR	Van Trojen Rd.	JE
Clallam Bay	Slip Point Light Station Keeper's Residence		WHR	North end of Frontier St.	CA
Cosmopolis	Cooney Mansion, Neil	Spruce Cottage	WHR/NR	802 E. Fifth St.	GH
Crescent Bay	Fort Hayden	Tongue Point	WHR	Tongue Point Rd.	CA
Discovery Bay	Uncas School	Discovery Bay School	WHR/NR	171 E. Uncas Rd. North	JE
Discovery Bay	Vancouver's Landing		WHR	On Contractor's Point, Section 36, Township 30 North, Range 2 West	JE
Duckabush	Duckabush River Bridge		WHR/NR	Spans Duckabush River	JE
Dungeness	Dungeness School		WHR/NR	657 Towne Rd.	CA
Dungeness	McAlmond House		WHR/NR	Twin View Dr. and McAlmond St.	CA
Dungeness Spit	New Dungeness		WHR	Base of Dungeness Spit	CA
Eldon	North Hamma Hamma River Bridge		WHR/NR	Spans North Hamma Hamma River	MS
Eldon	South Hamma Hamma River Bridge		WHR/NR	Spans South Hamma Hamma River	MS
Elma	Schafer State Park		WHR/NR	1365 W. Schafer Park Rd.	MS
Elwha	Elwha River Bridge		WHR/NR	Old WA 112	CA
Forks	Copeland House, Adam	First Federal Savings and Loan Log Cabin	WHR	215 Calawah Way	CA
Forks	Enchanted Valley Chalet		WHR/NR	13 miles upriver from Graves Creek trailhead: Quinault Subdistrict	JE
Forks	Fifteen-mile Shelter		WHR/NR	Approximately 12.4 miles from NPS boundary on North Fork Bogachiel River Trail; 19 miles east of US 101: Hoh Subdistrict	CA

City	Register Name	Common Name	Listing Status	Street Address	Co
Forks	Graves Creek Ranger Station	Graves Creek Guard Station, Graves Creek Ranger Station Historic District	WHR/NR	Approximately 22 miles NE of US Highway 101 on Quinault River Road: Quinault Subdistrict	JE
Forks	Happy Four Shelter		WHR/NR	Approximately 5.4 miles along Hoh River Trail: Hoh Subdistrict	JE
Forks	Hyak Shelter		WHR/NR	Approximately 15.4 miles from NPS boundary on North Fork Bogachiel River Trail, 22 miles east of US 101: Hoh Subdistrict	CA
Forks	Kestner Homestead	Kestner-Higley Homestead, Kestner Homestead Site	WHR/NR	Quinault River Valley (north side of river): Quinault Subdistrict	GH
Forks	North Fork Quinault Ranger Station	North Fork Guard Station, North Fork Quinault Ranger Station Historic District	WHR/NR	Approximately 18 miles NE of US 101 on North Fork Rd. off North Shore Quinault Rd.: Quinault Subdistrict	JE
Forks	Olympus Guard Station	OGS, Olympus Guard Station Historic District	WHR/NR	Approximately 9 miles from Hoh River trailhead at Hoh Ranger Station: Hoh Subdistrict	JE
Forks	Pelton Creek Shelter		WHR/NR	Approximately 15.5 miles up Queets River Trail: Kalaloch Subdistrict	JE
Forks	Smith-Mansfield House		WHR	Sixth Ave. NW	CA
Forks	Twenty-one-mile Shelter		WHR	18.6 miles from NPS boundary on North Fork Bogachiel River Trail, 25.2 miles east of US 101: Hoh Subdistrict	CA
Forks	Wedding Rock Petroglyphs		WHR/NR	Address Restricted	CA
Hadlock	Cultural Resources of Hadlock Bay		WHR	Address Restricted	JE
Hadlock	Methodist Episcopal Church of Port Hadlock	Barrett House	WHR/NR	Randolph and Curtiss Sts.	JE
Hadlock	Norman House	Colden House	WHR	Flagler Rd.	JE
Hadlock	Portage Canal Bridge	Bridge Number 116/5	WHR	WA 116 over Portage Canal	JE
Hadlock	Shibles House, Capt. Peter	Baumuck House, J. L.	WHR/NR	Curtiss St.	JE
Hadlock	Walan Point	Sherman Point	WHR	Address Restricted	JE
Hartstene Island	Harstine Island Community Hall		WHR/NR	North Island Dr. and Hartstene Island Dr.	MS
Hoodsport	Big Creek Archaeological Site (45ms100)	Big Creek Archaeological Site	WHR/NR	Address Restricted	MS

City	Register Name	Common Name	Listing Status	Street Address	Co
Hoodsport	Cushman No. 1 Hydroelectric Power Plant		WHR/NR	South end of Lake Cushman	MS
Hoodsport	Cushman No. 2 Hydroelectric Power Plant		WHR/NR	Skokomish River	MS
Hoodsport	Hamma Hamma Guard Station		WHR	Olympic National Forest	MS
Hoquiam	American Veterans Building--Hoquiam		WHR/NR	307 Seventh St.	GH
Hoquiam	Carnegie Library	Hoquiam Timberland Library	WHR/NR	621 K St.	GH
Hoquiam	Hodgdon House, Judge Charles W.		WHR/NR	717 Bluff St.	GH
Hoquiam	Hoquiam Olympic Stadium		WHR/NR	2811 Cherry St.	GH
Hoquiam	Hoquiam River Bridge		WHR/NR	North of US 12	GH
Hoquiam	Hoquiam's Castle	Lytle Mansion, Robert	WHR/NR	515 Chenault Ave.	GH
Hoquiam	Lytle Home, Joseph		WHR/NR	509 Chenault	GH
Hoquiam	Masonic Temple--Hoquiam		WHR/NR	510 Eighth St.	GH
Hoquiam	McTaggart House, Lachlin		WHR/NR	224 L St.	GH
Hoquiam	Polson House, F. Arnold, and Polson Grounds, Alex	Polson Park and Museum	WHR/NR	1611 Riverside Ave. (US 101)	GH
Hoquiam	Seventh Street Theater		WHR/NR	313 Seventh St.	GH
Hoquiam	US Post Office--Hoquiam Main		WHR/NR	620 Eighth St.	GH
Irondale	Irondale Jail		WHR/NR	Moore St.	JE
Irondale	Williams House, Hattie	Butts House	WHR/NR	Moore St.	JE
Kalaloch	Destruction Island Light Station		WHR/DOE	Salmon Beach	JE
Lake Ozette	Roose Homestead, Peter	Roose's Prairie, Peter Roose Homestead Historic District	WHR/NR	Along Indian Village Trail, approximately 1.5 miles north of trailhead: Ozette Subdistrict	CA
Lake Quinault	Lake Quinault Lodge	U.S.F.S. #cr-18-80a	WHR/NR	South Shore Rd.	GH
La Push	Coastie Head Lookout Cabin	Starbuck Creek Cabin	WHR	Approximately 2.4 miles south of Norwegian Memorial: Mora Subdistrict	CA
La Push	Olympic National Park Archaeological District		WHR/DOE	Address Restricted	JE
La Push	Ozette Indian Village Archaeological Site		WHR/NR	Address Restricted	CA
Lower Hadlock	Galster House	Ajax Café	WHR/NR	Water St.	JE
McCleary	McCleary Hotel, Old	Hotel McCleary	WHR/NR	42 Summit Rd.	GH
Montesano	Montesano City Hall		WHR	104 N. Main	GH

City	Register Name	Common Name	Listing Status	Street Address	Co
Montesano	US Post Office--Montesano Main		WHR/NR	211 Pioneer Ave. N.	GH
Neah Bay	Quimper's Landing at Neah Bay		WHR	Cape Flattery vicinity	CA
New Dungeness	Graveyard Spit		WHR	Address Restricted	CA
Nordland	Johnson House	Lybeck House	WHR/NR	7082 Flagler Rd.	JE
Nordland	Nelson House	Freeman House	WHR/NR	Freeman Rd.	JE
Nordland	Sole House, Tollef		WHR/NR	7013 Flagler Rd.	JE
Oakville	Oakville State Bank		WHR	201 Pine St.	GH
Olympia	Allen-Beals House		WHR	726 S. Percival	TN
Olympia	Allen House Hotel	Jefferson Apartments	WHR/NR	114-118 N. Jefferson	TN
Olympia	American Legion Hall		WHR/NR	219 W. Legion Hall	TN
Olympia	Barnes Building--Knights of Pythias	Oddfellows Hall	WHR	211 W. Fourth	TN
Olympia	Bigelow House, Daniel R.		WHR/NR	918 Glass St.	TN
Olympia	Black Lake School		WHR/NR	6000 Black Lake Blvd. SW	TN
Olympia	Capital National Bank Building	Rainier Bank	WHR	402 S. Capitol Way	TN
Olympia	Capitol Theater and Office Building		WHR	202-206 E. Fifth and 400 S. Washington	TN
Olympia	Chambers Prairie School	East Olympia School	WHR	8126 SE Normandy Dr.	TN
Olympia	Cloverfields	Stevens House and Grounds, Hazard	WHR/NR	1100 Carlyon Ave. SE	TN
Olympia	Daily Olympian Building, The		WHR	103 E. State, 120-122 N. Capitol Way	TN
Olympia	Delphi School		WHR/NR	7601 SW Delphi Rd.	TN
Olympia	Dofflemyer Point Light		WHR/NR	211 NE 73rd	TN
Olympia	Elks Building		WHR/NR	607-613 S. Capitol Way	TN
Olympia	Funk House		WHR/NR	1202 E. Olympia Ave.	TN
Olympia	General Administration Building		WHR/NR	210 11th Ave. SW	TN
Olympia	Georgia-Pacific Plywood Company Office	Washington State Department of Game	WHR/NR	600 Capitol Way North	TN
Olympia	Giles House, Charles		WHR	727 West Bay Drive	TN
Olympia	Hale House, Calvin and Pamela		WHR/NR	902 Tullis Street NE	TN
Olympia	Jeffers Studio		WHR/NR	500 and 502 S. Washington	TN
Olympia	Kearney House--YWCA Clubhouse		WHR	220 E. Union	TN
Olympia	Lane House, George B.	Seven Gables	WHR	1205 W. Bay Dr.	TN

City	Register Name	Common Name	Listing Status	Street Address	Co
Olympia	Lord Mansion, C. J.	State Capitol Museum	WHR/NR	211 W. 21st Ave.	TN
Olympia	Lotus, MV		WHR/NR	Fiddlehead Marina, B Dock	TN
Olympia	McCleary House, Henry		WHR/NR	111 W. 21st Ave.	TN
Olympia	Medicine Creek Archaeological Site (She Nah Nam)		WHR	Address Restricted	TN
Olympia	Meyer House		WHR/NR	1136 E. Bay Dr.	TN
Olympia	Millersylvania State Park		WHR/NR	12245 Tilley Rd.	TN
Olympia	Mottman Building		WHR/NR	101-105 N. Capitol Way	TN
Olympia	Old Capitol Building	Thurston County Courthouse–Washington State Capitol Building	WHR/NR	600 block of Washington St.	TN
Olympia	Old Olympia City Hall	Olympia Fire Department	WHR	W. State St. and N. Capitol Way	TN
Olympia	Olympia Downtown Historic District		WHR/NR	Roughly bounded by State Ave. on the north, Eighth Ave. on the south, Columbia St. on the west, and Franklin St. on the east	TN
Olympia	Olympia National Bank	Pacific First Federal	WHR/NR	422 S. Capitol Way	TN
Olympia	Olympia Public Library		WHR/NR	S. Franklin and E. Seventh	TN
Olympia	Patnude House, Charles		WHR/NR	1239 Eighth	TN
Olympia	Puget Sound Wesleyan Institute	Central School	WHR	317 E. Union and 1059 S. Adams St.	TN
Olympia	Reinhart-Young House	Byrd House, George	WHR/NR	1106 E. Olympia Ave.	TN
Olympia	Rudkin Homestead, Frank		WHR/NR	1005 E. Olympia Ave.	TN
Olympia	Sand Man, tugboat		WHR/NR	Percival Landing	TN
Olympia	Schmidt House, F. W.	34-421	WHR/NR	2831 Orange	TN
Olympia	South Capitol Neighborhood Historic District		WHR/NR	Roughly bounded by Capitol Lake, I-5, and 16th Ave.	TN
Olympia	Steele House, Alden Hatch		WHR/NR	1010 S. Franklin St.	TN
Olympia	Thurston County Courthouse	Old Thurston County Courthouse	WHR/NR	Capitol Way	TN
Olympia	Town Square	Sylvester Park	WHR/NR	Bounded by Seventh, Legion, Capitol Way, and S. Washington	TN
Olympia	US Post Office--Olympia Main	Federal Building	WHR/NR	801 Capitol Way	TN
Olympia	Washington State Capitol Historic District	Capitol Campus	WHR/NR	State Capitol and environs	TN

City	Register Name	Common Name	Listing Status	Street Address	Co
Olympia	Weyerhaeuser South Bay Log Dump Rural Historic Landscape	Woodard Bay Natural Resources Conservation Area	WHR/NR	609 Whitham Rd.	TN
Olympia	White House, William G.	Towerhouse Mansion, White House	WHR	1431 11th Ave. E.	TN
Olympia	Women's Club of Olympia		WHR/NR	1002 S. Washington St.	TN
Olympia	Zeigler's Welding and Hitch Shop, Inc.		WHR	322 N. Capitol Way	TN
Olympic National Park	Archaeological Site		WHR	Address Restricted	CA
Port Angeles	Altair Campground Community Kitchen	Altair Campground Community Kitchen	WHR/NR	Roughly 12 miles SW of Port Angeles, 4 miles S of US 101: Elwha Subdistrict	CA
Port Angeles	Bagley Lake Farm Tunnel		WHR	The End of Lake Farm Rd.	CA
Port Angeles	Blue Mountain School		WHR/NR	Blue Mountain Rd.	CA
Port Angeles	Botten Cabin	Wilder Patrol Cabin	WHR/NR	20.9 miles from Whiskey Bend trailhead on Elwha River Trail: Elwha Subdistrict	JE
Port Angeles	Clallam County Courthouse		WHR/NR	319 Lincoln St.	CA
Port Angeles	Dodger Point Fire Lookout		WHR/NR	Approximately 13 miles along Dodger Point Trail starting at Whiskey Bend trailhead: Elwha Subdistrict	CA
Port Angeles	Eagle Ranger Station	Eagle Guard Station, Sol Duc Ranger Station	WHR/NR	Approximately 11.6 miles south of US 101 on Upper Sol Duc Rd.	CA
Port Angeles	Ediz Hook Light Station	Port Angeles Coast Guard Air Station	WHR	Tip of Ediz Hook	CA
Port Angeles	Elkhorn Guard Station	Elkhorn Ranger Station Historic District	WHR/NR	Approximately 11.5 miles along Elwha River Trail from Whiskey Bend trailhead: Elwha Subdistrict	CA
Port Angeles	Elk Lick Lodge	Remann's Cabin	WHR/NR	13 miles on Elwha River Trail from Whiskey Bend trailhead: Elwha Subdistrict	JE
Port Angeles	Elwha Campground Community Kitchen		WHR/NR	Roughly 15 miles SW of Port Angeles, 3 miles south of US 101: Elwha Subdistrict	CA
Port Angeles	Elwha Ranger Station	Elwha Guard Station, Elwha Ranger Station Historic District	WHR/NR	Approximately 3 miles SW of US 101 on Olympic Hot Springs Rd.: Elwha Subdistrict	CA
Port Angeles	Elwha River Hydroelectric Power Plant		WHR/NR	North end of Lake Aldwell	CA
Port Angeles	Emery Farmstead	Chancellor-Emery Farmstead	WHR/NR	Emery Rd.	CA

City	Register Name	Common Name	Listing Status	Street Address	Co
Port Angeles	Glines Canyon Hydroelectric Power Plant		WHR/NR	North end of Lake Mills at Elwha River	CA
Port Angeles	Hayes River Fire Cache	Hayes River Patrol Cabin Shed	WHR/NR	Approximately 16.8 miles up Elwha River Trail: Elwha Subdistrict	JE
Port Angeles	Humes Ranch Cabin	Humes Ranch Cabin #699	WHR/NR	2.5 miles from Whiskey Bend trailhead: Elwha Subdistrict	CA
Port Angeles	I'e'nis, Clallam Indian Village	Hollywood Beach	WHR	Address Restricted	CA
Port Angeles	Masonic Temple--Port Angeles		WHR/NR	622 S. Lincoln St.	CA
Port Angeles	Michael's Cabin		WHR/NR	Along Elwha River Trail, approximately 2 miles from Whiskey Bend trailhead: Elwha Subdistrict	CA
Port Angeles	Naval Lodge Elks Building	Naval Lodge #353 BPOE Temple	WHR/NR	131 E. First St.	CA
Port Angeles	Olympic National Park Headquarters Historic District		WHR/NR	600 E. Park Ave.	CA
Port Angeles	Paris House, Joseph	Airplane House; Peace House	WHR/NR	101 E. Fifth St.	CA
Port Angeles	Port Angeles Civic Historic District		WHR/NR	205, 215, 217, and 319 S. Lincoln St.	CA
Port Angeles	Puget Sound Cooperative Colony		WHR	Ennis Creek	CA
Port Angeles	Pyramid Peak Aircraft Warning Service Lookout		WHR/NR	3.5 miles up Pyramid Peak Trail at end of Camp David Jr. Rd.: Lake Crescent Subdistrict	CA
Port Angeles	Rosemary Inn	Rosemary Inn Historic District	WHR/NR	Barnes Point, south shore of Lake Crescent, along US 101: Lake Crescent Subdistrict	CA
Port Angeles	St. Andrew's Episcopal Church	Salvation Army Citidel Corps	WHR/NR	206 S. Peabody St.	CA
Port Angeles	Singer's Lake Crescent Tavern	Lake Crescent Lodge, Lake Crescent Tavern, Lake Crescent Lodge Historic District	WHR/NR	Barnes Point, south shore of Lake Crescent, US 101: Lake Crescent Subdistrict	CA
Port Angeles	Storm King Ranger Station	Morgenroth Cabin, Storm King Guard Station	WHR/NR	Barnes Point, south side of Lake Crescent off US 101, 20 miles SW of Port Angeles: Lake Crescent Subdistrict	CA
Port Angeles	Three Forks Shelter		WHR/NR	Approximately 4.5 miles from Three Forks trailhead at Deer Park Campground: Hurricane Subdistrict	CA

City	Register Name	Common Name	Listing Status	Street Address	Co
Port Angeles	US Post Office--Port Angeles Main	Old Post Office/ Federal Building	WHR/NR	W. First and Oak Sts.	CA
Port Angeles	Wendel Property		WHR/NR	Piedmont District (5 miles north on East Shore Rd. off US 101): Lake Crescent Subdistrict	CA
Port Gamble	Port Gamble Historic District		NHL	On NW end of Kitsap Peninsula near entrance to Hood Canal, Puget Sound	KP
Port Ludlow	Swanson House, Hans		WHR/NR	Swansonville Rd.	JE
Port Townsend	Alexander's Castle		WHR	Fort Worden	JE
Port Townsend	Bartlett House, Frank		WHR/NR	314 Polk St.	JE
Port Townsend	Bash House, Henry		WHR/NR	718 F St.	JE
Port Townsend	Beecher Home, Herbert Foote		WHR	525 Walker St.	JE
Port Townsend	City Hall	Jefferson County Historical Society Museum	WHR/NR	Water and Madison Sts.	JE
Port Townsend	Coleman-Furlong House	Furlong House	WHR/NR	1253 Umatilla Ave.	JE
Port Townsend	De Leo Home, James		WHR	Taylor and Lawrence Sts.	JE
Port Townsend	Downs Residence, George W.		WHR	538 Fillmore St.	JE
Port Townsend	Edwards House, Joel		WHR/NR	913 25th St.	JE
Port Townsend	Fitzgerald House, Thomas		WHR/NR	832 T St.	JE
Port Townsend	Fort Flagler	Fort Flagler Historic District	WHR/NR	SE of Port Townsend on Marrowstone Island	JE
Port Townsend	Fort Worden	Fort Worden State Park	NHL	Cherry and W Sts.	JE
Port Townsend	Fowler House, Capt. Enoch S.		WHR/NR	1040 Jefferson St.	JE
Port Townsend	Gagen-Sherlock House		WHR/NR	1906 Cherry St.	JE
Port Townsend	Grave of Chief Chetzemoka		WHR	Laurel Grove Cemetery	JE
Port Townsend	Grave of James G. Swan		WHR	Laurel Grove Cemetery	JE

City	Register Name	Common Name	Listing Status	Street Address	Co
Port Townsend	Griffiths House, J. W.		WHR/NR	2030 Monroe Street	JE
Port Townsend	Harper House, F. C.		WHR/NR	502 Reed St.	JE
Port Townsend	Hastings Building		WHR	839 Water St.	JE
Port Townsend	House at 503 Fir Street		WHR/NR	503 Fir St.	JE
Port Townsend	House at 1723 Holcomb Street		WHR/NR	1723 Holcomb St.	JE
Port Townsend	House at 30 Tremont Street		WHR/NR	30 Tremont St.	JE
Port Townsend	Irondale Historic District		WHR/NR	Port Townsend Bay and Admiralty Inlet	JE
Port Townsend	James House, Francis Wilcox		WHR/NR	1238 Washington St.	JE
Port Townsend	Jefferson County Courthouse		WHR/NR	Jefferson and Case Sts.	JE
Port Townsend	Lake-Little House		WHR/NR	1607 Sheridan St.	JE
Port Townsend	Laubach House, J. N.		WHR/NR	613 F St.	JE
Port Townsend	Leader Building	Fowler Building, The	WHR/NR	226 Adams St.	JE
Port Townsend	Manresa Hall	Eisenbeis Castle, Manresa Inn	WHR/NR	Sheridan St.	JE
Port Townsend	McIntyre House, Capt. James		WHR	633 Van Buren St.	JE
Port Townsend	Morgan House, O. L. and Josephine		WHR/NR	1033 Pierce St.	JE
Port Townsend	Old Fort Townsend State Park		WHR	North of Irondale	JE
Port Townsend	Old German Consulate	Frank's Folly, Olsen-Hastings House	WHR/NR	313 Walker	JE
Port Townsend	Parrish House	Oldest Brick House in Port Townsend	WHR	641 Calhoun St.	JE
Port Townsend	Pearson House		WHR/NR	1939 27th St.	JE
Port Townsend	Petersen House, H. S.	Guiner House	WHR/NR	50th and Kuhn St.	JE
Port Townsend	Pettygrove House, Benjamin S.		WHR/NR	1000 G St.	JE

City	Register Name	Common Name	Listing Status	Street Address	Co
Port Townsend	Phillips House		WHR	Polk and Jefferson Sts.	JE
Port Townsend	Point Wilson Lighthouse		WHR/NR	On a point of land between Strait of Juan de Fuca and Admiralty Inlet	JE
Port Townsend	Port Townsend Art Gallery		WHR	725 Water St.	JE
Port Townsend	Port Townsend Carnegie Library		WHR/NR	1220 Lawrence St.	JE
Port Townsend	Port Townsend Fire Department Bell Tower		WHR	Tyler St.	JE
Port Townsend	Port Townsend Historic District		NHL	Roughly bounded by Scott, Blaine, Walker, and Taft Sts. and the waterfront	JE
Port Townsend	Ralston House, Judge		WHR/NR	1523 Madison St.	JE
Port Townsend	Rothschild House		WHR/NR	Taylor and Franklin Sts.	JE
Port Townsend	St. Paul's Episcopal Church		WHR/NR	Corner of Jefferson and Tyler Sts.	JE
Port Townsend	Saint's Rest, Tukey's Pioneer Cabin and Homestead House	Chevy Chase	WHR/NR	Chevy Chase Rd.	JE
Port Townsend	Saunders House, James C.	Holly Manor	WHR/NR	Sims Way	JE
Port Townsend	Schlager House, Ferdinand		WHR/NR	810 Rose St.	JE
Port Townsend	Starrett House	House of the Four Seasons	WHR/NR	744 Clay St.	JE
Port Townsend	Stegerwald House, Andrew		WHR/NR	1710 Fir St.	JE
Port Townsend	Tree of Heaven		WHR	Water and Polk Sts.	JE
Port Townsend	Trinity Methodist Church		WHR	602 Taylor St.	JE
Port Townsend	Trumbull House, John		WHR/NR	925 Wilson St.	JE
Port Townsend	Tucker House, Horace		WHR/NR	706 Franklin St.	JE
Port Townsend	US Post Office--Port Townsend Main	Port Townsend U.S. Customs House and Post Office	WHR/NR	1322 Washington	JE
Port Townsend	Victorian Residences in Port Townsend TR	Victorian Residences in Port Townsend	TH	Various	JE
Port Townsend	Ward House, Milo P.	Andrews House	WHR/NR	1701 Jackson St.	JE

Appendix F. National and State Registered Historic Landmarks

City	Register Name	Common Name	Listing Status	Street Address	Co
Potlatch	taba das	45MS50	WHR/NR	Address Restricted	MS
Pysht	Hoko River Archeological Site		WHR/NR	Address Restricted	CA
Quilcene	Oatman House, Earl		WHR/NR	Muncie St.	JE
Quilcene	Seal Rock Shell Mounds (45je15)		WHR/NR	Address Restricted	JE
Quilcene	Quilcene-Quinault Battleground Site		WHR/NR	Address Restricted	JE
Quilcene	Quilcene Ranger Station	Quilcene Lower Compound	WHR/NR	61 Herbert St.	JE
Quinault	Ole Mickelson Cabin		WHR/NR	Lot 46, south shore of Lake Quinault	GH
Sekiu	Hoko River Rockshelter Archaeological Site		WHR/NR	Address Restricted	CA
Sekiu	Sekiu School		WHR/NR	Rice St.	CA
Sequim	Sequim Opera House		WHR/NR	119 N. Sequim Ave.	CA
Sequim	Dungeness River Bridge		WHR/NR	Spans Dungeness River	CA
Sequim	Gierin Farmstead		WHR	219 Port Williams Road	CA
Sequim	Hyer Farm, John A.		WHR/NR	334 Grant Rd.	CA
Sequim	Manis Mastodon Site		WHR/NR	Address Restricted	CA
Sequim	New Dungeness Light Station		WHR/NR	Dungeness Spit	CA
Sequim	Port Williams		WHR	North of Washington Harbor	CA
Sequim	Sequim Town Hall	Sequim Public Works Department Building	WHR	152 W. Cedar St.	CA
Sequim	US Quarantine Station Surgeon's Residence		WHR/NR	101 Discovery Way, Diamond Point	CA
Shelton	Goldsborough Creek Bridge		WHR/NR	Washington Highway 3	MS
Shelton	High Steel Bridge		WHR/NR	Spans South Fork Skokomish River	MS
Shelton	Oakland Site	Oakland Site	WHR	3 miles NE of Shelton on WA 3	MS
Shelton	Shelton Public Library and Town Hall	Shelton Public Library	WHR/NR	Fifth St. and Railroad Ave.	MS
Shelton	Simpson Logging Company Locomotive No. 7 and Peninsular Railway Caboose No. 700	Tollie	WHR/NR	Third and Railroad Aves.	MS
Shelton	Vance Creek Bridge		WHR/NR	NW of Shelton	MS
Sol Duc Hot Springs	Canyon Creek Shelter	Sol Duc Falls Shelter	WHR/NR	Approximately 0.9 mile from Upper Soleduck River trailhead, approximately 42 miles SW of Port Angeles; Lake Crescent Subdistrict	CA

City	Register Name	Common Name	Listing Status	Street Address	Co
Sol Duc Hot Springs	North Fork Sol Duc Shelter		WHR/NR	Approximately 9.5 miles from North Fork Sol Duc trailhead, approximately 46 miles SW of Port Angeles: Lake Crescent Subdistrict	CA
Union	Dalby Waterwheel		WHR	Between milepost 7 and 6920 E. WA 106 at Dalby Creek	MS
Upper Hoh River	Huelsdonk Homestead		WHR	Approximately 8 miles west of Hoh Ranger Station	JE
Westport	Grays Harbor Light Station	Grays Harbor Lighthouse, Westport Lighthouse	WHR/NR	1020 West Ocean Avenue	GH
Westport	Old Westport Coast Guard Station		WHR	2201 Westhaven Dr.	GH

Bibliography

Alt, D., and D. Hyndman. 1994. *Roadside Geology of Washington*. Missoula: American Indians of the Pacific Northwest Collection. N.d. Retrieved 2010. content.lib.washington.edu/aipnw/index.html.

Amundson, M. 2003. *The Great Forks Fire*. Port Angeles: Western Gull Publishing.

{3em}. 2004. *Sturdy Folks*. Port Angeles: Western Gull Publishing.

Anderson, M. Kat, Ph.D. (2009). *The Ozette Prairies of Olympic National Park: Their Former Indigenous Uses and Management*. Davis, National Plant Data Center, USDA Natural Resources Conservation Service, University of California.

Atwater, B. F., and S. Musumi-Rokkaku. 2005. *The Orphan Tsunami of 1700*. Seattle: University of Washington Press.

Bailey, I. A. 1997. *Brisson, A Scrapebook of History*. Bremerton: Perry Publishing.

Barkan, F. 1987. *The Wilkes Expedition*. Olympia: Washington State Capital Museum.

Bawlf, S. 2004. *The Secret Voyage of Sir Francis Drake: 1577–1580*. New York: Penguin Books.

Bearden, J. 1994. *History of Hoodsport, Gateway to the Olympics*. Bremerton: Perry Publishing.

Bergland, E., J. Marr. 1988. *Prehistoric Life on the Olympic Peninsula*. Seattle: Pacific Northwest National Parks and Forests Association.

Boyd, R. 1999. *The Spirit of Pestilence*. Seattle: University of Washington Press.

Brown, B. 1990. *Mountain in the Clouds: A Search for the Wild Salmon*. Seattle: University of Washington Press.

Carlson, L. 2003. *Company Towns of the Pacific Northwest*. Seattle: University of Washington Press.

Center for the Study of the Pacific Northwest. N.d. Retrieved 2010. www.washington.edu/uwired/outreach/cspn/Website/index.html.

Chew, J. 2008. "Planning Behind Proposed Brinnon Mega-resort Sound, State Growth Board Rules." *Peninsula Daily News,* September 17. www.peninsuladailynews.com/article/20080917/NEWS/809170306&SearchID=73338339451571.

Crutchfield, J. 1995. *It Happened in Washington*. Helena, MT: Falcon Press Publishing.

Dalby, E. 2000. *Tales of Hood Canal*. Shelton, WA: Mason County Historical Society.

Dietrich, William. 1992. *The Final Forest: The Battle for the Last Great Trees of the Pacific Northwest*. New York: Penguin Books.

{3em}. 2003. *Natural Grace*. Seattle: University of Washington Press.

Dungeness.com. N.d. *Irrigation and Irrigation Festival.* Retrieved 2010 www.dunge-ness.com/river/index.htm.

Eells, M. 1985. *The Indians of Puget Sound.* Seattle: University of Washington Press.

ExploreHoodCanal.com. N.d. *Explore Hood Canal and South Puget Sound.* Retrieved 2010. www.explorehoodcanal.com/squaxin-island-tribe.html.

Ficken, R. E. 1987. *The Forested Land: A History of Lumbering in Western Washington.* Seattle: University of Washington Press.

Fredson, M. 1993. *Log Towns.* West Olympia: Minute Man Press.

Fredson, M. 2007. *Images of America: Hood Canal.* Charleston, SC: Arcadia Publishing.

Goin, D. 1998. *Salmon in the Dungeness.* Retrieved June 1998. www.olympus.net/community/oec/slmnd.htm.

Gulick, B. 2005. *Traveler's History: A Roadside Historical Guide.* Caldwell, ID: Caxton Press.

Hempton, G. 2009. *One Square Inch of Silence.* New York: Free Press.

History Link. N.d. *Mason County—Thumbnail History.* Retrieved 2011. historylink.org.

Hult, R. 1954. *Untamed Olympics: The Story of a Peninsula.* Portland: Binfords and Mort.

International Whaling Commission. N.d. Retrieved May 2010. www.iwcoffice.org/.

Jamestown S'Klallam Tribe. N.d. Retrieved 2010. www.jamestowntribe.org/jst-web_2007/index1024.htm.

Jewitt, J. 1987. *The Adventures and Suffering of John R. Jewitt, Captive of Maquinna.* Seattle: University of Washington Press.

Kirk, Ruth, and J. Franklin. 2001. *The Olympic Rain Forest: An Ecological Web.* Seattle: University of Washington Press.

Lackey, R., D. Lach, and S. Duncan. 2006. *Salmon 2010: The Future of Wild Pacific Salmon.* Bethesda, MD: American Fisheries Society.

Lavendar, D. 1985. *Westward Vision.* Lincoln: University of Nebraska Press.

Leighton, C. 1995. *West Coast Journeys, 1865–1879.* Seattle: Sasquatch Books.

LeMonds, J. 2001. *Deadfall: Generations of Logging in the Pacific Northwest.* Missoula: Mountain Press Publishing.

Lichatowich, J. 1999. *Salmon Without Rivers.* Washington, DC: Island Press.

Lien, Carsten. 2000. *Olympic Battleground: The Power Politics of Timber Preservations.* Seattle: The Mountaineers Books.

Lien, Carsten. 2001. *Exploring the Olympic Mountains: Accounts of the Earliest Expeditions 1878–1890.* Seattle: The Mountaineers Books.

Louter, D. 2006. *Windshield Wilderness: Cars, Roads, and Nature in Washington's Na-

tional Parks. Seattle: University of Washington Press.

Lund, J., and W. Smyth. 1999. *Olympic Peninsula Loop, Heritage Corridor Tour.* Olympia: Northwest Heritage Resources

Majors, H. 1975. *Exploring Washington.* Holland, MI: Van Winkle Publishing.

Mann, C. C. 2005. *1491: New Revelations of the Americas Before Columbus.* New York: Vintage Books.

Mapes, Lynda. 2005. "Unearthing Tse-whit-zen." *The Seattle Times.* Retrieved 2010. seattletimes.nwsource.com/news/local/klallam/index.html.

Mapes, Lynda. 2009. *Breaking Ground.* Seattle: University of Washington Press.

Marr, C. J. N.d. *Assimilation Through Education: Indian Boarding Schools in the Pacific Northwest.* Retrieved 2010. content.lib.washington.edu/aipnw/marr.html.

McKee, B. 1972. *Cascadia: The Geologic Evolution of the Pacific Northwest.* New York: McGraw-Hill.

Menzies, G. 2001. *1421: The Year China Discovered America.* New York: HarperCollins Publishers.

Miller, H., and M. Reece. N.d. *Indians and Europeans on the Northwest Coast, 1774–1812.* Retrieved 2010. www.washington.edu/uwired/outreach/cspn/Website/Resources/Curriculum/Natives%20Contact/Natives%20Main.html.

Morgan, Murray. 1955. *The Last Wilderness.* Seattle: University of Washington Press.

Morgenroth, C. 1991. *Footprints in the Olympics, an Autobiography.* Fairfield, WA: Ye Galleon Press.

Nisbet, Jack. 2009. *The Collector.* Seattle: Sasquatch Books.

Norse, E. A. 1990. *Ancient Forests of the Pacific Northwest.* Washington, DC: Island Press.

Peterson, G., and G. Schaad. 2005. *High Divide: Minnie Peterson's Olympic Mountain Adventures.* Forks, WA: Poseidon Peak Publishing.

{3em}. 2007. *Women to Reckon With: Untamed Women of the Olympic Wilderness.* Forks, WA: Poseidon Peak Publishing.

Philbrick, N. 2003. *Sea of Glory: America's Voyage of Discovery, the U.S. Exploring Expedition 1838–1842.* New York: Penguin Books.

Port Gamble S'Klallam Tribe. N.d. *The Port Gamble S'Klallam Tribe History.* Retrieved 2010. www.pgst.nsn.us/land-and-people-and-lifestyle/history.

Quileute Nation. N.d. Retrieved 2010. quileutenation.org/.

Roberts, G., and J. Roberts. 1999. *Discover Historic Washington State.* Baldwin Park, CA: Gem Guide Books.

Rooney, J. R. 2007. *Frontier Legacy: History of the Olympic National Forest 1897 to 1960.* Seattle: Northwest Interpretive Center.

Ruby, R. H., and J. A. Brown. 1976. *Myron Eells and the Puget Sound Indians.* Seattle: Superior Publishing.

Schalk, R. 1988. *The Evolution and Diversification of Native Land Use Systems on the Olympic Peninsula.* Seattle: Institute for Environmental Studies, University of Washington.

Skokomish Indian Tribe. N.d. *Culture and History of the Skokomish Tribe.* Retrieved 2010. www.skokomish.org/frame.htm.

Smithson, M., and P. O'Hara. 1993. *Olympic Ecosystems of the Peninsula.* Helena, MT: American and World Geographic Publishing.

SquaxinIsland.org. N.d. *Squaxin Island Tribe.* Retrieved 2010. www.squaxinisland. org/index.html.

Stilson, M. L., D. Meatte, and G. W. Robert. 2003. *A Field Guide to Washington State Archeology.* Olympia: State of Washington.

Sturtevant, W. C. 1990. *Handbook of the North American Indians, Vol. 7: Northwest Coast.* Washington, DC: Smithsonian Institution.

Tabor, Ron. 1975. *Guide to the Geology of Olympic National Park.* Seattle: University of Washington Press.

US History.com. N.d. *Skokomish Indian Tribe.* Retrieved 2011. www.u-s-history.com/ wa/s/skokintb.htm.

Van Syckle, E. 1980. *They Tried to Cut It All: Grays Harbor, Turbulent Years of Greed and Greatness.* Aberdeen, WA: Friends of the Aberdeen Public Library.

Washington State. 2007. *Revisiting Washington* [compact disc]. Olympia: State of Washington.

Washington State Department of Fish and Wildlife. 2008. Dungeness National Wildlife Refuge. Retrieved March 25. www.fws.gov/washingtonmaritime/ dungeness/.

Whitney, Steven, and Rob Sandelin. 2003. *Field Guide to the Cascades and Olympics.* 2nd ed. Seattle: The Mountaineers Books.

Wikipedia. N.d. *Klallam.* Retrieved 2010. en.wikipedia.org/wiki/Klallam.

Wood, Robert. 1995. *The Land that Slept Late.* Seattle: The Mountaineers Books.

Wray, J. 2002. *Native Peoples of the Olympic Peninsula.* Norman: University of Oklahoma Press.

Wray, J., and D. Taylor. 2006. *Postmistress Mora, Wash. 1914–1915.* Seattle: Northwest Interpretive Association.

Wright, T. 2006. *A History of Treaties and Reservations on the Olympic Peninsula, 1855–1898.* Retrieved 2010. content.lib.washington.edu/curriculumpackets/ treaties/Treaties-and-Reservations.pdf.

ACKNOWLEDGMENTS

First and foremost, Cherylee, my wife, has to be recognized as my biggest supporter. She continuously gave me the space to bring this book from distant idea to fruition. Second, a special thanks to my children, Maxwell and Hailey, whom I dragged on more trips to the Peninsula for "field research" than I can remember.

Ricki and Doug McGlashan were the first to actually use this book as it was intended way back when it was version 0.3. They supplied very valuable feedback to both the direction and the content. David Middleton taught me that in order to be a published photographer, one has to know how to write. Looks like I learned how to write way better than photograph. Georgia and Hank Scott gave me access to their expansive library of books on the Peninsula.

Early in my research, the staff of the State Capital Museum, in Olympia, was very generous to stay open one night while I peppered them with more questions than I am sure they wanted to answer. Pat Clemons, of Chehalis Valley Historical Museum, shared my fascination with William O'Leary, the first pioneer on the Peninsula. Dale Croes, the archaeology expert from South Puget Sound Community College, provided valuable insight into the Peninsula's earliest inhabitants. Rowland Tabor is a Geologist Emeritus with the USGS who literally wrote the book on the local geology. He was always generous with his energies and answered many of my newbie questions as an excellent and generous teacher would. Rob Sandelin provided invaluable initial guidance and encouragement. Tim McNulty shared more than natural history with me; he gave valuable insights to what it is to be a writer. Lynda Mapes was very encouraging in spite of my inexperience with a project such as this. L.A. Heberlein was helpful even right at conception of this project and encouraged me all along the way. Jim Dickmeyer helped put many of the final touches on my draft by professionally proofreading it. All the good people with the Olympic Peninsula Audubon Society helped with the birding locations and species list. The Fulsaas sisters are indeed wizards in helping me bring my manuscript from rough draft to the printing press.

Others include, but are not limited to, Janet Strong from the Chehalis River Basin Land Trust; Dann Sears of the Aberdeen Museum of History; Annie Stradler from the Washington State Department of Archaeology and Historic Preservation; Curt Pavola, program manager, Department of Natural Resources Natural Areas Program; Bellevue College's Dr. Michael Hanson whose enthusiasm for botany is infectious; and Jeffrey Duda, a USGS research ecologist with many answers on the Elwha. I am grateful to everyone who helped, yet any errors remain mine.

About The Author

Christopher Chapman has lived in the Seattle area for more than twenty-five years and has always been fascinated with what lies on the other side of Puget Sound. He has hiked many of the trails among the large trees in the forest and the beautiful sea stacks on the beach.

He lives in Woodinville, a suburb of Seattle, with his wife and daughter. After obtaining a bachelor's degree in biology from the University of Colorado and an MBA from the University of Michigan, he spent most of his work life in the finance and accounting fields. Later in life, a sense of adventure swept him to fully explore all the wonder that is so close by. One hiking trip from Hurricane Ridge led to a backpacking trip on the Pacific beach, and, from there, to explorations of as much as he could see on the Peninsula.

Inspired by how much there is to experience for the casual car-bound traveler but with no adequate guidebook available, he decided to write his own. Leveraging his background in the natural sciences, he began to gather information that he was interested in and thought others would be also. A chance reading of a Captain Cook biography revealed to him all the history that should be included (it also awakened his inner historian). You can learn more at www.roadsideolympicpeninsula.com.

Maps, Illustrations and Photographs

All maps were created by Lori Fulsaas except the following:

Page 64 *A Chart shewing part of the Coast of N.W. America.* (courtesy of University of Washington Libraries, Special Collections, uwm 96, originally published in 1798)

Page 80 *Preston's sectional and county map of Oregon and Washington.* (courtesy of University of Washington Libraries, Special Collections, UW 35577, originally published in 1856)

Page 98 *Map of the automobile roads of the State of Washington* (courtesy University of Washington Libraries, Special Collections, UW 35548, originally published in 1919)

All other images were created by the author except the following:

Page 20 *Quinault sea otter derrick, on beach between Copalis and Point Grenville, Washington, in drawing made ca. 1885* (Sarah Willoughby, courtesy University of Washington Libraries, Special Collections, NA 4041)

Page 22 *Stellar Jay* (Kellie Sagen)

Page 22 *A volunteer aiding in the clean-up* (Heidi Walker)

Page 54 *Makah Indians cutting up whale carcass, with three pieces of blubber laid out on the beach at Neah Bay, Washington, 1910* (Asahel Curtis, 1910, courtesy University of Washington Libraries, Special Collections, CUR2052)

Page 58 *Quinault men netting and spear fishing at low tide, mouth of the Quinault River* (Sarah Willoughby, 1886, courtesy of University of Washington Libraries, Special Collections, NA 4042)

Page 88 *Men, possibly loggers, standing at base of large cedar tree, ca. 1904* (courtesy University of Washington Libraries, Special Collections, UW17190)

Page 90 *Team of oxen hauling logs along skid road* (courtesy University of Washington Libraries, Special Collections, UW 1683)

Page 91 *Logging crew and vertical spool donkey engine* (courtesy University of Washington Libraries, Special Collections, UW12167)

Page 105 *Hydroelectric power plant and dam on the Elwha River near Port Angeles* (Asahel Curtis, 1914, courtesy of University of Washington Libraries, Special Collections, A. Curtis 28530)

Acknowledgements

Page 110 *High lead logging* (courtesy University of Washington Libraries, Special Collections, UW35582)

Page 112 *Northern Spotted Owl* (David Middleton)

Page 176 *Port Townsend, Washington, ca. 1890* (courtesy University of Washington Libraries, Special Collections, UW1940)

Page 248 *Aberdeen, Washington, ca. 1910* (courtesy University of Washington Libraries, Special Collections, UW23296z)

INDEX